UNITED STATES TO 1877

Nova Britannia.

OFFERING MOST

Excellent fruites by Planting in VIRGINIA.

Exciting all such as be well affected to further the same.

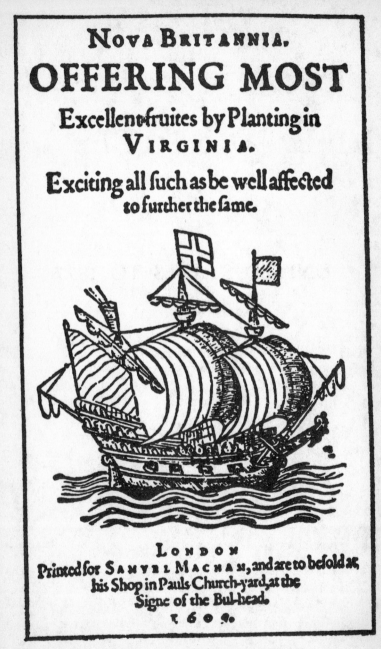

LONDON
Printed for Samuel Macham, and are to be sold at
his Shop in Pauls-Church-yard, at the
Signe of the Bul-head.
1609.

PAMPHLET OF THE LONDON COMPANY
SEEKING COLONISTS FOR VIRGINIA

UNITED STATES
TO 1877

Seventh Edition, Revised

JOHN A. KROUT
Formerly Vice President
Columbia University

BARNES & NOBLE BOOKS
A DIVISION OF HARPER & ROW, PUBLISHERS
New York, Cambridge,
Philadelphia, San Francisco, London,
Mexico City, São Paulo, Sydney

ABOUT THE AUTHOR

John A. Krout received his A.B. degree from the
University of Michigan and his A.M. and Ph.D.
degrees from Columbia University. From 1922 until
his retirement in 1962 he served at Columbia University successively as instructor in, to professor of,
history, Dean of Graduate Faculties, and Vice
President. He is a trustee of the Museum of the
City of New York and of the New York State
Historical Association, and belongs to numerous
other historical groups—among these being the
American Historical Association and the Society
of American Historians. He was also a member by
presidential appointment of the Civil War Cen-
tennial Commission. His published works include
*The Origins of Prohibition, Annals of American
Sport, American History for Colleges* (with D. S.
Muzzey), *Approaches to American Social History*
(W. E. Lingelbach, editor), *The Completion of
Independence* (with D. R. Fox), *Great Issues in
American History,* and *United States since 1865* (a
companion College Outline).

PREFACE

United States to 1877 is designed as an introduction to the history of the American people from the period of European expansion overseas to the rebuilding of the nation after the conflict that tested the durability of the Federal Union. For many citizens of the United States the Centennial Exposition of Philadelphia in 1876 symbolized the emergence of "modern America." The beginnings of social and economic recovery in the South coincided with the expansive thrust of commerce, industry, and transportation in the North. The new day was born, not so much because of the victories of Union armies as out of the achievements of American business enterprise.

This Outline does not follow any one textbook; it should therefore provide a plan for the organization of the information which the student acquires from both textbook and collateral reading. The author hopes that students will regard the Outline as a guide to the most reliable secondary sources, rather than as an easy short cut to historical knowledge. With this objective in view, the general Bibliography consists of a selected list of titles with which every serious student of the history of the United States should become acquainted. Their use will be rewarding.

JOHN A. KROUT

TABLE OF CONTENTS

MAPS AND CHARTS

UNITED STATES TO 1877

Chapter I

OPENING A NEW WORLD

The story of the people of the United States opens with opportunity granted to a generation of Europeans to make a new beginning in a New World. How they transplanted their ideas about science, economics, politics, religion, and all the other aspects of civilization to a wilderness environment is the heroic theme of that story.

EARLY EUROPEAN EXPANSION

Late in the fifteenth century there began a great movement of Europeans which within five hundred years carried them into every part of the world. One phase of this migration of Europe's population was the creation of the United States of America.

Forerunners of Expansion—The Vikings. Out of northern Scandinavia in the ninth and tenth centuries had come the Vikings, a resourceful people for whom the sea held few terrors. In Iceland they established a commonwealth more than a thousand years before American military forces used the island as a base in the Second World War. They left frontier settlements in Greenland and then sailed on to Vinland the Good, which may have been on the North American coast just south of Labrador. If the Norse sagas are correct, Leif the Lucky, son of Eric the Red, discovered Vinland about A.D. 1000. Norsemen who later sang of his exploits stirred the imagination of Europeans for a time, but their songs soon became mere legends.

The Lure of the Orient. In spite of the remarkable prowess of Norse mariners, the history of the American begins not in the dark forests of North America but on the shores of the sunlit Mediterranean.

CONTACTS BETWEEN EUROPE AND ASIA. Europeans faced east over the centuries for a longer period of time than they have faced west, but it was the remarkable attraction of the Orient that finally brought them to the Americas.

Impact of the Crusades. Though the roads between eastern Europe and western Asia had fallen into disrepair, they were usable by the crusaders in those religious-military expeditions which strove to regain the Holy Land, particularly Jerusalem, from the Turks who had won it in A.D. 1071. Many a glowing tale of the Levant and eastern Asia was told by courageous knights returning from the recurrent Crusades before the opening of the fourteenth century.

Revival of Asian Trade Routes. Missionaries, such as the Franciscans who knew Persia, India, China, and finally Japan, and merchants, like the Polos, Nicolo, Maffeo, and young Marco, who visited in the thirteenth century the fabulous court of the Great Khan of China, stirred the imagination of Europeans and revived an east-west trade that had almost disappeared. By 1400 luxuries of the Orient—silks, precious stones, silver and gold—as well as such necessities as spices and drugs, were being carried by the sea to the head of the Persian Gulf, thence by camel caravan through Baghdad to the Mediterranean. Northern routes came from China to the Caspian, and branched into several minor roads terminating along the shores of the Black Sea.

Commerce of the Italian Cities. This growing trade with the Levant and the Orient in the Italian city-states—Venice, Genoa, Florence—chiefly enriched middlemen who became merchant princes, controlling an economic domain based on the spices of the East Indies, silks and cashmeres of India, porcelain from China, rugs of Persia, and lacquer ware from Japan.

BEGINNINGS OF THE COMMERCIAL REVOLUTION. During the fifteenth century the emerging nations of western Europe—Portugal, Spain, France, and England—became increasingly dissatisfied with the conditions under which they secured the products of the Levant and the Far East. It seemed imperative that they find a new way to tap the trade of the Orient.

Disadvantages of Western Europe. Several factors were operating against the best interests of western European nations: (1) the drain of gold and silver eastward to settle unfavorable trade balances; (2) the costly and dangerous methods of transportation and the uncertainty about trade routes, especially after the Turks captured Constantinople (1453); and (3) the monopoly of the Mediterranean commerce by the merchant princes of the Italian city-states.

Opportunities for New Commerce. The revolutionary changes in Europe's trade were stimulated by: (1) accumulation of knowledge concerning the Oriental sources of supply provided by missionaries, travellers, and traders; (2) more exact geographical information; (3) improved methods of navigation and changes in ship construction and design; and (4) expansion of credit facilities based on accumulation of capital by moneylenders and bankers.

COMMERCIAL EMPIRES

European commercial expansion, which first became evident in Portugal and Spain, soon involved most of the western European nations. By the seventeenth century these national states were engaged in establishing colonial empires.

The Age of Exploration. The discovery and exploration of a new world overseas worked a revolution in the ideas and aspirations of western Europeans during the sixteenth and seventeenth centuries.

PORTUGAL'S LENGTHENING REACH. Portugal was the first European nation to establish direct contact with the Far East. Her mariners, trained in the school established by Prince Henry the Navigator (1418), pushed down the western coast of Africa. In 1488 Bartholomew Diaz rounded the Cape of Good Hope, and ten years later Vasco da Gama reached India. By the early decades of the sixteenth century Portuguese traders had established posts in India, China, Japan, and the East Indies, from which Lisbon reaped rich rewards. In Africa, likewise, commerce was Portugal's prime objective. In America, Brazil, discovered by Cabral in 1500, was brought under the control of the Portuguese monarchs (1515–1570).

SPAIN'S AMERICAN EMPIRE. Unlike Portugal, Spain turned west rather than east.

Early Explorers. In 1492 Christopher Columbus, an Italian seaman and geographer, was financed by Ferdinand and Isabella of Spain to make a westward voyage in search of a new route to Asia. In this and three later voyages he discovered parts of the Americas, eventually recognized as a New World. Soon other explorers were seeking either new lands or new ways to old lands. By the Papal Line of Demarcation (1493), modified a year later by the Treaty of Tordesillas between Spain and Portugal, Spain was given control over all "heathen lands" lying west of a line drawn from North to South Pole, 370 leagues to the west of the Cape Verde Islands. For Spain, Balboa,

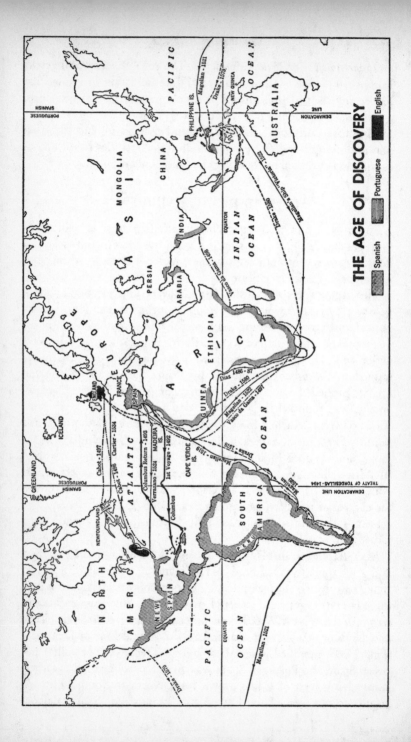

THE AGE OF DISCOVERY

crossing the Isthmus of Panama, reached the Pacific (1513); the same year Ponce de León landed in Florida; Magellan carried the flag to the Philippines, and one of his ships completed the first trip around the globe (1519–1522).

Conquistadors and Colonists. Spanish noblemen and gentlemen adventurers (conquistadors) followed quickly. Cortez in Mexico (1520), Pizzaro in Peru (1531), Mendoza in the Argentine (1535), DeSoto along the Mississippi (1539–1542), Coronado beyond the Rio Grande (1540), and Menendez in Florida (1565) pushed out the frontiers of Spanish territory. By 1575 approximately 175,000 Spaniards, organized politically in the viceroyalties of New Spain and Peru, were exploiting the resources of the Americas, Christianizing thousands of the natives, and sending a steady stream of gold and silver to Europe.

The Challenge to Spain and Portugal.
By the time Spain had conquered Mexico, France had become a force in European power politics, and Francis I (1515) served notice that he would not permit Spain and Portugal to divide the New World between them.

THE BEGINNINGS OF NEW FRANCE. Frenchmen based their claims on the activities of French fishermen in American waters and the explorations of Verrazano, who sailed along the coast of North America (1524), and Jacques Cartier, who tried unsuccessfully to establish settlements along the St. Lawrence (1534–1535). It was not until 1608 that Samuel de Champlain, under orders from a monopoly granted by Henry IV, founded the little trading post of Quebec, which was to become the capital of New France.

THE DUTCH COMMERCIAL EMPIRE. The Dutch provinces of the Netherlands, which broke away from Spanish control (1581), preyed upon Spanish commerce with America and despoiled the Portuguese in their Asian and African trading posts. As Dutch commerce grew in the early seventeenth century, the New Netherland Company and the West India Company sponsored settlements in South America (Guiana), the West Indies, and the valley of the Hudson River, which Henry Hudson had discovered in 1609. The first short-lived trading post in the Hudson Valley was established in 1614, and a decade later Dutch settlers began to arrive on Manhattan Island, forming the port of New Amsterdam (later New York).

SWEDES AND DANES IN THE NEW WORLD. Swedish commercial power in the Baltic countries grew rapidly in the seventeenth century. Sweden's merchants established a trading post on the Delaware

River (1638), but it was not well supported, and its struggle against great odds ended in 1655, when it was conquered by the Dutch. Greenland and the Virgin Islands were Denmark's closest contacts with the continent of North America.

REVIEW QUESTIONS

1. Explain the significance of the term "Commercial Revolution."
2. Why did the nations of western Europe consider the Oriental trade so important?
3. What was the contribution of Prince Henry the Navigator to the age of discovery?
4. Explain the ability of the rising national states to break the Mediterranean monopoly held by the merchants of the Italian city-states.
5. How do you account for the leadership of Portugal and Spain in exploration and colonization during the fifteenth and sixteenth centuries?
6. What characteristics of the Spanish colonial empire distinguished it from that of Portugal?
7. What was the effect of royal supervision upon the French dominions overseas?
8. What were the principal interests of the Dutch West India Company in the Hudson Valley settlements?

CHAPTER II

THE COMING OF THE ENGLISH

Though England began her empire building later than Portugal, Spain, and France, she became the greatest of all the European nations in the planting and governing of colonies overseas. Her insularity, her flourishing commerce, her expanding navy, and the growing strength of her middle classes were great assets in the struggle for world-wide power.

THE PROCESS OF ENGLISH COLONIZATION

The English government never participated in colonial ventures as directly as did the governments of Spain and France; yet the English Crown from the days of Elizabeth I to the closing years of Charles II gave encouragement to Englishmen who were willing to adventure in foreign parts.

The Motives for Expansion. Statesmen and publicists who advocated the planting of English colonies in the New World were inspired by a wide range of motives. Most important were: (1) the desire to weaken Spain and France; (2) the eagerness of merchant adventurers to secure higher profits from foreign trade; (3) the belief that England was overpopulated and needed to send surplus laborers abroad; (4) the desire to win converts to Protestant Christianity; and (5) the determination to increase the nation's prestige by ensuring its economic self-sufficiency within the borders of its own empire.

EXPLORERS, COLONIZERS, AND ELIZABETHAN SEADOGS. From the year 1497, when John Cabot sailed from Bristol to Cape Breton Island and skirted the coast of North America southward, English mariners kept up the search for a shorter route through America to the Orient. Unspectacular as their achievements were, they added to Europe's knowlege of geography. Late in the sixteenth century the deeds of Captain John Hawkins in despoiling the Spanish slave trade, and of Sir Francis Drake in raiding the Spanish colonies and the Spanish galleons carrying precious metals to Europe won special rewards from Queen Elizabeth. The Queen also encouraged Sir Humphrey Gilbert, who tried unsuccessfully to establish a settlement in Newfoundland (1583) and Sir Walter Raleigh, who sent out several ventures, culminating in the Lost Colony of Roanoke (established in 1587, it had disappeared by 1590, when English ships returned to it).

MIGRATION OF THE DISCONTENTED. Most English settlers sought the New World as a release from their troubles in the Old World. Some, like the Calvinistic dissenters from the Church of England, fled from the Stuart policy of religious uniformity or, like the Roman Catholics, sought refuge from possible persecution in England. After the Restoration of the Stuarts to the throne, supporters of the parliamentary cause emigrated to escape the divine-right pretensions of the monarchy. Most, however, were the victims of economic changes in England. Out of work, they were willing to risk the only capital they possessed, their lives, in the hope that they would find a new prosperity across the sea for themselves and their children.

Methods of Establishing Colonies.

The English government authorized the use of two agencies to promote the establishment of settlements overseas—the chartered trading company and the proprietorship. Both, long known to the landholding and commercial leaders of England, proved to be well adapted to the work of colonization.

THE CHARTERED TRADING COMPANY. These commercial joint-stock companies, operating under royal charters, were composed of "adventurers" (stockholders) who shared pro rata the profits and losses of the colonial venture. Political control of the colony was at first vested in the directors of the company, who were usually more interested in profits than in settlers. Most charters provided that colonists should have all the rights and privileges of Englishmen and that their governing bodies should pass no law contrary to the laws of England.

Virginia and Massachusetts. Two of the colonies which later became the United States were established by English chartered trading companies: the settlement at Jamestown, Virginia, by the London Company (1607) and the Puritan colony in Massachusetts by the Massachusetts Bay Company (1630). In 1620 the Pilgrims (separatists from the Church of England) arrived and settled in Plymouth, Massachusetts. The colony was self-governing under the Mayflower Compact * until 1691, when William III brought the Plymouth settlement under the governorship of the Massachusetts Bay Colony. Virginia become a royal province in 1624, when the London Company, having failed in its attempt to exploit the colony's resources, surrendered its charter to the Crown. The stockholders of the Massachusetts Bay company migrated to America, thus making the colony corporate or self-governing. So it remained until the Crown annulled the charter in 1691 and appointed a royal governor.

New York and Delaware. Two of the thirteen original colonies were initiated by non-English joint-stock companies: New Netherland, later New York, by the Dutch West India Company in 1623 and Delaware by a Swedish company in 1638. New York was captured by the English in 1664 and became a royal province when its proprietor, James, Duke of York, became king in 1685. Delaware fell under the control of the Penn family as a proprietary province.

THE PROPRIETORSHIP. The proprietary charters normally granted huge tracts of land to an individual or a group of persons on terms reminiscent of feudal tenure.

Political and Economic Growth. In the proprietorships, political control was theoretically in the hands of those who received the royal grant, but power was actually delegated in part to representatives chosen by the colonists. The owners usually invested their personal fortunes in developing their lands. They encouraged settlers to take small holdings from them, expecting to reap their profits from quitrents paid to the proprietor by those who tilled the soil.

Seven Proprietary Grants. Of the thirteen English colonies, seven were founded as proprietorships: Maryland by Lord Baltimore (1632); New Hampshire by Captain John Mason (1635); New Jersey by Sir William Berkeley and Sir George Carteret in 1663; the Carolinas by friends of Charles II (1663); Pennsylvania by William Penn in 1682; and Georgia by a board of trustees, headed by James Oglethorpe in 1732. All except Pennsylvania and Maryland had become royal provinces before the outbreak of the Revolution.

THE CORPORATE COLONIES. The chief characteristic that distin-

---

* This agreement was signed on board ship at the behest of Bradford and other leaders ("Saints") who realized that the territory they had reached was out of the jurisdiction of the Virginia Company (which had granted their patent) and who feared rebellion by the non-Pilgrims ("Strangers") attached to the group.

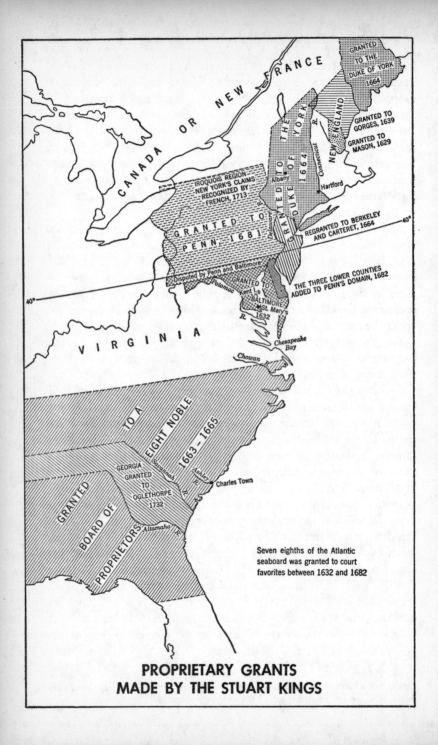

CANADA OR NEW FRANCE

GRANTED TO THE DUKE OF YORK 1664

GRANTED TO GORGES, 1639

GRANTED TO MASON, 1629

NEW ENGLAND

Connecticut R.

IROQUOIS REGION — NEW YORK'S CLAIMS — RECOGNIZED BY FRENCH, 1713

GRANTED TO PENN, 1681

GRANTED TO THE DUKE OF YORK 1664

Albany

Hartford

Delaware R.

40°

REGRANTED TO BERKELEY AND CARTERET, 1664

Disputed by Penn and Baltimore

40°

VIRGINIA

Potomac R.

GRANTED TO BALTIMORE 1632

Kent I. o

★St. Mary's

THE THREE LOWER COUNTIES ADDED TO PENN'S DOMAIN, 1682

Chesapeake Bay

Chowan R.

GRANTED

TO A

EIGHT NOBLE

1663 – 1665

BOARD OF

PROPRIETORS

GEORGIA GRANTED TO OGLETHORPE 1732

Savannah R.

Ashley R.

Charles Town

Altamaha R.

Seven eighths of the Atlantic seaboard was granted to court favorites between 1632 and 1682

PROPRIETARY GRANTS
MADE BY THE STUART KINGS

guished the corporate colony from others in English America was the large measure of self-government which it enjoyed. The qualified voters in the colony chose the governor, the governor's council, and the legislative assembly. Massachusetts, as we have seen (p. 9), was a corporate colony until it lost its charter in 1691. Connecticut (1662) and Rhode Island (1663), originally settled by dissident groups from Massachusetts, were fortunate in securing royal charters which conferred upon the colonists control of their own government.

THE FRUITS OF ENGLISH COLONIZATION

Between 1607 and 1732 English men and women had established permanent settlements along the eastern coast of North America from New Hampshire to Georgia, which were organized into thirteen separate political units.

The Distribution of Land. The opportunity to become a landowner was the great loadstone that drew most settlers to the English colonies in America.

Land Tenure in New England. During the seventeenth century the New England legislatures tried to establish many small towns of freeholders, who were either church members or regular church attendants. To accomplish this, they granted tracts of land to "proprietors," who were responsible for laying out the town. Each settler belonging to the dominant religious group received a home lot and additional arable land for a farm. He became an outright owner of his home and farm and a joint owner with his fellow townsmen of the common meadow and wooded land belonging to the whole town. As a result, small farms owned as freeholds, rather than great estates, became typical of New England. This system of land distribution broke down in the eighteenth century as speculators persuaded the legislatures to grant larger tracts in which the grantees might sell lots for profit.

The Quitrent System. Freeholds, similar to those in New England, existed in parts of the middle Atlantic and southern colonies, but generally the system of landholding was based upon semifeudal grants by an overlord, who had received his holdings from the Crown. Such were the manorial estates in New York, Pennsylvania, and Maryland, and the extensive holdings that developed under individual grants from colonial legislatures in Virginia and the Carolinas. Farms were apt to be larger than in New England, and were held not as freeholds but as grants from the original owner, subject to the annual payment of a quitrent. However small the quitrent might be, it came to be resented and caused disturbances in some provinces. Many colonial farmers learned how to evade payment when enforcement was attempted.

LAND SPECULATION. The wooded, but fertile, acres beyond the western fringe of settlement attracted not only pioneer farmers, eager to occupy them, but also shrewd speculators, determined to hold them for future increase in value. Every colony, even in New England, had its land companies and great proprietors who secured large tracts along the frontier. They aroused the hostility of actual settlers, anxious to acquire homes, unless the speculators were willing to sell farms, free of quitrent or other feudal obligations.

The Organization of Production.

English America in colonial days was essentially a land of farmers and planters; but there were differences in the organization of production determined by natural resources, land tenure, and labor supply.

THE MARITIME PROVINCES. The New England colonies showed certain similarities in the processes of their economic life that distinguished them from other sections of English America.

Agriculture. Characteristic of the region northeast of the Hudson Valley was the diversified farming of small freeholds. Despite the handicaps of a short growing season and rocky soil, many crops were grown successfully. Among the chief products were corn, oats, rye, barley, and fruit. Cattle, sheep, horses, and poultry were also raised.

Fisheries. Fishing, as a commercial enterprise, was virtually confined to New England. By 1765, 10,000 persons were employed in catching, cleaning, and preserving cod, mackerel, bass, halibut, and other deep-sea fish, which had become an important factor in Anglo-American trade with Europe and the West Indies. New Englanders hunted whales in the Atlantic from the Arctic to the coast of Brazil. Some 360 vessels were engaged in the whaling industry at the outbreak of the Revolution.

Commerce and Shipbuilding. In the maritime sections of New England, seafaring surpassed farming. Her shipbuilders and mariners played a role in foreign trade far greater than is indicated by the proportion of New England's products in that commerce.

Manufacturing. Domestic production in New England, as elsewhere, was supplemented by the output of small handicraft industries. Woolen textiles, leather goods, household utensils, and iron implements were important, but in the eighteenth century the distillation of rum from West Indian molasses became New England's chief manufacturing industry. It was part of the profitable trade in molasses, rum, and slaves which brought gold and silver into the maritime provinces.

THE PROVISION PROVINCES. New York, New Jersey, and Pennsylvania were largely responsible for supplying New England with raw materials, and have aptly been called the provision provinces.

Agriculture. Diversified farming, not unlike that of New England, was more rewarding in the fertile valleys of the middle colonies. Wheat, corn, and other grains, cattle, sheep, swine, vegetables, and fruits were the foodstuffs which bulked large in the export trade of this section.

Manufacturing. The wheat areas of the provision provinces were dotted with flour mills. The presence of skilled workmen in Pennsylvania and New Jersey enabled the section to make important contributions to the production of textiles, paper, glass, and iron.

Fur Trade. The trade in furs, especially that which passed through the Iroquois country into Albany, was important during the seventeenth century, but it declined rapidly in New York after 1715.

THE PLANTATION PROVINCES. During the eighteenth century the area from Maryland to Georgia became increasingly interested in the production of great staple crops.

Agriculture. Though the southern colonies produced grains and fruits, the farmers and planters of the section relied upon tobacco (Maryland, Virginia, and North Carolina), rice, and indigo (South Carolina and Georgia) as their commercial crops. Before the Revolution, Maryland and Virginia were raising fifty million pounds of tobacco annually, whereas South Carolina was exporting five hundred thousand pounds of rice a year.

Lumber and Naval Stores. The forests of the Carolina uplands furnished lumber for shipbuilding and "naval stores"—pitch, tar, and turpentine—for the British navy.

Fur Trade. In the eighteenth century Carolina and Georgia traders did a thriving business in furs, Augusta becoming one of the important trading centers in furs in America.

Manufacturing. The southern colonies had fewer manufacturing establishments than the other sections of the country. The iron industry was important in Maryland and Virginia, but most of the work of blacksmiths, tanners, cobblers, weavers, etc., was done on the plantations for domestic consumption.

The Scarcity of Labor. The colonial farmers, merchants, and manufacturers were generally in search of laborers, for the ease with which newcomers in English America acquired land meant that industrious colonists could soon become landlords in their own right. Indentured servants and enslaved Negroes and Indians constituted the most important labor force.

INDENTURED SERVANTS. These bondsmen, under contract for a limited term of service, usually five years, were particularly numerous in the colonies from New York southward to Virginia. The voluntarily indentured, or "redemptioners," were sometimes skilled artisans, occasionally persons with professional training. The unskilled laborers were often recruited by kidnappers operating in European ports; many others were transported by English courts for political and religious offenses, as well as for misdemeanors and crimes.

NEGRO SLAVES. Late in the seventeenth century the white indentured servants were rapidly replaced in Virginia and the Carolinas by enslaved Africans. The first shipload of African Negroes arrived in Virginia in 1619, but the labor force of the Southern colonies throughout the seventeenth century was chiefly recruited from the poor whites, both free and indentured. Negro slavery, however, increased rapidly after 1713, when England and Spain signed the *Assiento* (see p. 32), which gave England the exclusive right for thirty years to bring Africans into the Spanish possessions. By 1760 it was estimated that there were 400,000 Negroes in English America, of whom three quarters were in the South. In some communities of South Carolina and Georgia they exceeded the white population in number.

The First Americans. Everywhere that the European penetrated the continent of North America he found the American Indians. They may have been descendants of primitive Asians who had crossed Bering Strait from Siberia to the headlands of Alaska. By the fifteenth century they roamed the high plains, hunted the mountain valleys, and farmed along the rivers from the Pacific to the Atlantic. Divided into scores of tribes and speaking hundreds of languages, they bore a striking resemblance to their Mongolian ancestors. Without their aid, the first Europeans might not have survived in the New World. In the process of European conquest, the Indian lost his "happy hunting grounds" to the white man. Often he was cruelly deceived and dispossessed by the Europeans to whom he had shown the way to combat the wilderness and tame its resources.

REVIEW QUESTIONS

1. What circumstances delayed England's participation in the competition for colonial possessions?
2. How did England's rivalry with Spain affect her attitude toward the New World?
3. Discuss the struggle between the Stuarts and Parliament as a motive for English migration.
4. What groups of religious dissenters were most eager to seek their fortunes overseas?
5. Why was the trading company an acceptable instrument of colonization?
6. What advantages accrued to the recipient of a proprietary grant from the Crown?
7. How was the Massachusetts Bay Company transformed into a body politic?
8. In what respect did the corporate colony, such as Connecticut, differ from the proprietorship, such as Pennsylvania?

CHAPTER III

PROVINCIAL AMERICA

To men and women from the Old World the American colonies presented a new social environment, requiring adjustment to new conditions of life, but also offering the opportunity to put new ideas into practice, unhampered by the traditions of Europe.

THE EMERGENCE OF AN AMERICAN CULTURE

Many of the old ways of life and habits of thought were retained by the early settlers, but the eighteenth century saw the beginnings of a distinctive American culture.

Social Life. The details of everyday life in English America varied according to place, time, and social status.

THE CITIES. The major colonial cities—Boston, Newport, New York, Philadelphia, and Charleston—were all ports. Beginning as tiny settlements of a few wooden houses, they rapidly developed into commercial centers in which merchants, artisans, mechanics, and professional people lived a life not unlike that which they had left behind in Europe. Between these colonial cities communication at first was mainly by sea because roads through the forests were poor. For a time the seaports were more closely in touch with England, six weeks away by sea, than they were with one another.

THE FRONTIER. Compared to the relative comfort of the cities, life on the frontier was crude and hazardous. Families generally moved westward in groups to establish new settlements and immediately built a stockade as protection against Indian raids before clearing the land. By the eighteenth century the log cabin was the standard dwelling; clothing was often made from the skins of animals; food at first was obtained chiefly by hunting and fishing. Recreation usually took the form of useful community enterprises, such as log-rollings, house raisings, and husking bees.

THE FAMILY. The family was basic in the pattern of colonial society. Marriages took place at an early age and families were large, particularly on the frontier, where each new pair of hands counted. The position of women, who had an almost completely dependent status under English common law, improved rapidly in English America, where women were few; and they were often accepted by men as equal partners in the social and business affairs of the family.

SOCIAL STATUS. Though the primitive conditions of life along the frontier tended to make all men equal in their wilderness environment, class distinctions were obvious in the seaport cities and the older village settlements. A relatively small upper class, having close connections with England, consisted of colonial governors, clergymen, wealthy merchants and planters, and professional men. Much larger and increasing steadily was a middle class of prosperous tradesmen, thrifty farmers, mechanics, and laborers. Of the two groups of bond servants, those under indenture were decreasing in number late in the eighteenth century, while the number of slaves was increasing.

The Religious Scene. Although the desire for freedom of worship had inspired many nonconformist religious groups to move from England and the European continent to the New World, religious toleration and the separation of church and state were difficult to achieve in the English colonies.

THE ESTABLISHED CHURCHES. Few English colonists at the outset were concerned to separate authority in their political affairs from authority in their religious organizations. By the middle of the eighteenth century nine of the original thirteen colonies had established churches in the sense of support of a particular religious denomination by general taxation.

The Anglicans. Virginia was the first of the English colonies to give legislative sanction to the Church of England. Prior to the Revolution, Maryland, New York, the Carolinas, and Georgia had also recognized the Anglican Church by voting to support its parishes out of taxes. There was no resident bishop of the Church of England in colonial America, and the Anglican clergy, handicapped by difficulties of travel and communication among scattered settlements, never gained a dominant position; but in Virginia and other Southern colonies membership in the Church of England was politically and socially advantageous.

Puritanism. Calvinistic Puritanism was influential in all parts of

English America, but nowhere did it become so powerful as in Massachusetts and later Connecticut, through the establishment of the Congregational Church. The Puritan Congregationalists believed that their members had been divinely "elected" for salvation, and they imposed rigid controls to insure "godly" living. In the early years of Massachusetts only church members could vote, and to become a church member one had to have his spiritual worth approved by the minister and the congregation. The clergy dominated the political magistrates, and the government of the colony could best be described as a theocracy. Conformity was not easy to maintain. Church membership requirements were relaxed, and in its second century the colony permitted the establishment of some Anglican chapels, adopted a policy of co-operation with Presbyterian Calvinists, and authorized such dissenting sects as Baptists and Methodists to use funds derived from taxes for the support of their own ministers.

THE MULTIPLICATION OF RELIGIOUS SECTS. In the eighteenth century, thousands of European Protestants who were neither Congregationalists nor Anglicans came to America. Along the frontier particularly, Baptists, Presbyterians, Methodists, and Quakers increased their membership. Lutherans, Dutch Reformed, Moravians, and Huguenots found a haven in the middle colonies, especially Pennsylvania and New Jersey.

ADVANCE TOWARDS RELIGIOUS FREEDOM. Such examples of tolerance as Roger Williams' separation of church and state in Rhode Island (which he had founded as a religious refugee from Massachusetts); the approval by Lord Baltimore, a Roman Catholic, of the Maryland Toleration Act of 1649; the freedom of conscience provision in New Jersey in 1665; and the broad invitation to all religious sects sent out by the Quaker William Penn in settling his province of Pennsylvania, contributed to a slow movement against intolerance and religious bigotry. The New England theocracies, pressed by the demands of the growing non-English population, made notable concessions to dissenters. The Massachusetts charter of 1691, for example, removed the church membership requirement for the right to vote. In 1708 Connecticut accepted the Presbyterians as virtually full partners with Congregationalists in missionary work.

THE GREAT AWAKENING. During the early decades of the eighteenth century the growth of secular interests and the influence of the ideas of the European Enlightenment greatly weakened men's belief in an arbitrary and vengeful God. Churchmen deplored a general religious apathy in the English colonies. To combat it some gave their support to an evangelical revival known as the Great Awakening. Led by Jonathan Edwards (1734), a fiery New England Congregational minister, and George Whitefield, an evangelical Anglican from England, the revival deeply stirred both port towns and countryside. It caused a split among religious leaders into *Old Lights,* who condemned emotionalism and took a more rationalistic approach to theology, and *New Lights,* who encouraged evangelical fervor.

Education in the Colonies. Education was early a compelling concern of the English colonists, especially in New England.

Elementary Schooling. In 1647, for example, the Massachusetts School Law required every town of fifty householders to maintain a grammar school. In the Middle Colonies schools were dependent on religious societies and other private organizations. In the South the tidewater families employed private tutors or relied on the clergy to conduct secondary schools. Among the working classes education took the form of apprenticeship rather than schooling, and for Negro slave children there was little opportunity to learn to read or write. Most elementary schools were for boys exclusively, but girls began to be admitted in the eighteenth century.

Colleges and Professional Training. Before the Revolution nine colleges had been founded: Harvard (1636), William and Mary (1693), Yale (1701), the "Academy" in Philadelphia, which developed into the University of Pennsylvania (1740), the College of New Jersey, now Princeton (1746), King's College, later Columbia (1754), Brown (1764), Rutgers (1766), and Dartmouth (1769). The first colleges were established primarily for the training of ministers, and the curriculum, which emphasized theology and the classics, followed that of the English liberal arts colleges. By 1720 Natural Philosophy (science) was being taught and modern languages were considered worthy of study. The latter part of the eighteenth century saw the founding of medical schools at the College of Philadelphia and at King's College. This association of professional schools with colleges was the basis of our present university system.

Beginnings in Literature and Art. In spite of colonial dependence on Europe, it was clear by the last quarter of the eighteenth century that English America was beginning to produce artists and cultural institutions of its own.

Newspapers and Magazines. Beginning with the *Boston News*

Letter (1704), over fifty newspapers were published in the colonies. They generally contained comment on the news from abroad; local news; literary pieces copied from English journals, and as the conflict with Britain approached, heated pieces against the restrictions imposed by the mother country. The few magazines published in the colonies showed a remarkable breadth of interest.

LIBRARIES AND LEARNED SOCIETIES. The eighteenth century witnessed a large increase in the number of books imported to America as well as in the number printed in the colonies from the time the first printing press was in operation in Massachusetts in 1639. Private libraries grew in size and public subscription libraries were founded on the model of Benjamin Franklin's in Philadelphia (1731). The American Philosophical Society (1743), under Franklin's leadership, strove to unite scientists and philosophic thinkers.

FINE ARTS. Painting in the colonies reached a high point at the end of the eighteenth century in the work of four artists recognized in Europe as well as at home: John Singleton Copley, Benjamin West, Charles Wilson Peale, and Gilbert Stuart. Music was frowned upon by the Puritans, but in Charleston and Philadelphia singing societies were founded after 1740, and chamber concerts were popular among the well-to-do. The Moravians of Pennsylvania were outstanding for their compositions and performance of church music in the German tradition. The only important composer in the colonial period was the hymn writer, Francis Hopkinson.

THE EUROPEAN HERITAGE

It is easy to exaggerate the cultural achievements of such a frontier society as English America at the close of the eighteenth century. Long after the colonies won their political independence, they were deeply in debt, intellectually and spiritually, to the peoples of Great Britain and continental Europe.

Non-English Influences. Waves of settlers who had never lived in England began to reach American shores, and they brought ideas and traditions that steadily modified the predominantly English manners and mores.

FRENCH HUGUENOTS. Fleeing religious and political persecution after Louis XIV revoked the Edict of Nantes (1685), these industrious French Calvinists were highly successful as merchants and craftsmen in the growing American ports. Boston, New York, and particularly Charleston felt the impact of French styles in architecture, house furnishings, and dress. Probably not more than fifteen thousand Huguenots came before the Revolution, but one glimpses their influence on American life in such family names as Bowdoin, DeLancey, Devereux, Delano, Jay, Faneuil, and Revere.

THE GERMANS. One of the largest streams of continental Europeans flowing into the English colonies after 1700 was from the German provinces. Many were hard-working peasants, dispossessed by the successive wars of France's Louis XIV. Others had been trained as skilled artisans or professional men in the Old World. Pennsylvania was the center of German settlements, but they carried into the Shenandoah Valley and the Piedmont region of Virginia and North Carolina their commitments to a "pietistic" theology, their belief in good schools, and their confidence in the power of the press. Probably 200,000 Germans were in the colonies in 1775.

THE SCOTCH-IRISH. Quite as influential as the Germans were the descendants of Presbyterians from the Scottish Lowlands who had been colonized in northern Ireland early in the seventeenth century. Shortly after 1700 these Scotch-Irish, driven by religious and economic grievances, left Ulster in large numbers for Pennsylvania and the colonies south of that province. Drawn westward along the fertile river valleys by the magnet of cheap land, these people developed on the colonial frontiers a society that was individualistic, resourceful, and self-reliant. It is estimated that almost 300,000 Scotch-Irish came to America before the Revolution.

OTHER NON-ENGLISH GROUPS. Less important numerically than the Scotch-Irish and Germans were other groups that fled Europe to escape religious or political persecution or economic hardship—the Scots in Virginia and South Carolina, the Swiss in North Carolina, the Catholic Irish in Maryland and Pennsylvania, the Welsh Quakers in Pennsylvania and New England, and small groups of Jews from Spain and Portugal in most port cities. Along the Hudson the impact of early Dutch settlement was still obvious in speech, dress, and building construction as late as the opening of the nineteenth century.

The English Tradition. Despite the differences in ethnic origin, economic circumstances, and cultural backgrounds, colonial Americans possessed a common bond in their rich inheritance from England.

LANGUAGE AND LITERATURE. On the eve of the Revolution, Americans were more predominantly English in thought and aspiration than the large numbers of continental Europeans in the population seemed to indicate. Except among the German groups in Pennsylvania, English was the speech of the overwhelming majority in every community. A further bond of unity for the citizens of the thirteen separate colonies was their common literature, expressing the historic ideals of Englishmen. Even the rationalistic philosophy of the French Enlightenment had come to them through the refinements of English commentators.

LAW AND POLITICS. Nowhere in English America had the presence of large groups of settlers from continental Europe changed legal codes or governmental institutions or political practices from their English prototypes. The first American representative assembly, the Virginia House of Burgesses, met in 1619; it was followed by assemblies in all of the colonies with the lower house in each elected. English common law and judicial procedures were established. The British tradition of personal liberty that had been the essence of the British revolutions of the seventeenth century gained new meaning and emphasis in colonial America.

REVIEW QUESTIONS

1. How did colonial conditions modify the transplanted English landholding systems?
2. The colonial farmer has been called a "jack-of-all-trades." Explain.
3. What is meant by an "established church"? Where was the Anglican church established?
4. How did the increase of evangelical Protestant sects affect the traditional doctrine of the union of church and state?
5. What was the character and purpose of the early American colleges?
6. Why did the English heritage constitute a strong bond of union among the thirteen colonies?
7. Where were some of the major non-English groups influential in English America at the close of the eighteenth century?

Chapter IV

PROBLEMS OF IMPERIAL CONTROL

For more than a century and a half after Jamestown was settled, English officials, at home and in the colonies, tried to formulate a system of imperial administration that would benefit all parts of the expanding empire.

POLICIES OF THE STUARTS

From the accession of James I (1603), to the unceremonious departure of James II (1688), the Stuart kings devised various methods of imposing the royal will on their American colonies, only to be repeatedly thwarted by the shifting fortunes of political factions in Great Britain.

Royal Administration. James I, who regarded America as an extension of the royal domain, created administrative agencies which he hoped would maintain the Crown's authority over the colonies. He appointed a Council of Trade (1622) to see that English laws were enforced in America, and he revoked the charter of the London Company (1624), thus making Virginia a royal province. His successor, Charles I, gave large powers over the colonies to a commission of twelve members of his Privy Council (1634).

Puritan Revolution. The activity of the Privy Council in colonial affairs was cut short by the Puritan revolt (1642) against Stuart authority which resulted in the execution of Charles I and the establishment of a Commonwealth. Though the Long Parliament tried to maintain continuity of control by naming a special board of six noblemen and twelve commoners (1643), little was accomplished during the period of Parliamentary ascendancy. The colonies were on the whole left to develop their local institutions, and learned useful lessons in self-government.

The Restoration. When Charles II returned from exile to take

TABLE OF ENGLISH COLONIES

NAME (the thirteen original states in italic)	FOUNDED BY	DATE	CHARTER	ASSEMBLY	MADE ROYAL	STATUS IN 1775	REMARKS
Virginia	London Company	1607	{1606–1609–1612}	1619	1624	Royal	
Plymouth	Separatists	1620		1639	1691		Merged with Massachusetts in 1691
Massachusetts	Puritans of the Mass. Bay Co.	1628	1629	1634	1684	Royal	Only royal colony to have its charter restored (1691)
Maryland	Lord Baltimore	1634	1632	1634		Proprietary	A royal province, 1690–1715
Rhode Island	Roger Williams	1636	1663	1647		Self-governing	{Frustrated Andros's attempt to take away charters, 1686–1687
Connecticut	Emigrants from Massachusetts	1636	1662	1637		Self-governing	
New Haven	Emigrants from Massachusetts	1638		1643			Merged with Connecticut, 1662
Maine	F. Gorges	1641	1639		1691		Bought by Massachusetts, 1677
North Carolina	Eight nobles	1663	1663	1669	N. 1729	Royal	{Informally separated, 1691; formally separated with different governors, 1729
South Carolina					S. 1729	Royal	
New York	(Duke of York)	1664	1664	1683–1685	1685	Royal	Dutch colony of New Netherland, 1622–1664
New Hampshire	John Mason	1664	1639	1680	1679	Royal	Towns absorbed by Massachusetts, 1641–1679
New Jersey	Berkeley and Carteret	1664		1664	1702	Royal	Under the governor of New York till 1738
Pennsylvania	William Penn	1681	1680	1681		Proprietary	A royal province, 1692–1694
Delaware	Swedes	1638		1702		Proprietary	{Conquered by Dutch, 1655; by English, 1664 / Merged with Pennsylvania, 1682
Georgia	Jas. Oglethorpe	1732	1732	1733	1752	Royal	Separate governor (1691) and assembly (1702)

the throne, he promptly reasserted royal authority in America (1660). Seeking the advice of his favorites among the nobility and the wealthier merchants, he named two advisory bodies—a Council for Foreign Plantations and a Council for Trade (1660)—which were merged in 1674 into a standing committee of the Privy Council for "Trade and Foreign Plantations." Charles's comprehensive plans never accomplished his purpose because his administrative associates were diverted by domestic strife and foreign wars.

The Dominion of New England. The advisers of Charles II finally resorted to a radical scheme to curb the tendency toward self-government which they had detected in Massachusetts and neighboring provinces. In 1684 they secured the revocation of the Massachusetts charter. Two years later they persuaded James II to proclaim the establishment of the Dominion of New England, which in 1688 was extended to include New York and the Jerseys,* under Sir Edmund Andros as royal governor. The creation of the Dominion was represented as a measure of defense against possible military attack by an unfriendly foreign nation, but Americans generally regarded it as a device to impose royal authority on the colonies. The Dominion collapsed when James II was driven from the throne by the "Glorious Revolution" (1688).

PARLIAMENT AND THE EMPIRE

While the Stuarts were failing in their attempts to make royal control of the colonies effective, Parliament was staunchly defending the theory that colonial affairs could be guided through commercial regulation, which was, therefore, of parliamentary concern.

Mercantilism. The English legislators, like other European statesmen, generally accepted the politico-economic theory of *mercantilism,* holding that a nation's prosperity depended upon the amount of precious metals which it could accumulate through favorable trade balances. Colonies, therefore, were believed to be valuable only if they furnished raw materials that the colonizing nation needed, and a market for its finished products, thus enabling the mother country to sell to foreign countries much more than it needed to buy.

The Acts of Trade. The English legislation which embodied the major theories of the mercantilists consisted of a series of trade

* From 1676 to 1701 there were two Jersey colonies.

acts passed in the second half of the seventeenth century and is generally described as the "Old Colonial System." Initially designed to destroy the commerce of Dutch merchants whose ships were on every sea and in every port, they became important in England's effort to win commercial leadership for its empire.

Navigation Act of 1651. Parliament decreed that all goods entering England must be carried in ships owned and in major part manned by British subjects, including colonials, or in ships of the country producing the goods. By this arrangement the Spanish could bring to England their olives and the Portuguese their wines, but Dutch ships carrying such products were barred. The Netherlands retaliated with war (1652–1654) which further enhanced the prestige of England's navy and merchant marine.

Enumerated Commodities Act (1660). In this law most of the provisions of the original Navigation Act were re-enacted and the English colonies were forbidden to export certain commodities such as tobacco, sugar, cotton, indigo, and dyes to any country except England or other English colonies. The list was made to include rice, molasses, and naval stores in 1706, and in 1722 it was further extended to copper, ore, and skins. Since the commodities enumerated were much in demand in England and since the colonies had been established to serve the mother country, English political leaders held that the act was justified.

The Staple Act (1663). Designed to protect English merchants against foreign competition in American markets, this Act provided that all European imports into the American colonies, with a few exceptions, must first be brought into English ports and there be reshipped, after the payment of duty.

The Duty Act (1673). This was an important step toward enforcement of the earlier legislation through the appointment of customs collectors, resident in the colonies but directly responsible to the commissioners of customs in England.

The Enforcement Act of 1696. The American colonies, regarding the Acts of Trade as inconsistent with their rights and destructive of their growing commerce, found many ways to evade them. Customs officials, notably Edward Randolph in Massachusetts (1680), could get slight help in carrying out their duties. As a result, the law of 1696 contained stringent clauses to break up smuggling, requiring that all English and colonial ships be registered, and authorizing customs officials to search ships, wharves, and warehouses and to seize unlawful goods. Admiralty courts to handle enforcement proceedings were established in all the colonies.

Effects of Commercial Regulation. Historians have long debated whether the English restrictions on trade hit the pride rather than the purses of the colonists.

DISADVANTAGES. The colonists insisted that they had a right to dispose of their own produce in ways that they judged to be most advantageous. They strongly resented a policy based on the idea that the colonial establishments existed primarily to serve the colonizing nation. Furthermore, they maintained that the "enumeration" of commodities which must be carried to England before they could be offered for sale in any other ports reduced their profits and hindered their commercial development.

BENEFITS. English merchants and officials of the government argued that the Navigation Acts in their entirety conferred important benefits on the colonial producers and shippers. (1) The British navy could give them better protection against pirates and enemy ships if ship captains followed the trade routes prescribed in the Acts of Trade; (2) the British government paid a bounty to colonial producers for some of the "enumerated commodities" and gave the colonial merchants a monopoly of the English markets for such products as tobacco, tar, and naval stores; (3) colonists who were compelled to buy supplies in the English ports often got the commodities at prices lower than those charged to English consumers. Whatever the economic effect of the Navigation Acts, they served to bind the colonies to each other and to England in ways that helped to defeat Britain's foes in Europe.

THE "WHIG COMPROMISE"

Although the "Glorious Revolution" of 1688 subordinated the Crown to Parliament in England, the victorious Whigs continued their effort to dominate the colonists in America through officials appointed by the King.

Increasing Imperial Control. The determination of the royal ministers to strengthen the bonds of imperial control was revealed in various ways: (1) the frequent use of the royal veto over acts of the colonial legislatures; (2) attempts to regulate certain colonial industries (including wool and iron manufacture) to reduce competition with those of England; (3) the strict regulation of the issuance of colonial currency; (4) the extension of the right of appeal from colonial courts to the Privy Council; and (5) the conversion of chartered colonies to royal provinces. Between 1682 and 1752 eight charters were annulled, and the number of royal officials increased in all the colonies.

Colonial Conflicts with British Officials. While British statesmen insisted that the King in Parliament was the supreme legislative authority for the colonies, the American colonists were equally determined that royal officials should not control their elected assemblies.

THE ROYAL PROVINCE. By 1775 all of the English provinces except Connecticut, Rhode Island, Pennsylvania, Delaware, and Maryland conformed to the royal pattern of government. In each the Crown was represented by a royal governor, advised by a Council, usually named by the Crown, and dependent for his salary on a legislature chosen by the qualified voters of the province. The governors generally appointed the judges of the colonial courts.

ROYAL GOVERNORS VERSUS COLONIAL ASSEMBLIES. The colonial assembly stood as the representative of the people against the encroachments of royal prerogative. There were frequent quarrels between the governors and their assemblies over control of appropriations, provision for frontier defense, enforcement of the Navigation Acts, and payment of the governor's salary.

CUSTOMS AGENTS VERSUS MERCHANTS AND SHIPPERS. Prosperous merchants, like Peter Faneuil and John Hancock, defied the British customs officials and throve on illicit trade. Other merchants, less influential, followed their example; and lawsuits, arising out of alleged violations of the Acts of Trade, were frequent and bitter. There was constant dispute concerning the jurisdiction of the admiralty courts in cases involving trade.

REVIEW QUESTIONS

1. How did the vicissitudes of English politics in the seventeenth century interfere with the establishment of an effective control in the new world?
2. What politico-economic theories were embodied in the Acts of Trade?
3. To what extent did these theories endanger the commercial prosperity of the colonies?

4. What was the purpose of the Dominion of New England? Why was it a failure?
5. By what means did Parliament in the eighteenth century seek to establish a stricter control over the American colonies?
6. Was there any justification for the assumption of financial power by the colonial assemblies?
7. What was the effect in the colonies of the lax enforcement of British commercial regulations?

CHAPTER V

ANGLO-FRENCH STRUGGLE
FOR SUPREMACY

From the Glorious Revolution of 1688 to the Peace of Paris (1763), the development of English America was in large part determined by the contest for power waged by England and France in every part of the world.

THE "GALLIC PERIL"

Early in the eighteenth century royal officials in the colonies, as well as in England, sounded a warning against the danger that French forts and trading posts might encircle the English settlements along the Atlantic coast.

French Policy. The monarchy in France seemed determined to conquer the English colonies and to destroy the institutions which Englishmen were slowly establishing in America.

THE WESTWARD THRUST. From their settlements at Quebec and Montreal on the St. Lawrence, the French during the seventeenth century pushed up the river toward the Great Lakes. Their "empire" was little more than a series of trading posts, missions, and forts strung along the route of the fur traders from the St. Lawrence to Lake Superior.

MARQUETTE AND JOLIET. In 1763 Father Marquette, the adventurous Jesuit missionary, and Louis Joliet, a successful fur trader, managed to "turn the corner" from Lake Michigan to the tributaries of the Mississippi, then sailed southward on that great river to the mouth of the Arkansas.

FRONTENAC AND LA SALLE. Count Frontenac, then governor of New France, realizing the strategic importance of control of the Mississippi, gave strong support to the daring of La Salle. In 1682 La Salle's little band of French and Indians formally claimed the whole

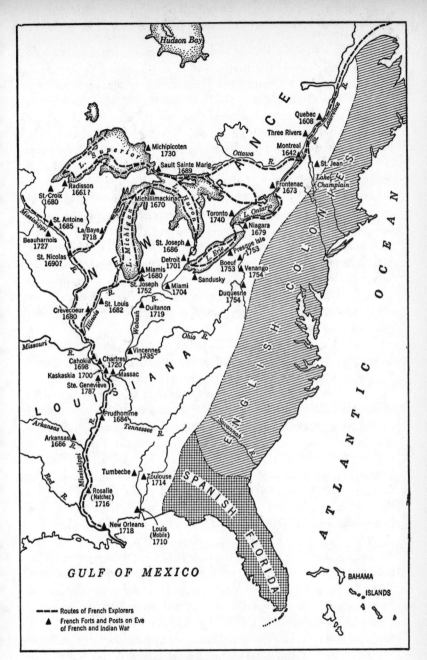

THE ENCIRCLING FRENCH

Mississippi Valley for France and began to erect forts which would bar the English and their Iroquois allies to the east of the River.

Wars to Win a Continent. The military conflict between English and French in America was but one aspect of a world-wide struggle between the two nations that was waged from Canada to the West Indies, on the high seas, and through Europe and Asia. For the English and French colonists in America the important stakes were control of the fur trade, supremacy in the North Atlantic fisheries, and possession of the great Ohio-Mississippi basin.

KING WILLIAM'S WAR (1689–1697). Known in Europe as the War of the League of Augsburg, this war's American phase was marked by raids out of Canada in which the French had the aid of their Indian allies, the Hurons. Settlements at Dover, New Hampshire, and Schenectady (1690) were destroyed. The English took Port Royal in 1690, but failed in a later attempt, with their Iroquois allies, to capture Quebec. Hostilities ended in the inconclusive Treaty of Ryswick (1697), but Huron and Iroquois continued to raid each other's villages.

QUEEN ANNE'S WAR (1702–1713). Starting in Europe because of Louis XIV's desire to place his own candidate on the throne of Spain, Queen Anne's War brought victory to British arms. Though the French in America won the Iroquois away from their close alliance with the English, the province of Acadia was lost to the French (1710). The dispersal of its inhabitants inspired Longfellow in a later generation to write *Evangeline*. On European battlefields the brilliant leadership of the Duke of Marlborough was decisive for the British. By the Treaty of Utrecht (1713) Great Britain secured the Hudson Bay Region, Newfoundland, and Nova Scotia (Acadia). Spain yielded to British merchants a monopoly of the slave trade to Spanish America (Assiento).

A TROUBLED TRUCE. For thirty years after the Treaty of Utrecht the French and English were busy establishing trading posts, building strategic forts, arranging agreements with the Indian tribes most active in the fur trade, and developing their trade routes with the West Indies. In this competition the French were more aggressive.

KING GEORGE'S WAR (1745–1748). Bitter rivalry broke into war first in Europe in the War of the Austrian Succession (1744). There, and in America the conflict was inconclusive. New Englanders captured Louisbourg but it was returned to France by the Treaty of Aix-la-Chapelle. The frontier friction in the colonies continued.

THE FRENCH COLLAPSE

The contest for world dominion reached its climax in the war which was known in Europe as the Seven Years' War. In Asia and America, as well as on the European continent, England finally broke the power of France and her allies.

The French and Indian War (1754–1763). War came to America two years earlier than to Europe and Asia. The bone of contention was control of the Ohio Valley, which stood as a buffer zone between the English settlements along the Alleghenies and the French posts in the Mississippi Valley.

STRENGTH OF THE BELLIGERENTS. The French had several advantages at the outbreak of hostilities: (1) unity of action as a result of royal control over New France; (2) a small but well-disciplined standing army in America; (3) strategic forts in a great arc from Quebec, along the St. Lawrence and the Great Lakes to the Mississippi; (4) powerful Indian allies, especially among the Hurons. Britain's power flowed from (1) a population in its colonies fifteen times as great as that of New France and far more consolidated; (2) control of the seas; (3) vast material resources in America; (4) support from the Iroquois.

BRITISH DIFFICULTIES. At first the French and Indian war went badly for the British. Braddock's regulars, supported by Virginia militiamen under Washington, were put to rout on their expedition against Fort Duquesne. In America, the French captured Fort Oswego, while in Europe Russia, Austria, and Sweden joined France in defeating England's ally, Frederick of Prussia.

WILLIAM PITT'S VICTORIOUS LEADERSHIP. At the low point in British fortunes, William Pitt brought a new spirit into the war. As England's prime minister, he established effective control of military forces and foreign policy and rallied his countrymen with eloquent and patriotic speeches. He stirred the colonists to greater efforts. His friend Horace Walpole enthusiastically wrote: "It is necessary each morning to inquire what victory there is, for fear of missing one."

"TWO WONDERFUL YEARS." In 1758 a colorful army of English, Scots, and Americans, led by Jeffery Amherst and James Wolfe stormed the French fortress of Louisbourg. Later that year John Forbes's troops cut their way across Pennsylvania and blew up Fort Duquesne, erecting Fort Pitt on its ruins. Young General James

Wolfe gave his life on the Plains of Abraham, as his daring soldiers vanquished the gallant Montcalm, who tried in vain to save Quebec for the French Crown. By 1760 Montreal had fallen to the British and the war in America was over.

The Peace of Paris (1763). The nations that signed the peace treaty in Paris accepted the complete victory of English arms.

THE APEX OF BRITISH POWER. Britain ended the influence of France in India. She gave Cuba and the Philippines back to Spain, but received Florida in return. In America the boundaries of her colonies were pushed out to include Canada and all of France's territory east of the Mississippi except New Orleans.

REMNANTS OF FRANCE'S EMPIRE. France was compelled to cede to Spain the port of New Orleans and the rest of Louisiana that lay west of the Mississippi. The French empire in America was reduced to Martinique and Guadeloupe in the West Indies and half of Hispaniola. Off Newfoundland her fishing folk had bases in the little islands of Saint Pierre and Miquelon.

Consequences of Britain's Triumph. The removal of the "Gallic Peril" from North America was a momentous fact for English America. It made the colonies less dependent on Great Britain for military defense, and it opened the eyes of the colonists to many defects in the imperial system.

INTERCOLONIAL CO-OPERATION. The wars with the French had convinced many colonial leaders of the great value of intercolonial co-operation, not only in military matters but also in handling Indian relations and in promoting commercial contacts.

THE ALBANY CONGRESS (1754). Even before the opening clash of the French and Indian War, delegates from seven colonies met in Albany to discuss the possibility of a closer union among the English provinces. The Congress accepted Benjamin Franklin's suggestion that a federation be formed with a federal council chosen by the colonial assemblies and a president-general appointed by the Crown. The Council was to provide for common defense, guide Indian negotiations, and levy taxes for general purposes. The Albany Plan was rejected by the British government and received little support in the colonial assemblies.

RISING PRESTIGE OF COLONIAL LEGISLATURES. The Anglo-French conflict emphasized the growing importance of the colonial legislative bodies, for these local units in the British imperial system maintained their control of the purse, appropriating sums for military expedi-

OWNERSHIP OF THE CONTINENT, 1682-1783

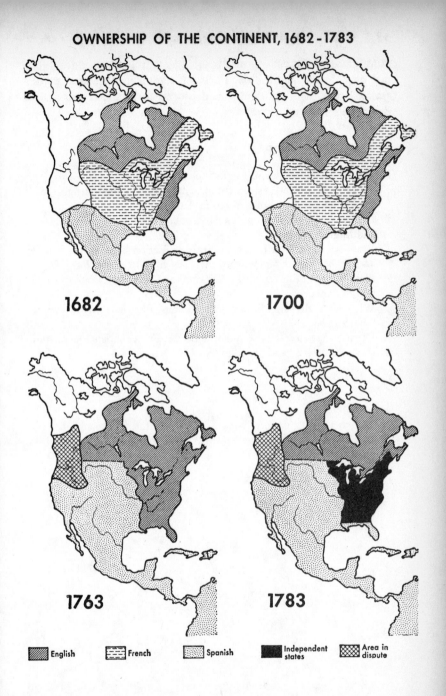

1682

1700

1763

1783

English · French · Spanish · Independent states · Area in dispute

tions, granting supplies to the British forces, and exercising supervision over the colonial militia. Their self-confidence increased as they realized that their militiamen had proved to be the equals of the British regulars.

REVIEW QUESTIONS

1. Compare the French and English colonial systems.
2. What great advantages did the British possess in their struggle with the French for dominance in North America?
3. Explain the effect of European dynastic rivalries upon the French and English colonists.
4. What were the most important areas of friction between the English and French at the outbreak of the French and Indian War?
5. How did the mistakes of the British War Office complicate the situation in America?
6. What was the significance of William Pitt in Anglo-American relations?
7. Discuss the effect of the removal of the French upon the relations between England and her colonies.

Chapter VI

CONFLICT OF INTERESTS
WITHIN THE EMPIRE

The global extent of the British Empire made necessary its careful economic and political reorganization, a task which seemed to be beyond the wisdom of the British statesmen who were close to King and Parliament.

IMPERIAL REORGANIZATION

New problems were complicated by the failure to reconcile conflicting attitudes of policy-makers, so that the result too often was merely confusion.

The Western Frontier. The most pressing problem was that of the new territories, where questions of Indian relations, fur trade, land policy, and political administration had to be solved.

PONTIAC'S UPRISING (1763). The western frontier exploded into war when a chief of the Ottawa tribe formed his followers into a confederacy to drive English settlers out of the Ohio Valley. Though this attempt to block English expansion was soon crushed, it convinced British administrators that a permanent standing army in America was necessary.

PROCLAMATION LINE OF 1763. Four new governments were created by royal edict: Granada in the West Indies, East Florida, West Florida, and Quebec. The proclamation reserved the region between the Alleghenies and the Mississippi from Florida to 50° north latitude for the use of Indian tribes, and ordered the colonists to remain east of a line drawn along the crest of the Alleghenies. Moreover, those who had already settled in the region were forced to withdraw. The promulgation of this line aroused a storm of protest in America from traders, frontier settlers, and land speculators.

The Regulation of Trade. British merchants complained that the American colonists had long evaded the Acts of Trade with impunity, and that colonial merchants had made handsome profits during the French wars by supplying the enemy with foodstuffs and other materials. Parliament was pressed by a powerful mercantile lobby to enforce commercial regulations strictly in the colonies.

The Imperial Budget. Merchants and landlords in Parliament demanded that the burden on British taxpayers be lightened by compelling the colonies to bear a larger share of imperial expenses. Great Britain's debt had doubled between 1756 and 1764, while the cost of maintaining the civil and military establishments in America had increased fivefold after 1748. Although a few of the American colonies had met the requisitions imposed by the British government, most had contributed little to the costs of the French wars.

BRITISH ATTEMPTS TO RAISE REVENUE

For a dozen years after 1763 royal officials and parliamentary leaders were concerned, so far as they manifested any interest in America, with various efforts to secure increasing revenue from the colonies.

Grenville's Policies. George Grenville, the able and conscientious Chancellor of the Exchequer, thought he knew how to help George III solve the financial problems that beset him.

CATERING TO BRITISH MERCHANTS. By enforcing the trade laws scrupulously, Grenville hoped to force the colonies to pay for a larger share of imperial expenses.

Writs of Assistance. These general search warrants, against which James Otis of Boston had made his famous plea in 1761, were used ever more frequently to locate illegal shipments and to collect customs duties that had formerly been lost through smuggling.

The Sugar Act (1764). An enlarged customs service was charged with enforcing the Molasses Act of 1733, imposing almost prohibitive duties on rum, spirits, sugar, and molasses imported into the colonies from foreign sources, which had long been evaded. In 1764 the duty on foreign molasses was slightly reduced, that on refined sugar was increased, and new taxes on wines, silks, and other luxuries were imposed.

The Currency Act (1764). At the solicitation of British creditors, Parliament forbade further issuance of paper money in the colonies, thus preventing colonial debtors from settling their accounts in depreciated currency.

The Stamp Act (1765). Grenville hoped to secure considerable revenue from the law providing that all official and legal documents, newspapers, almanacs, and pamphlets that were circulated in the colonies must bear stamps showing that a tax on them had been paid.

The Quartering Act (1765). An attempt was made to reduce the cost of the military establishment by compelling the colonists to furnish lodging and supplies for British troops if colonial barracks were inadequate.

YIELDING TO COLONIAL PROTESTS. The resistance of the colonists to the Grenville legislation was much more violent than any government official had expected.

Boycotts and Mobs. Aroused by the threat to their lucrative West Indian trade, implicit in the Sugar Act, colonial merchants used nonimportation and nonconsumption agreements, which became more effective after the resentment over the Stamp Act had stirred some colonials to direct action. In Boston, New York, and other ports the more radical element, often organized as the Sons of Liberty, held public demonstrations, terrorized the stamp collectors, and destroyed the stamps.

Retreat from Grenville's Policy. Delegates from nine colonies, who assembled in New York in 1765 to protest the Stamp Act, challenged the right of Parliament to impose any taxes on the American colonies. They asserted that they could be constitutionally taxed only by their own representatives. It was the decline of American trade with Great Britain, however, that persuaded the new Rockingham ministry to repeal the Stamp Act and to reduce the duties imposed by Grenville in 1764. At the same time Parliament reasserted its right to tax the colonies as it saw fit.

The Townshend Program. Charles Townshend, the brilliant but erratic Chancellor of the Exchequer who succeeded Grenville, persuaded Parliament to make a new attempt to secure revenue from America through comprehensive regulation of trade.

THE TOWNSHEND LEGISLATION. In 1767 Parliament passed a Duty Act imposing duties on glass, lead, tea, paper, and painters' colors, to be collected by British commissioners in America. Enforcement of the existing laws was emphasized; for example, the New York Assembly was suspended for refusing to comply with the Quartering Act of 1765. In 1768 the Massachusetts legislature was dissolved for issuing a "circular letter" calling for united resistance to Parliamentary taxation, and the Virginia House of Burgesses was dissolved for endorsing the letter.

COLONIAL PROTESTS. The imposition of the Townshend duties was answered by a strong renewal of nonimportation and nonexportation agreements in the colonies. Violence subsided in favor of argument; but customs officials in Boston, Newport, and New York were roughly handled at times.

THE BOSTON MASSACRE (1770). Two regiments of British troops were quartered in Boston to assure enforcement of the laws. A slight brawl between the "Redcoats" and a street crowd developed into mob action; the British troops unwisely fired at the shouting civilians, killing five and wounding several others.

Lord North and Conciliation. When King George's favorite minister, Lord North, took over the control of governmental policy, he promised to heal the breach that had been developing between the colonies and the mother country.

REPEAL OF TOWNSHEND ACTS. Parliament in 1770 was persuaded to repeal all duties on colonial imports except a small tax on tea.

ORGANIZING THE RADICALS. Lord North's conciliatory attitude strengthened the conservatives in the American colonies, who wished to avoid trouble; but the radicals, who distrusted North, prepared to meet any future infringement of their political and economic rights.

THE BOSTON TEA PARTY. Lord North and his colleagues in 1773 blundered in an attempt to help the British East India Company to sell its surplus tea in America, and thus to save the Company from financial disaster.

The Tea Act of 1773. Parliament relieved the Company of the duty which it had paid on importing tea into England and granted it a monopoly of the transport of tea to America, where it was subject to a small tax and could be sold only by Company agents.

Destruction of Tea. In Boston a crowd, disguised as Indians, boarded the East India Company's ships and dumped the tea into the harbor. Elsewhere the colonies either refused the Company permission to unload its tea or prevented the sale, while the tea spoiled in storage.

Answering Coercion with United Resistance. The decision of the British government to punish Boston for the destruction of the

East India Company's property destroyed the hopes of the moderates both in England and America.

THE INTOLERABLE ACTS. Parliament passed a series of measures to punish the town of Boston and the province of Massachusetts, which were labeled in America the "Intolerable Acts."

Boston Port Bill. The port of Boston was closed to all commerce until the province of Massachusetts had paid for the destroyed tea.

Massachusetts Government Act. The Charter of 1691 was suspended, the members of the Council and other officials were made appointees of the Crown, and town meetings were forbidden to assemble without permission from the royal governor.

The Administration of Justice Act. Any British official, charged with a capital offense in enforcing the law, was granted the right of a trial in England.

The Quartering Act. The province of Massachusetts was ordered to provide lodging and food for British soldiers stationed there.

THE QUEBEC ACT. The area west of the Alleghenies and north of the Ohio River was annexed to the Province of Quebec, to be governed directly by British officials. This act proved distasteful to several colonies which claimed the region.

THE FIRST CONTINENTAL CONGRESS (1774). The colonial response to the Intolerable Acts was the meeting in Philadelphia of the first congress representing colonies moving toward unity. Its members, chosen by Committees of Correspondence, Committees of Safety, and provincial mass meetings from every colony except Georgia, were critical of the conservative view of imperial problems.

Ratification of the Suffolk Resolves. The Continental Congress, after rejecting Joseph Galloway's proposal for a colonial congress which could accept or reject legislation enacted by the British Parliament, endorsed the resolves of Suffolk County, Massachusetts, which declared the Intolerable Acts unconstitutional.

Appeals to Britain. The Continental Congress also sent to Great Britain the "Declaration of Rights and Grievances," asserting the rights of the colonists under the English constitution and demanding a return to the status of 1763. It petitioned the King and appealed directly to the people of Great Britain for redress of political and economic grievances.

The Continental Association. The most important action of the Congress was to urge the American colonies to join in an agreement, "the Association," to boycott both import and export trade with

Great Britain. Detailed methods were worked out for the enforcement of such an agreement in all the colonies.

REVIEW QUESTIONS

1. How did the results of the French and Indian War complicate the problem of British imperial organization?
2. Why was the period after 1763 too late for the formulation of a comprehensive system of imperial control?
3. Would the Americans have been satisfied with a system of taxation imposed by a Parliament in which they had minority representation? Why?
4. Why did the Stamp Act meet with such unexpected and violent opposition?
5. Discuss the significance of the radical patriot in the period from 1763 to 1774.
6. Why did Lord North's attempt to aid the British East India Company culminate in the Boston Tea Party?
7. What were the "Intolerable Acts"?
8. How radical were the members of the First Continental Congress, as judged by the work of the Congress?

Chapter VII

REVOLUTION: POLITICIAL
AND SOCIAL

The American Revolution was more than a severing of the political ties between Great Britain and thirteen of its colonies in North America. It set those colonies on the path which led toward a more democratic society.

THE ROAD TO INDEPENDENCE

Few Americans in 1775 thought that the mounting quarrel with the British government would lead to independence for the English colonies. As "reluctant rebels," they hoped for a modification of imperial regulations that would satisfy their demand for a greater measure of self-government.

The Appeal to Arms. After the adjournment of the First Continental Congress, the radicals among the colonial leaders created Committees of Safety to enforce the nonimport and nonexport features of the Association agreement. Though Lord North's ministry offered a compromise on the issue of taxation, this overture was nullified by Parliament's Restraining Act (March, 1775) designed to destroy New England's commerce.

Lexington and Concord. Before the Second Continental Congress assembled in Philadelphia in the spring of 1775 the Massachusetts minutemen had fought the British regulars at Lexington and Concord. The clashes occurred when General Gage ordered his troops to destroy military stores in the hands of Americans, and to arrest such leaders of the colonists as John Hancock and Samuel Adams.

Siege of Boston. Militia from all the New England provinces promptly surrounded Gage's regiments in Boston, while Massachusetts leaders appealed to all other colonies for aid.

The Second Continental Congress. In response to these appeals the members of the Second Continental Congress, while sending a final "Olive Branch" petition to the King, took steps to raise and equip an army, appointed Washington commander in chief, issued a "Declaration of Causes for Taking up Arms," and began seeking alliances with France and other European nations.

Defeat of the Moderates by Radicals. The movement for political separation from England grew slowly but steadily among Americans.

DELAY IN DECLARING INDEPENDENCE. Fighting in the colonies had been going on more than a year before the Continental Congress decided in favor of independence. There were several reasons for this hesitation: (1) the sentimental attachment of most of the colonists to the mother country; (2) the fear that either anarchy or despotism might take the place of British authority; (3) the hope of some colonial leaders that the English Whigs might offer to abandon the policies against which Americans were in revolt; (4) the reluctance of colonial merchants to lose trade privileges which they enjoyed under the British flag; and (5) the inertia of many colonials and their failure to give specific instructions to their delegates in the Continental Congress.

DEVELOPING DESIRE FOR POLITICAL SEPARATION. The colonists were incensed by the policy of the British government in hiring foreign mercenaries to fight Englishmen in America, and by the attempts of Britain's agents to incite Indian raids against frontier settlements. Press and pulpit agreed with Thomas Paine's argument in his pamphlet *Common Sense* that it was inconsistent to pretend to be loyal to Great Britain, while fighting British troops on American soil. One of the most persuasive arguments for independence was the fact that the colonies needed foreign aid to win, and that aid would come from France if Americans broke their political ties with Great Britain.

The Irrevocable Step. During the spring of 1776 several colonial legislatures instructed their delegations in the Continental Congress to work and vote for independence.

LEE'S RESOLUTIONS. On June 7, 1776, Richard Henry Lee of Virginia moved that "these united colonies are, and of right ought to be free and independent states." The Congress responded by naming a committee—Thomas Jefferson, Benjamin Franklin, John Adams, Roger Sherman, and Robert R. Livingston—to draft a declaration of independence.

THE DECLARATION. Largely the work of Thomas Jefferson, the Declaration of Independence was accepted by the Congress on July 2 and was formally signed by most of the delegates on July 4, 1776. The document falls logically into two parts: first, a preamble containing an admirable statement of the natural rights philosophy, championed by John Locke and the English liberals of the late seventeenth century; and second, a severe indictment of the policy of the British government in America, containing a bill of particular grievances.

THE EFFECT OF THE DECLARATION. The Declaration was designed to strengthen the radical cause in America and to win foreign support for the American rebellion.

Patriots and Loyalists. The patriots now had a definite creed by which they could test the loyalty of their fellow countrymen to the revolutionary movement. The distinction between Whigs and Tories (or Patriots and Loyalists) was, therefore, more sharply defined.

French Aid. The French government, little interested in the quarrel of the colonists with Great Britain, was willing to aid secretly, if the quarrel led to the disruption of the British Empire.

THE SINEWS OF WAR

The realization of independence was a task which required energy and efficiency in the government, as well as victory on the field of battle.

Supporters of the Revolution. Reliable estimates indicate that only one third of the colonial population energetically supported the movement for independence. In the northern colonies this group was recruited from the farmers, mechanics, and petty tradesmen. In the plantation districts it included many of the tidewater planters, who had quarreled with British officials over land and financial policies and who were deeply indebted to British merchants. Along the frontier a majority apparently supported the Revolution.

The Problem of the Loyalists. Probably one third of the people in the colonies actively worked for or favored the British cause.

DEFENDERS OF BRITISH POLICIES. The Loyalists were recruited from: (1) the great landowners in the North; (2) the wealthier merchants; (3) the Crown officials: (4) the Anglican clergy and laity; and (5) the professional classes and others dependent upon wealthy merchants or landlords.

THE PUNISHMENT OF THE LOYALISTS. The state governments created under the impetus of the revolutionary movement dealt severely with the Loyalists. Thousands were imprisoned, sent to detention camps, tarred and feathered, or banished. Many more voluntarily emigrated to Canada or England.

THE CONFISCATION OF LOYALIST PROPERTY. Many of the states confiscated the real estate and personal property of Loyalists. New York, for example, probably got one third as much from the sale of Loyalist property as it collected in taxes during the war years.

Revolutionary Finances. The Continental Congress did not have the power of taxation; therefore, it resorted to various devices to raise revenue.

PAPER MONEY. By 1780 almost $242,000,000 had been issued in Continental bills of credit (paper money). It depreciated rapidly, about half of it finally being redeemed at one fortieth of its face value.

REQUISITIONS ON THE STATES. The requests for specific sums, which the states were inclined to ignore, brought only $6,000,000 in coin into the Continental treasury.

DOMESTIC AND FOREIGN LOANS. Certificates similar to modern bonds were sold through loan offices in the various states. Foreign loans, totalling approximately $8,000,000, were placed in France, Holland, and Spain.

FINANCIAL ADMINISTRATION. After experimenting with several committees and treasury boards, Congress in 1781 selected Robert Morris as superintendent of finance.

The Military Establishment. George Washington, as commander in chief of the Continental armies, had serious difficulties not only in conducting campaigns in the field, but also in persuading the committees of the Continental Congress to permit him to organize an effective fighting force.

THE ARMY. The congressional leaders relied upon the state militias until October, 1776, when they finally yielded to Washington's pleas that a national army be created. The nucleus of Continental troops, however, did not solve such difficulties as the inexperience of militia levies, the lack of competent officers, and the jealousies between the various states over military affairs. Too many of the hardships of the armies were caused by incompetent or negligent officials, bad management, and the refusal of the people to sell food and clothing for depreciated paper money.

THE NAVY. Although American privateers wrought great havoc

among British merchantmen, sending insurance rates soaring, and although John Paul Jones won several naval engagements and for a time terrorized the North Sea, the rebellious colonists had no sea power worthy the name until the French navy came to their aid in 1780. Some two thousand privateers and thirty-four commissioned ships of war constituted the naval force in the early years of the war.

THE DISRUPTION OF BRITAIN'S EMPIRE

In spite of Washington's courageous leadership and the numerous military blunders made by British leaders, it would have taken the Americans a long time to win independence if they had not received aid from France.

The Field of Battle. Few of the British generals were men of military ability. Sir William Howe and his brother, Admiral Richard Howe, for example, were unsympathetic with the purposes of the Tory ministry in England and failed to conduct a vigorous campaign in 1776.

THE BATTLE OF LONG ISLAND. On August 27, 1776, the British defeated Putnam's division of Washington's army on Brooklyn Heights, but failed to prevent the escape of the American forces across the East River. Howe leisurely followed Washington northward, content to fight light skirmishes at Harlem Heights and White Plains.

THE RETREAT ACROSS NEW JERSEY. The Americans were compelled to abandon Forts Washington and Lee on the Hudson River. Washington fell back across New Jersey, while Howe distributed certificates of loyalty to many who were willing to desert the patriot cause.

TRENTON AND PRINCETON. On Christmas night, 1776, Washington surprised the Hessians at Trenton, taking a thousand prisoners. Outwitting Cornwallis, he defeated the British at Princeton and then went into winter quarters at Morristown.

THE BRITISH SCHEME TO SEVER THE COLONIES (1777). The British tried in 1777 to carry out their plan to capture the state of New York and split the colonies. Three British armies were to meet near Albany: General John Burgoyne was to move southward from Canada via Lake Champlain; Colonel Barry St. Leger was to advance eastward from Lake Ontario by way of the Mohawk Valley; and General Howe was to send an army north from the port of New York.

Howe's Attack on Philadelphia. Howe failed to carry out his part in this campaign. Instead, he decided to capture Philadelphia. Having overcome Washington's stubborn resistance at Brandywine Creek and Germantown, he quartered his army comfortably in the Pennsylvania capital, while the Americans went into winter quarters at Valley Forge.

St. Leger's Failure. American troops under General Nicholas Herkimer managed to check St. Leger's advance eastward at Fort Stanwix, and the British commander abandoned his attempt to reach Albany.

Burgoyne's Surrender at Saratoga. Burgoyne had fought his way south of Fort Ticonderoga, while embattled farmers from New York and New England harassed his regiments and broke his lines of communication. On October 17, 1777, he surrendered to General Horatio Gates at Saratoga the five thousand men who remained in his army.

The Turning Point: The French Alliance. The news of the American victory at Saratoga induced the French government to sign a formal treaty of alliance with the United States.

Secret French Aid. American agents—Silas Deane, Arthur Lee, and Benjamin Franklin—had found the French willing to give secret aid to the revolting American colonies. Ammunition, clothing, shoes, and other supplies went from France in a steady stream during 1777.

Franklin and Beaumarchais. In the versatile Beaumarchais, playwright and amateur diplomat, who urged the French foreign minister, Vergennes, to form an alliance with the United States, Franklin had an invaluable ally in promoting the cause of his country in France.

The Treaty of 1778. On February 6, 1778, France recognized the independence of the United States and signed a military alliance and a treaty of commerce with the new nation. Spain and Holland followed France in declaring war on Great Britain.

The Military Stalemate. The Franco-American alliance caused Great Britain to redouble its efforts, but neither side for three years was able to deliver a decisive blow.

Washington's Strategy. After the terrible winter (1777–1778) at Valley Forge, where his troops suffered from lack of food, clothing, and military supplies, Washington took the offensive, fighting the indecisive Battle of Monmouth (June, 1778), and then occupying a strong position in the highlands of the Hudson. For three years he fought no important engagement.

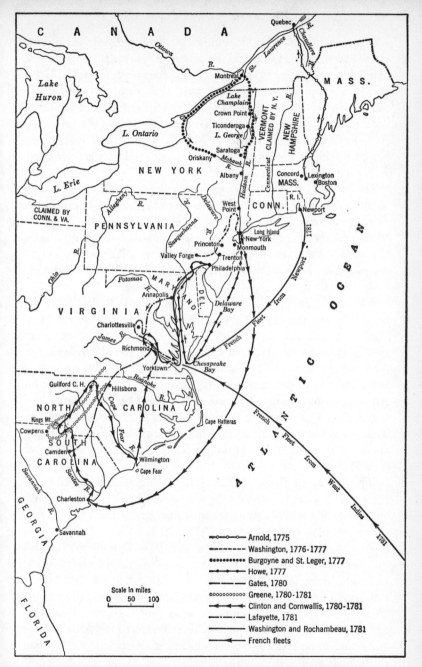

THE REVOLUTIONARY WAR ON THE ATLANTIC SEABOARD

Legend:

- ⊸⊸⊸ Arnold, 1775
- –––––– Washington, 1776-1777
- ●●●●●● Burgoyne and St. Leger, 1777
- ●●●●●● Howe, 1777
- –– –– Gates, 1780
- ○○○○○ Greene, 1780-1781
- ◄—◄— Clinton and Cornwallis, 1780-1781
- —·—·— Lafayette, 1781
- ———— Washington and Rochambeau, 1781
- ◄——— French fleets

THE WAR IN THE SOUTH. Hoping to win support from the Loyalists of the Carolinas and Georgia, the British transferred the war to the South. They captured Savannah (1778), occupied Charleston (1780), and won a brilliant victory under Lord Cornwallis at Camden. Although the British managed to hold the seaport towns in the Carolinas, they were unable to make their control effective because of the work of such guerrilla leaders as Marion, Sumter, and Pickens. At King's Mountain the British and their Loyalist allies were decisively defeated by the Carolina frontiersmen.

THE WEST (1777–1779). The gloomy years of British campaigning in the South were relieved by the success of American troops in the Northwest. Virginia's outpost, Kentucky, had been ravaged by Indian raids, and the Kentuckians were eager to strike the British posts northwest of the Ohio River. George Rogers Clark led American troops against Kaskaskia and Vincennes (1778–1779) and broke British power in that area.

YORKTOWN. Meanwhile in the East, American leaders were depressed by the attempt of General Benedict Arnold to deliver West Point to the enemy for a price. They were, however, heartened in 1780 by the success of Lafayette, who had volunteered his services to the American cause, in persuading Louis XVI to send Rochambeau and a French army to America. Additional French troops came with Admiral de Grasse in 1781. Late in the summer Washington and Rochambeau, co-operating with de Grasse, struck a decisive blow. They trapped Cornwallis at Yorktown, Virginia, after his Carolina and Virginia campaigns, and compelled him to surrender on October 19, 1781.

The Peace of Paris (1783). The closing years of the Revolutionary War were marked by the vigorous efforts of Great Britain's enemies to destroy British power in Europe and America.

PROPOSALS OF THE ROCKINGHAM MINISTRY. By 1782 England was eager to make peace with her American colonies in order to deal with her European foes. As the Rockingham Whigs took over political leadership from Lord North's ministry, they found their country at war with France, Spain, and Holland, and facing the possibility of trouble with the Armed Neutrality of the North (Russia, Denmark, and Sweden). In this situation Rockingham urged the Americans to agree to a settlement on the basis of imperial relations as they had existed before 1763.

DIPLOMATIC NEGOTIATIONS. The Americans who represented the

Continental Congress in Paris (Benjamin Franklin, John Adams, and John Jay), refused to consider any peace proposals unless Britain first recognized the independence of the American colonies. Although France supported the American demand for independence, the French government agreed with Spain that the new nation should be limited to the region east of the Alleghenies. Aware of French policy, the Americans, in violation of the terms of the French alliance, went forward with negotiations with the British, ignoring the French foreign minister, Vergennes.

THE TREATY. Great Britain in the final treaty recognized the independence of the United States and its claim to the territory westward to the Mississippi and from the Canadian border to Florida (which was returned to Spain by a separate treaty). The Americans were confirmed in their fishing privileges off Newfoundland and adjacent territories. From the United States the British secured pledges that: (1) no legal impediments would be placed in the way of British creditors seeking to collect sums owed by American debtors; (2) Congress would urge the states to restore to the Loyalists their confiscated property; and (3) navigation of the Mississippi from source to mouth would be open to subjects of Great Britain and the United States.

REVIEW QUESTIONS

1. How do you explain the fact that fifteen months elapsed after the outbreak of hostilities before the Declaration of Independence was adopted?
2. What was the source of the political theory contained in the Declaration of Independence?
3. Discuss the statement that the American Revolution was the work of an energetic minority.
4. What effect did the Declaration of Independence have upon the efforts of Americans to secure an alliance with France?
5. Explain the attitude of the British Whigs toward the American Revolution.
6. Discuss the relations of England, France, Holland, and Spain during the Revolutionary War.
7. What factors complicated the peace negotiations for the American representatives?
8. How do you account for the success of the American negotiators in their discussions with the British delegates in 1782–1783?

Chapter VIII

ESTABLISHING THE NEW NATION

Before their independence had been officially recognized in the peace treaty of 1783, the American people had started the long and difficult task of building a new government.

UNITED IN NAME ONLY

Although the conflict with Great Britain had forced the thirteen colonies into united action, most Americans still regarded themselves as citizens of the particular state in which they lived. Nationalism was to grow slowly.

The Independent States. The overwhelming majority of the three and a quarter million people in the United States were tillers of the soil, living within two hundred miles of the Atlantic Coast from Maine to Georgia.

THE RESULTS OF THE REVOLUTION. The social consequences of the Revolution were quite as important as the political. The economic upheaval of war was either directly or indirectly responsible for: (1) the enrichment of certain groups through privateering, speculation, and profiteering in army contracts; (2) the stimulation of manufacturing; (3) the tendency to break up large estates into small holdings; (4) the revision of laws of inheritance; (5) the removal of British restraints on industry and commerce; (6) the growth of the spirit of religious toleration.

THE STATE GOVERNMENTS. In May, 1776, the Continental Congress recommended that the colonies set up new frameworks of government. Already New Hampshire and South Carolina had adopted new constitutions. These written fundamental laws were in some instances merely revisions of the colonial charters. They generally stressed the "natural rights" philosophy of the period, contained an elaborate "bill of rights" guaranteeing the rights of the governed, and provided for a division of powers among executive, legislative, and judicial departments. Most provided for relatively strong legislative and weak executive branches. Control of government continued to be in the hands of the property holders.

The Articles of Confederation. As soon as the colonies decided to take the path to independence, the Continental Congress, which served as an intercolonial steering committee for the war, authorized a committee of thirteen to draft articles of more permanent union.

PRECEDENTS FOR INTERCOLONIAL UNION. The colonies had made tentative ventures in federation in the New England Confederation (1643), the Albany Congress (1754), and the First and Second Continental Congresses.

STRUCTURE OF THE CONFEDERATION GOVERNMENT. The Articles of Confederation provided for a league between sovereign states. Each state had one vote in the federal Congress, and unanimous consent was necessary for amendment. Congress was empowered to borrow money, regulate the currency, establish a postal service, regulate Indian affairs, and settle interstate disputes. The Confederation Congress assumed all financial obligations of the Continental Congress.

DEFECTS OF THE POLITICAL SYSTEM. The failure of the fundamental law to confer adequate powers upon Congress became apparent soon after the Articles were ratified. The serious omissions were: absence of a federal executive and judiciary; the failure to give Congress power to levy taxes, to regulate foreign and interstate commerce, or to enforce its laws.

Creation of a National Domain. Ratification of the Articles of Confederation, which were drafted in 1777, was not secured until 1781. Maryland refused to agree to the federal arrangement until the states claiming western lands consented to cede them to the central government.

WESTERN LAND CLAIMS. The colonial charters of six of the states had granted them indefinite westward extension. When the Revolution wiped out the Proclamation Line of 1763 and the Quebec Act of 1774, these states sought to extend their authority to the Mississippi. New York, basing its claims on treaties with the Iroquois, led the way in surrendering its western claims in 1780. The other states followed suit. All cessions were not concluded, however, until 1802.

ORDINANCE OF 1784. As soon as the Treaty of Paris had confirmed the title of the United States to the region between the Alleghenies and the Mississippi, the Confederation Congress adopted an ordinance, proposed by Thomas Jefferson, guaranteeing that the territory should be divided into states, each to be admitted into the Union as soon as it had sufficient population.

LAND ORDINANCE OF 1785. Eager to secure revenue from the public domain, Congress authorized surveys to divide the land northwest of the Ohio River into townships and each township into thirty-six sections of 640 acres to be sold at public auction for a minimum price of $1.00 per acre. Section 16 in each township was set aside for the support of public schools.

THE NORTHWEST ORDINANCE (1787). As a result of the effective lobbying of Manasseh Cutler, who had secured a grant of five million acres for his company, Congress provided for the government of the Northwest Territory. There were to be not less than three nor more than five states carved out of the area northwest of the Ohio River, as soon as population warranted such division. Meanwhile, territorial administration was provided for. The Ordinance banned slavery from the Northwest Territory, made provision for public education, and guaranteed to the settlers civil rights and freedom of religion. The states were to be admitted to the Union as full equals of the original states.

Facing the European Powers. The American government under the Articles of Confederation was often scorned by the statesmen of Europe. It required skill and patience to win favorable treatment from Great Britain and Spain.

HOSTILITY OF GREAT BRITAIN. In violation of the treaty of 1783 the British refused to abandon the fur-trading posts that their officials had established along the southern shores of the Great Lakes. In justification of its refusal to cede the western posts, the British government claimed that the United States had failed to indemnify the Loyalists and to pay the debts owed the British merchants. Britain refused to open her West Indian ports to American ships or to send a diplomatic representative to the United States.

SPAIN'S WESTERN INTRIGUES. From their colonies in the Floridas, the Spanish tried to win the western frontiersmen away from their loyalty to the new American nation and to bring them under the Spanish flag. Since Spain held the mouth of the Mississippi, and thus controlled the commerce of the great river which was indispensable to American settlers, the Spanish threat was serious. John Jay, as Secretary of Foreign Affairs, tried to settle these difficulties with the Spanish diplomat Diegode de Garquodi; but their agreement of

1786, by which the United States would have relinquished her claims to navigation on the Mississippi in return for commercial privileges, was not ratified by Congress, and the settlers in Kentucky and Tennessee threatened either to leave the Union or to wage war on the Spaniards.

Economic Changes. The critical years from 1783 to 1789 were filled with economic problems created by the postwar deflation and the need for reorganization of business activity in all the states.

GOVERNMENTAL FINANCES. Without the power of taxation Congress had to rely upon requisitions, which the state governments frequently failed to meet. The national debt steadily increased, while sums were borrowed to pay current operating expenses. So low was the credit of the government in 1786 that domestic and foreign loans could be obtained only with great difficulty and at exorbitant interest rates. Congress could not induce the states to grant it adequate sources of revenue.

COMMERCIAL DEPRESSION. The fictitious prosperity of the war years collapsed within a year of the treaty of peace.

Foreign Trade. The heavy importation of European goods immediately after the war drained specie from the country. The means of replenishing it were lacking, because Great Britain barred American ships and many American products from her ports in the West Indies and in Europe. Spain and France also closed their West Indian islands to American ships.

Interstate Commerce. Lack of a uniform currency handicapped the merchants interested in domestic markets. Paper money was uncertain in value and easily counterfeited. Specie was scarce and made up of bewildering varieties of coins. Between the states tariff barriers hindered rather than encouraged trade.

The Debtor's Plight. With the depression came a fall in prices and a rise in the value of money. Debtors found themselves unable to secure funds with which to pay interest, settle mortgages, or meet tax assessments. In Rhode Island they secured control of the government and cheapened the currency with large issues of paper money.

Shays' Rebellion. In Massachusetts the debtor classes failed to protect their interests through legislation. Under the leadership of Daniel Shays and others, some farmers and mechanics staged riots in 1786, known as Shays' Rebellion. They attempted to prevent the courts from issuing judgments against debtors and from conducting proceedings that might lead to the foreclosure of mortgages. When troops were dispatched to the troubled towns, the revolt quickly collapsed; but it had aroused the country to a realization of the dangers of weak government.

PLANNING A CENTRAL GOVERNMENT

The political, economic, and diplomatic difficulties of the nation in the critical, postwar years contributed to the strength of the movement to revise the Articles of Confederation.

Campaign for a New Basic Law. The refusal of the state legislatures to approve amendments designed to give Congress larger powers over commerce and finance persuaded many that an entirely new basis for the central government would have to be written.

ECONOMIC INTERESTS. Among the propertied classes the desire for governmental reform was voiced by such groups as: (1) holders of government securities, who desired a government able to meet its financial obligations; (2) manufacturers, who desired a monopoly of the home market behind adequate tariff walls; (3) merchants, who desired a government powerful enough to secure commercial concessions from foreign governments; (4) financiers, who feared the inflationist tendencies of the state legislatures; and (5) land speculators, who demanded that the government quiet Indian troubles on the frontier and open their lands to settlement.

PRELIMINARY CONFERENCES. In March, 1785, committees from the Maryland and Virginia legislatures met at Mount Vernon to discuss navigation of the Potomac River and Chesapeake Bay. They decided to invite all the states to confer on commercial problems of the Confederation. The Annapolis Conference (1786) was attended by delegates from five states, who adopted a report by Alexander Hamilton, calling a convention of all the states to meet at Philadelphia in May, 1787, to devise an adequate constitution for the federal government. The Confederation Congress tardily endorsed this call.

THE PHILADELPHIA CONVENTION OF 1787. The fifty-five men who attended the meetings at Philadelphia were among the "first characters" of the country. They were aware of the problems that needed to be solved, and most of them had already distinguished themselves in the service of their respective states.

Leadership of the Convention. There was a general high level of competence in the Convention, and certain delegates revealed special ability in the discussions. From Virginia came James Madison and George Mason; from Pennsylvania came Benjamin Franklin, James Wilson, and Gouverneur Morris. Other leaders were John Dickinson of Delaware, Luther Martin of Maryland, William Paterson of New Jersey, the Pinckneys of South Carolina, and Alexander Hamilton of New York. George Washington presided. Absent were the "radical" revolutionary leaders, Thomas Paine, Patrick Henry, and Samuel Adams. Jefferson, then Minister to France, was in Paris.

Plans for Governmental Reorganization. The delegates were agreed that, whatever the form of federal government they devised, it must be able to levy taxes, regulate commerce, protect private property, pay the national debt, coin and borrow money, and provide for the national defense. Two major plans were presented:

VIRGINIA PLAN (LARGE STATES)	NEW JERSEY PLAN (SMALL STATES)
This provided for a two-house legislature with representation apportioned to the states on the basis of population. The lower house was to be elected by popular vote and the upper house by the lower house.	This provided for a single legislative body in which the states would be equally represented.
The executive was to be chosen by the national legislature.	The executive was to consist of a committee chosen by the national legislature.
The judiciary of a supreme court and the inferior courts was to be chosen by the legislature.	A national judiciary was created.
The national legislature was to have power to pass upon the constitutionality of laws enacted by the states.	The national legislature was to have power to compel the states to obey its laws, and all acts of the national legislature were binding upon the courts of the various states.

The "Connecticut Compromise." The delegates from Connecticut suggested that the differences between the large and small states could be reconciled by creating a national legislature in which the lower house, or House of Representatives, would represent the states according to population, and the upper house, the Senate, would be based upon equal representation of the states.

The Constitution. The delegates at Philadelphia concluded their secret deliberations on September 17, 1787, and promptly made public the document which had been put into literary form by Gouverneur Morris.

THE STRUCTURE OF GOVERNMENT. The completed document, known as the Constitution, provided for a government of three branches: executive, legislative, and judicial. The President was to be named by a college of electors chosen in such fashion as the legislatures of the various states might direct. The Congress was to consist of two houses: the lower composed of popularly elected representatives apportioned according to population (including three fifths of the slaves) and elected by persons eligible to vote for the most numerous branch of the state legislature; the upper composed of two senators from each state, elected by the state legislature. The judiciary was to consist of a Supreme Court and such inferior courts as Congress might create, the judges to be appointed for life or good behavior by the President with the consent of the Senate.

THE ROLE OF THE STATES. Under the Confederation the states had been able to ignore or defy the measures of Congress with impunity. This defect was remedied in the Constitution by obliging the officials of every state to take an oath to support the Constitution, by pledging the state courts to recognize the Constitution and the laws and treaties made under it as the supreme law, and by bringing the citizens of every state under the direct authority of the United States through the federal courts.

THE POWERS OF CONGRESS. The strength of the new federal government was implicit in the extensive powers, exclusive and concurrent, which were given to Congress. Particularly important were the powers of taxation, regulation of interstate and foreign commerce, control of the army and navy, and supervision of foreign relations.

The Campaign for Ratification. There was immediate and widespread opposition to the new Constitution, necessitating an intensive campaign in many states in order to secure its ratification by the special conventions to which it was submitted.

CRITICISM OF THE CONSTITUTION. Among the numerous arguments against ratification of the work of the Philadelphia Convention the following were significant: (1) the proposed government had been secretly fashioned by the representatives of a propertied aristocracy; (2) the delegates had gone beyond their powers in writing a new framework of government; (3) the document contained no "bill of rights" to protect the citizen against tyranny; (4) the powers granted to the central government were so great that the states would be reduced to dependent provinces; and (5) the rights of property and not the rights of man were emphasized in the Constitution.

THE STRENGTH OF THE FEDERALISTS. The Federalists, as the supporters of the proposed Constitution were called, were able to mobilize powerful forces in the struggle over ratification. They enlisted most of the business and financial interests, the professional classes, and the influential newspaper editors. They had money, they were well organized, and they were led by some of the most prominent men in the country, including Alexander Hamilton, James Madison, and John Jay, authors of *The Federalist,* a collection of essays providing the most cogent analysis and defense of the Constitution.

BITTERNESS OF THE CONTEST. Delaware, Connecticut, New Jersey, and Georgia ratified promptly, while the victories for ratification in Maryland and South Carolina were large. But in Massachusetts, Virginia, Pennsylvania, and New York the fight was close and bitter. North Carolina and Rhode Island had not yet ratified when Washington took the oath of office in 1789.

REVIEW QUESTIONS

1. What is the importance of the Articles of Confederation in United States constitutional history?
2. Explain how the federal government came into the possession of a national domain.
3. Discuss the economic conditions of the country during the "critical years."
4. What groups were eager for the continued inflation of the currency? Why?
5. Why was Shays' Rebellion an important factor in spurring on the leaders who demanded a new framework of government?
6. What economic interests were represented at the Philadelphia Convention of 1787?
7. By what device were the provisions of the Constitution made binding upon the citizens of the various states?
8. Who opposed the ratification of the Constitution in New England? In New York? In Virginia?

Chapter IX

THE FEDERALIST REGIME

Fortunately for the American people, the testing of the Constitution during the early years of the Republic was conducted by officials who were determined to see the new government succeed and who demonstrated that a stronger central government was workable.

ESTABLISHING PRECEDENTS

As unanimously elected first President of the United States, George Washington faced many problems which American leaders had never before had to solve. His decisions set precedents for his successors in the presidential office, and in some cases determined the course of governmental business that is followed to this day.

Starting the Governmental Machine. The first Congress under the Constitution (1789) speedily turned to the task of providing necessary legislation to establish departments, create federal courts, and provide federal revenues.

Congressional Legislation. Having decided to secure most of its revenues through customs duties, Congress passed the Tariff Act of 1789. It created the executive departments of State, Treasury, and War, and other administrative offices. In the Judiciary Act (1789) it provided for the organization of the Supreme Court and the erection of federal circuit and district courts.

Constitutional Amendments. From more than one hundred proposed amendments to the Constitution, Congress selected twelve that had been especially urged by the states and referred them to the state legislatures for possible ratification. Ten of these had been ratified by 1791. Known as the "Bill of Rights," they protect the citizen against the possibility of tyranny or infringement of civil rights by the federal government. (Judicial interpretation of the

Fourteenth Amendment has extended some of these restrictions on power to state and local governments as well.)

PRESIDENTIAL APPOINTMENTS. President Washington named Thomas Jefferson, Secretary of State; Alexander Hamilton, Secretary of the Treasury, and Henry Knox, Secretary of War. For his legal adviser, he chose Edmund Randolph, making him Attorney General. John Jay was appointed first Chief Justice of the Supreme Court.

The Hamiltonian System. So brilliantly did young Alexander Hamilton handle the financial problems of the new government that his proposals concerning the public credit came to be known as the Hamiltonian System. More than any other leader of his generation he realized the need to create strong economic support for the nation.

HANDLING THE NATIONAL DEBT. Hamilton's plans concerning the debt, which had been incurred during the Revolution and the Confederation period, called for the payment at full face value of all federal obligations, those held by foreigners as well as by citizens of the United States. With considerable help from Thomas Jefferson, he also persuaded Congress to assume payment of the debts of the several states, on the ground that such indebtedness had been incurred chiefly during the Revolution by colonies fighting in a common cause.

PROVIDING THE REVENUE. Through systematic refunding and payment of the national debt, Hamilton managed to reduce interest charges and thus effected a saving for the government. To secure the income needed to meet expenses, he outlined in detail proposals for: (1) customs duties on imports; (2) excise taxes on domestic goods, especially distilled liquor; and (3) procedures for the rapid sale of lands in the national domain.

ESTABLISHING THE BANK AND THE CURRENCY. In order to establish a sound currency, Hamilton suggested, and Congress after a long and sometimes bitter debate passed, a bill for the chartering of a Bank of the United States (1791), with $10,000,000 capital stock, one fifth subscribed by the government and the remainder by the public. (Jefferson, arguing that such an act was unconstitutional, advocated a strict interpretation of the Constitution; but Hamilton's theory that the government had "implied" powers, as well as delegated ones, prevailed.) The Bank was authorized to issue notes, that is, paper money, backed in part by gold and silver but chiefly by government bonds. The Mint Act of 1792 followed Hamilton's proposal that the government mint gold and silver coins at a ratio of fifteen to one. The gold dollar, which was the standard, was to contain 24 ¾ grains of pure gold.

ENACTING A PROTECTIVE TARIFF. Hamilton's *Report on Manufactures* strongly urged the adoption of a protective tariff to aid American industries and to stimulate new industries which might develop under favorable conditions. The Revenue Act of 1792, however, failed to place the rates as high as he desired them to be.

Emerging Political Parties.

The battle in Congress over such issues as the assumption of state debts, the Bank, the excise duties, and the protective tariff emphasized the growing differences between the financial and commercial interests on one side and the farmers and mechanics on the other.

OPPOSING FACTIONS. The political distinctions between the groups which tended to support Hamilton (Federalist) and those which backed Jefferson (Democratic-Republican) may be summarized as follows:

FEDERALIST	DEMOCRATIC-REPUBLICAN
a. Merchants, bankers, manufacturers, and holders of large estates.	a. Farmers, artisans, mechanics, and small shopkeepers.
b. Strong in the commercial towns and the tidewater plantations of the South.	b. Strong in the farming communities of the North and the frontier sections of the South.
c. Supporting a broad interpretation of the Constitution to give the central government more power.	c. Inclined toward a strict interpretation of the Constitution to limit the powers of the central government.
d. Friendly toward Great Britain in foreign policies.	d. Friendly toward France in foreign policies.

FIRST TRIALS OF STRENGTH. The Hamiltonian system went before the electorate for endorsement in the election of 1792, at a time when business activity was declining. Though Washington was re-elected, the Federalists lost control of the House of Representatives and had a majority of only twenty-three electoral votes for their Vice-President, John Adams.

Protecting the Frontier.

One of the most pressing problems for the Washington administration was the control of the Indian tribes along the frontier. While some tribes were conciliatory, others continued to raid border settlements in their attempt to halt the westward advance of the whites.

DEVELOPMENT OF POLITICAL PARTIES

	1796	1800	1804	1808	1812	1816	1820	1824	1828	1832
Elected President	Adams Fe 71	Jefferson D-R 73	Jefferson D-R 162	Madison D-R 122	Madison D-R 128	Monroe D-R 183	Monroe D-R 231	J. Q. Adams NP(A) 84	Jackson JD 178	Jackson JD 219
Alabama							D-R 3	NP(J) 5	JD 5	JD 7
Connecticut	Fe 9	Fe 9	Fe 9	Fe 9	Fu 9	Fe 9	D-R 9	NP(A) 8	NR 8	NR 8
Delaware	Fe 3	Fe 3	Fe 3	Fe 3	Fu 4	Fe 3	D-R 4	NP(A) 1 Ca(C) 2	NR 3	NR 3
Georgia	D-R 4	D-R 4	D-R 6	D-R 6	D-R 8	D-R 8	D-R 8	Ca(C) 9	JD 9	JD 11
Illinois							D-R 9	NP(A) 1 NP(J) 2	JD 3	JD 5
Indiana						D-R 3	D-R 3	NP(J) 5	JD 5	JD 9
Kentucky	D-R 4	D-R 4	D-R 8	D-R 7	D-R 12	D-R 12	D-R 12	NP(C) 14	JD 14	NR 15
Louisiana					D-R 3	D-R 3	D-R 3	NP(A) 2 NP(J) 3	JD 5	JD 5
Maine							D-R 3	NP(A) 9	NR 8 JD 1	JD 10
Maryland	Fe 7 D-R 4	Fe 5 D-R 5	Fe 2 D-R 9	Fe 2 D-R 9	Fu 5 D-R 6	D-R 8	D-R 11	*	NR 6 JD 5	NR 5 JD 3
Massachusetts	Fe 16	Fe 16	D-R 19	Fe 19	Fu 22	Fe 22	D-R 15	NP(A) 15	NR 15	NR 14
Mississippi							D-R 2	NP(J) 3	JD 3	JD 4
Missouri							D-R 3	NP(C) 3	JD 3	JD 4
New Hampshire	Fe 6	Fe 6	D-R 7	Fe 7	Fu 8	D-R 8	D-R 7 IR 1	NP(A) 8	NR 8	JD 7
New Jersey	Fe 7	Fe 7	D-R 8	D-R 8	Fu 8	D-R 8	D-R 8	NP(J) 8	NR 8	JD 8
New York	Fe 12	D-R 12	D-R 19	D-R 13 IR 6	Fu 29	D-R 29	D-R 29	**	NR 16, JD 20	JD 42
North Carolina	Fe 1 D-R 11	Fe 4 D-R 8	D-R 14	Fe 3 D-R 11	D-R 15	D-R 15	D-R 15	NP(J) 15	JD 15	JD 15
Ohio			D-R 3	D-R 3	D-R 7	D-R 8	D-R 8	NP(C) 16	JD 16	JD 21
Pennsylvania	Fe 1 D-R 14	Fe 7 D-R 8	D-R 20	D-R 20	D-R 25	D-R 25	D-R 24	NP(J) 28	JD 28	JD 30
Rhode Island	Fe 4	Fe 4	D-R 4	Fe 4	Fu 4	D-R 4	D-R 4	NP(A) 4	NR 4	NR 4
South Carolina	D-R 8	D-R 8	D-R 10	D-R 10	D-R 11	D-R 11	D-R 11	NP(J) 11	JD 11	ID(F) 11
Tennessee	D-R 3	D-R 3	D-R 5	D-R 5	D-R 8	D-R 8	D-R 7	NP(J) 11	JD 11	JD 15
Vermont	Fe 4	Fe 4	D-R 6	D-R 6	D-R 8	D-R 8	D-R 8	NP(A) 7	NR 7	A-M 7
Virginia	Fe 1 D-R 20	D-R 21	D-R 24	D-R 24	D-R 25	D-R 25	D-R 25	Ca(C) 24	JD 24	JD 23
Losing Parties Votes	Jefferson D-R 68	Adams Fe 65	Pinckney Fe 14	Pinckney Fe 47 / G. Clinton IR 6	DeW Clinton Fu 89	R. King Fe 34	J. Q. Adams IR 1	Jackson NP(J) 99 / Crawford Ca(C) 41 / Clay NP(C) 37 / †	J. Q. Adams NR 83	Clay NR 49 / Floyd ID(F) 11 / Wirt A-M 7

Fe = Federalist
D-R = Democratic-Republican
IR = Independent Republican
Fu = Fusion
NP(J) = No Party (Jackson)
NP(A) = No Party (J. Q. Adams)
Ca(C) = Caucus (Crawford)
NP(C) = No Party (Clay)
JD = Jacksonian Democrats
NR = National Republicans
ID (F) = Independent Democratic (Floyd)
A-M = Anti-Masonic

*NP(A) 3, NP(J) 7, Ca(C) 1   **NP(A) 26, NP(J) 1, Ca(C) 5, NP(C) 4
† Inasmuch as no candidate received majority of electoral vote, J. Q. Adams was chosen president by House of Representatives

RESTLESSNESS IN THE NORTHWEST TERRITORY. British influence at the fur-trading posts along the Great Lakes was not conducive to peaceful relations between American settlers and the tribes that still roamed over the Northwest Territory. General Arthur St. Clair, trying to open up the region south of Lake Erie, suffered a severe defeat in 1791, but three years later "Mad Anthony" Wayne led federal troops to a decisive victory in the Battle of Fallen Timbers. In 1795 Wayne persuaded the leading chiefs to sign the Treaty of Greenville, whereby the Indians surrendered their claims to most of the area that is now Ohio.

THE SOUTHWEST. Spanish agents operating out of Florida and Louisiana kept the Creeks, Cherokees, and Seminoles on the warpath, though they had reached agreements with representatives of the United States in 1791. The attacks on border settlements increased the desire of Washington's advisers to reach a settlement with Spain.

TESTING DIPLOMATIC STRENGTH

The diplomatic difficulties of the American republic were greatly aggravated during Washington's second administration by the war in Europe between the French Republic and a coalition of powers headed by Great Britain.

Defending Neutrality. Though the terms of the treaty of alliance (1778) with France provided that Americans would aid the French in protecting the French West Indies against British attack, the Washington administration refused to be drawn into Europe's wars.

GENÊT'S MISSION. Edmond Genêt, rash minister of the French Republic, landed in Charleston early in April, 1793. Calling upon the United States to fulfill the terms of its alliance with France, he started to fit out privateers, enlist seamen, and carry out belligerent plans before he had presented his credentials.

WASHINGTON'S PROCLAMATION. Though President Washington received Genêt, he issued a proclamation forbidding United States citizens to "take part in any hostilities on land or sea with any of the belligerent powers." When Genêt failed to abide by the Proclamation, the administration demanded that he be recalled. Hamilton defended this policy on the ground that the alliance of 1778 was with the government of Louis XVI, not with the revolutionary forces, and that it pledged the United States to defend France in the West Indies, not to support a France proclaiming a general war against European monarchies.

Jay's Diplomatic Mission. In order to secure a settlement of American grievances against Great Britain, Washington sent John Jay on a special mission to London.

BRITISH OFFENSES. The catalogue of Britain's offenses included: (1) her refusal to evacuate the northwestern fur posts under the terms of the treaty of 1783; (2) her policy of keeping the Indian tribes hostile to the American government; (3) her failure to open her West Indian ports freely to American commerce; (4) her seizures of United States ships trading with the French West Indies; and (5) her impressment of American seamen into British naval service.

UNSATISFACTORY NEGOTIATIONS. Jay's discussions with Lord Grenville resulted in a treaty in which the British (1) agreed to surrender the fur posts by June, 1796; (2) opened their East Indian ports to the United States; and (3) made meager concessions in the West Indian trade. No mention was made of the seizure of American ships or the impressment of seamen. The question of debts owed to British creditors by Americans and of American claims for damages to shipping were referred to arbitral commissions. The treaty was so unpopular that the Federalists had difficulty both in getting the Senate to ratify it and in getting the House to provide appropriations to carry it out.

PINCKNEY'S TREATY. The negotiations of Jay at London convinced the Spanish government that the United States and Great Britain were drawing closer together, and Spain hastened to settle her differences with the United States. Thomas Pinckney in October, 1795, negotiated the Treaty of San Lorenzo whereby Spain (1) recognized the 31st parallel as the boundary of Florida; (2) promised to restrain the Indians from attacking United States borders; and granted the United States free navigation of the Mississippi with the right of deposit at New Orleans free of duty.

Controversy with France. The news of the Jay Treaty aroused intense indignation in Paris, where the American representative, James Monroe, had been trying to establish more friendly relations.

THE XYZ AFFAIR. The French government refused to permit Charles C. Pinckney, who succeeded Monroe in Paris (1797), to remain on French soil. President Adams finally sent John Marshall (Federalist) and Elbridge Gerry (Republican) to join Pinckney

(Federalist). This commission was waited upon by three agents of the French foreign minister, Talleyrand (X, Y, and Z), who demanded a bribe to secure a favorable treaty with France.

THE UNDECLARED WAR (1798). News of the insult to the American commissioners stirred the country to war fever. Harbors were fortified, frigates built, the army enlarged, Washington called to chief command. During 1798 more than eighty French armed vessels were seized by United States privateers and warships.

THE CONVENTION OF 1800. Neither the French Directory nor President Adams wanted war. A new commission (William Vans Murray, Oliver Ellsworth, and William R. Davies) was appointed and reached France in 1800. Napoleon, now in power, signed a convention permitting the United States to abrogate the treaty of alliance of 1778 and providing for the regulation of commerce and maritime relations between the two nations.

THE DECLINE OF THE FEDERALISTS

While American diplomats were slowly winning recognition for the United States in the family of nations, political events at home were weakening the strength of the Federalists and transferring power to the groups who accepted the leadership of Thomas Jefferson.

The Rising Jeffersonians. In 1793 Jefferson resigned from Washington's cabinet and began to organize the voters who were hostile to the Federalist program, into the political party which at first was called Democratic-Republican.

THE WHISKEY REBELLION (1794). When the farmers of western Pennsylvania, who distilled their grain and sold the liquor, revolted against the payment of Hamilton's excise tax, the Jeffersonians criticized the government's part in the affair at every point. They argued (1) that the excise was an unnecessarily burdensome tax imposed on the farmers for the benefit of the capitalists; and (2) that the government had magnified a local riot into an assault on the nation's security by sending troops to quell the disturbance.

RESENTMENT OVER THE JAY TREATY. The Republicans were quick to denounce what they considered the Federalists' policy of yielding to Great Britain. Jefferson's newspaper supporters pictured the Jay treaty as an alliance with England, which had alienated America's real friend, France.

THE ADAMS-HAMILTON FEUD. Although Adams defeated Jefferson by three votes in the electoral college in 1796, there was serious dissension in the Federalist party. The followers of Hamilton, including Pickering, Wolcott, and McHenry in Adams' cabinet, were hostile to the President and sought to minimize his leadership in the party.

THE ALIEN AND SEDITION LAWS (1798). During the war fever of 1798 the Federalists passed a series of laws which became a boomerang against them. (Since the laws were based on the theory that they were a wartime necessity, the peaceful settlement with France removed the reason for their enactment.) The laws were: (1) a Naturalization Act requiring all aliens to live fourteen years in the country before they could become citizens; (2) Alien Acts giving the President power to remove from the country any alien deemed dangerous to the country; and (3) a Sedition Act providing for the punishment with fines or imprisonment of persons conspiring to oppose the execution of the laws or publishing false and malicious writings concerning the President or the government. The Republicans immediately condemned this legislation.

THE KENTUCKY AND VIRGINIA RESOLUTIONS. The Kentucky Resolutions, written by Jefferson, and the Virginia Resolutions, prepared by Madison, declared that the alien and sedition laws of 1798 were void and of no effect, because they violated the Constitution. The resolutions, claiming that the states could prevent the federal government from exercising unwarranted powers, became campaign material for the Jeffersonians.

The Political Revolution of 1800. The presidential campaign was bitterly contested by the Federalists, torn with factional strife, and the Democratic-Republicans, ably led by Jefferson.

RESULT IN THE ELECTORAL COLLEGE. The electioneering brought unprecedented numbers to the polls, as Jefferson waged a campaign to "get out the vote." Adams carried New England, New Jersey, Delaware, and parts of Maryland and North Carolina. He had sixty-five electoral votes to seventy-three for Jefferson.

THE BURR INTRIGUE. Since all the Republican electors had voted for both Jefferson and Burr, the two were tied in the electoral vote. The election was thus thrown into the House, where certain Federalist leaders connived with Burr to attempt to prevent the election of Jefferson. Thirty-six ballots were required before Jefferson was elected President and Burr, Vice-President. The Twelfth Amendment, ratified in 1804, changed the method of electing the President and thus prevented the recurrence of the tie of 1800.

THE SIGNIFICANCE OF JEFFERSON'S ELECTION. The election of Jefferson was more than the substitution of a Republican administration for a Federalist one. It meant the repudiation of government by "the rich, the well-born, and the able" and the triumph of the theory that government could safely be entrusted to the mass of the people who were being educated in democracy.

REVIEW QUESTIONS

1. Discuss the justice and practicability of Hamilton's plan for establishing the credit of the United States on a sound basis.
2. What was the nature and purpose of the First Bank of the United States?
3. What were the important issues between the Federalists and the Republicans (1793–1799)?
4. Why was the United States on the verge of war with Great Britain in 1794? How was it averted?
5. Explain Spain's reasons for meeting Pinckney's demands in 1795. What were the chief provisions of the Treaty of San Lorenzo?
6. What was the significance of the Whiskey Rebellion? Why were such extensive arrangements made to suppress the riots?
7. How did the Alien and Sedition laws weaken the Federalist party?
8. What were the reasons for the dissension within the Federalist ranks, 1796–1800?
9. Discuss the significance of the election of 1800.

Chapter X

THE JEFFERSONIANS

Though the followers of Thomas Jefferson were more inclined than the Federalists to trust the judgment of the American people in political matters, there was little that could be called "radical" in their philosophy or their program. Many of the Federalist precedents were scrupulously followed.

PROSPERITY AND PEACE

Though the Federalists had insisted that Jefferson's election would inaugurate a turbulent era, the first four years of Republican rule were tranquil and relatively prosperous.

Presidential Leadership. Thomas Jefferson avoided the aristocratic tone which had been set up by his predecessors, but more than either Washington or John Adams he used the power of the presidential office to make sure that his program would be put into effect.

PARTY SOLIDARITY. Jefferson's followers, who had begun to call themselves simply Republicans, were well organized as a political party when he entered the White House.

Cabinet Members. James Madison, Jefferson's close friend and political disciple, was named Secretary of State; and Albert Gallatin, who had rallied western Pennsylvania for Jefferson, became Secretary of the Treasury. Both accepted the doctrine that the first responsibility of the new administration was the "encouragement of agriculture and of commerce as its handmaid."

The Patronage. Determined that there should be harmony in his administration, Jefferson appointed no Federalist to high office. He removed some who had been appointed by Washington and John Adams, complaining that few died and none resigned, and whenever he had a vacancy to fill, he named a Republican.

FINANCIAL RETRENCHMENT. Gallatin in the Treasury Department co-operated with Jefferson in a program of economy. Under their leadership the financial policy included: (1) the repeal of the internal revenue taxes; (2) retrenchment in military and diplomatic expenditures; (3) strict accounting in the expenditure of all appropriations; (4) rapid reduction of the principal of the national debt. Gallatin's plan to cut naval expenditures was halted by the Tripolitan War (1802–1805) to punish the Barbary states of North Africa for their plundering of American commerce.

RESTRAINING THE JUDICIARY. The Republicans, regarding the federal judiciary as the stronghold of Federalism, were hostile to the growing power of the courts and their Federalist judges. The Judiciary Act of 1801, which had created new judicial posts, was repealed. Impeachment proceedings were launched against several Federalist judges. John Pickering of the Federal District Court in New Hampshire was removed; Samuel Chase, justice of the Supreme Court was impeached, but acquitted.

The Louisiana Purchase. Jefferson's first administration was notable for the extension of the United States national domain to the Rocky Mountains.

AMERICAN INTEREST IN LOUISIANA. Expansionists looked upon the territory west of the Mississippi as an area for future growth of the United States. Its possession was important in determining control of the Mississippi Valley, a control which vitally affected the commerce of 50,000 Americans in the valleys of the Ohio and the Tennessee. The news that Louisiana had been ceded by Spain to France alarmed Jefferson, who feared that the port of New Orleans might be closed.

NAPOLEON'S COLONIAL SCHEME. Spain's cession of Louisiana to France by the secret Treaty of San Ildefonso (1800) was part of Napoleon's plan to re-create the French colonial empire in America. His plans did not materialize; and in 1802, as he saw the possibility of renewal of war with Great Britain, he was ready to sell the entire province at the moment that Jefferson was trying to purchase the port of New Orleans.

THE TREATY OF CESSION (1803). Congress appropriated $2,000,000 for the acquisition of New Orleans and named Monroe to join Robert R. Livingston in Paris. On May 2, 1803, a treaty was signed whereby the United States secured the province of Louisiana for $14,500,000.

THE TERRITORY OF ORLEANS. Although Jefferson doubted the constitutionality of the purchase, he put aside his scruples and asked

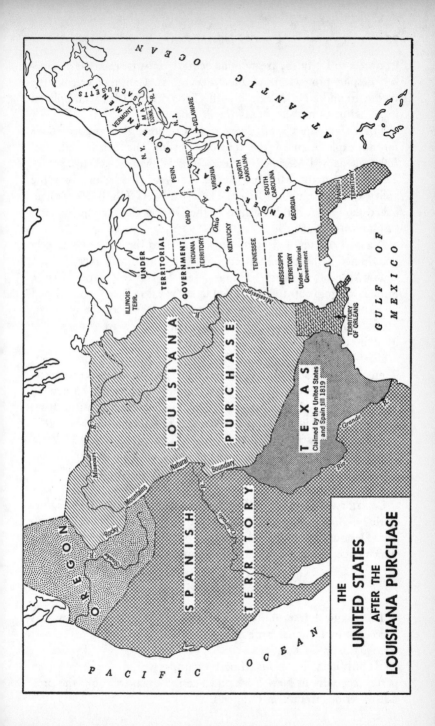

THE
UNITED STATES
AFTER THE
LOUISIANA PURCHASE

Congress to ratify the treaty. The acquisition was immensely popular, despite protests from some Federalists. Congress erected the region around New Orleans into the Territory of Orleans and placed its government in the hands of the President.

THE LEWIS AND CLARK EXPEDITION. Congress appropriated funds for an exploration of the territory beyond the Mississippi, and Jefferson named Meriwether Lewis and William Clark to lead an expedition up the Missouri, across the great divide and into the valley of the Columbia River. These explorers (1804–1806) established the best American claims to the Oregon Country in the later dispute with England.

Naval Policies. Jefferson's attitude toward the navy was largely determined by his desire for economy in governmental expenditures.

THE "MOSQUITO FLEET." He proposed the construction of a large number of gunboats to be manned by a "naval militia," which could be hastily recruited when danger threatened. Many of the gunboats proved to be unseaworthy, but nine of them were sent to the Mediterranean in 1805.

THE WAR WITH TRIPOLI. The unscrupulous rulers of Algiers, Tunis, and Tripoli had long preyed upon Mediterranean commerce, offering to spare the ships of those countries which paid them an annual tribute. Jefferson determined to put an end to the humiliating system by a show of force. An American squadron between 1802 and 1805 successfully challenged these Barbary pirates, and Bainbridge, Somers, and Decatur, with the aid of William Eaton, American consul in Tunis, finally secured a treaty providing for "peace without tribute."

COMMODORE DECATUR. With the outbreak of war in 1812, the Barbary corsairs once more challenged the United States. Commodore Decatur, sent to the African coast in 1815, finally dictated terms which ended for a long period the payment of ransom or tribute.

PARTY BATTLES

The political tranquility of Jefferson's first administration was succeeded by factional strife and political intrigue during his second term in the presidency.

Republican Factions. Local quarrels within the Republican party, especially in New York and Pennsylvania, were but the prelude to serious trouble in Congress.

JOHN RANDOLPH OF ROANOKE. This contentious Virginian, angered because Jefferson had pursued a conciliatory policy toward the Federalists, led a small group of anti-administration Republicans in the House.

DISPUTE OVER WEST FLORIDA. Randolph crossed swords with Jefferson over the West Florida controversy. The President insisted that the boundaries of Louisiana included the Spanish province of West Florida, but while he was trying to force Spain to admit his claim, he was urging Congress to grant him $2,000,000 to buy the province. Randolph bitterly attacked the President's proposal (see p. 80).

THE YAZOO CONTROVERSY. Randolph was more successful in his opposition to Jefferson's plan to handle the Yazoo land claims. When Georgia ceded her western claims to the federal government, the United States inherited numerous law suits filed by purchasers of land from Yazoo land companies, whose original grants had been annulled by the Georgia legislature on the ground that they had been fraudulent. Jefferson favored an appropriation of public land to satisfy bona fide purchasers from the Yazoo companies. For ten years Randolph and his supporters blocked all settlement.

Federalist Intrigues. The New England Federalists, aware that the center of political power had shifted to the South and West, doubted the value of maintaining the Union.

THE COALITION WITH BURR. In the hope of joining New England and New York in an Eastern confederacy, the "die-hard" Federalists supported Burr for governor of New York in 1804. Their plot was defeated, however, through Hamilton's influence in the Federalist party. The unfortunate sequel for Hamilton was the fatal duel with Burr. For Burr the sequel was his romantic plotting in the West which terminated in his trial for treason in 1807. Though he was acquitted, his political career ended.

THE ESSEX JUNTO. The inner council of New England Federalists, known as the Essex Junto, even deliberated upon the possibility of a union with Canada in order to escape from policies framed by Southern planters and Western farmers.

THE PERILS OF NEUTRALITY

As Napoleon strove to overcome Great Britain and her allies and to control all Europe, the United States vainly struggled to maintain her maritime rights as a neutral.

British Maritime Policies. British mercantile interests became alarmed at the rapid growth of American commerce and shipping after the termination of the Peace of Amiens (1803), when Europe had once more been plunged into war.

THE ESSEX DECISION (1805). This interpretation of the Rule of 1756 (a rule which forbade belligerents to open to neutrals trade routes which were closed in peacetime) was aimed at the American carrying trade. It held that a neutral ship laden with enemy goods, destined ultimately for an enemy port, could not change the character of the voyage by landing in a neutral port and making a pretense of transshipping the goods. American ships loading in French or Spanish West Indies with goods destined for France or Spain could not make the shipment a neutral one by breaking the voyage at an American port.

ORDERS IN COUNCIL. Taking full advantage of her superior sea power, Great Britain issued several orders which crippled the neutral traders quite as much as the enemy. The Fox Blockade (April, 1806) closed the ports of Northern Europe from the mouth of the Elbe to Brest; an Order in Council (January, 1807) forbade coastwise trade between ports under the control of France or its allies; and an order of November, 1807, blockaded all European ports from which the British flag was excluded and forced neutrals to trade with the Continent through Great Britain.

IMPRESSMENT OF SEAMEN. Great Britain persisted in her attempts to apprehend deserters from the British navy and merchant marine by stopping and searching American ships and removing suspected seamen. A flagrant example was the case of the *Chesapeake* (1807).

Napoleonic Retaliation. The British policy was the occasion for retaliatory decrees issued by Napoleon, which seriously hindered neutral carrying trade. The Berlin Decree (November, 1806) forbade all commerce with the British Isles and ordered the seizure of ships coming from England or her colonies to ports under French control. The Milan Decree (December, 1807) declared that all ships which paid a tax to the British government or obeyed British Orders in Council were "good prize." By subsequent decrees, Bayonne (1808), Rambouillet (1810), and Trianon (1810), Napoleon sequestered American vessels in French ports and confiscated their cargoes.

Jefferson's Peaceful Coercion. The warfare of orders and decrees seriously injured, though it did not ruin, the American carrying trade. Jefferson was convinced that some form of economic boycott would bring the belligerents to the point of honoring American neutrality.

NONIMPORTATION ACTS (1806–1807). These measures excluded important British manufactures from United States ports.

THE EMBARGO (1807). The failure of Monroe and William Pinkney to secure a satisfactory treaty with Great Britain in the spring of 1807, the *Chesapeake* affair, and the new Orders in Council persuaded Congress to place an embargo on all foreign commerce of the United States. It remained in effect until March, 1809, arousing more protests from the merchants of New England than from the commercial classes in Great Britain and France. Difficulties of enforcement prevented the embargo from being completely effective.

NONINTERCOURSE WITH GREAT BRITAIN AND FRANCE (1809). Fearful that civil strife might ensue if the embargo was continued, Congress repealed the act and opened United States commerce with all the world except Great Britain and France.

Madison's Diplomacy. James Madison, who succeeded Thomas Jefferson in the presidency in 1809, hoped to negotiate a way out of the commercial impasse.

THE ERSKINE FIASCO. David Erskine, British minister at Washington, persuaded Madison and his Secretary of State, Robert Smith, that Great Britain would rescind her orders if the United States would reopen trade. Accordingly the President proclaimed resumption of commercial relations with Great Britain only to discover that Erskine had not stated all of the conditions demanded by the British ministry.

MACON'S BILL NO. 2. Congress with Madison's approval, passed a bill, submitted by Nathaniel Macon, which reopened trade with both France and Great Britain (1810), but stated that if either nation would cease "to violate the neutral commerce of the United States," nonintercourse would be resumed against the other Power.

REVIVAL OF NONINTERCOURSE AGAINST GREAT BRITAIN. Napoleon responded to Macon's Bill by announcing his intention of repealing his decrees. Thereupon Madison proclaimed nonintercourse with Great Britain unless she revoked her Orders.

THE SECOND WAR WITH BRITAIN

The accumulation of grievances against Great Britain forced Madison to adopt a war policy in 1812, but none of the important differences between the two countries was settled as a result of the conflict.

Causes of the War of 1812. The demand for war came not from New England shipping interests, but primarily from aggressive frontiersmen of the West and planters of the South.

THE INFLUENCE OF NAPOLEONIC WARS. Several aspects of the struggle between Great Britain and France strengthened the war factions. If the commercial interests were content to evade British and French regulations in the hope of extraordinary profits, many Americans deeply resented (1) the insolent diplomatic attitude of the British ministry; (2) the confiscation of American cargoes and interference with American trade; (3) the impressment of American seamen into the British navy.

THE "WAR HAWKS." Along the frontier the expansionists were eager to acquire territory. In the Northwest the "war hawks" championed a conflict with England as a means of enabling them to realize such ambitions as: (1) the disruption of the understanding between the Canadians and the Indians which menaced the Western settlements; (2) the control of the British fur trade; (3) the conquest of Canada. In the South and Southwest, the "war hawks" were attracted by the possibility of securing Florida from Spain, now an ally of Great Britain.

TECUMSEH'S CONFEDERACY. The attempt of the Shawnee chief Tecumseh and his brother Tenskwatawa to unite the Indians from the Great Lakes to the Gulf in opposition to the encroachments of the white man convinced the Westerners that British influence was responsible for their troubles. When William Henry Harrison's troops, who defeated the Indian forces at Tippecanoe (1811), reported that the Indians had English guns and ammunition, the frontier was aflame with war enthusiasm.

The Field of Battle. The insistence of the war party in Congress, led by Henry Clay of Kentucky, John C. Calhoun of South Carolina, Felix Grundy of Tennessee, and Peter B. Porter of western New York, finally compelled Madison to send in a war message in June, 1812.

LACK OF PREPAREDNESS. The country was utterly unprepared for war. The army was small, poorly equipped, and handicapped by incompetent leaders. The state militia proved generally unreliable. Financial disorder followed the failure to recharter the Bank of the United States (1811), and the government's credit collapsed during the war.

THE OFFENSIVE AGAINST CANADA (1812–1813). The first attack on Canada was a failure. Hull surrendered Detroit; Smythe and Van Rensselaer failed at Niagara; Dearborn never crossed the border in his attack on Montreal. In 1813, however, Perry's victory on Lake Erie and Harrison's invasion of Canada recovered the Northwest.

THE WAR ON THE SEA. In the first six months of the war American frigates forced five British ships to strike their colors and American privateers took three hundred British merchantmen as prizes. But superior sea power finally enabled the British to blockade the chief ports of the United States and cripple her commerce.

THE FRUSTRATION OF THE BRITISH OFFENSIVE (1814). The elaborate plans of the British government to win the war in 1814 failed. At Niagara, Jacob Brown stopped Drummond's invasion; on Lake Champlain, MacDonough won a naval victory which compelled Prevost, the British commander, to retreat to Canada; Washington was taken by the British under Ross, but the resistance of Fort McHenry prevented Ross's troops from entering Baltimore; in the Southwest Andrew Jackson's frontiersmen repulsed Pakenham's British regulars in their assault on New Orleans, the battle being fought actually after the treaty of peace had been signed in Ghent, Belgium.

THE HARTFORD CONVENTION. Opposition to the War of 1812 was widespread in New England. The states refused to furnish militia for the Canadian campaigns; the financial interests boycotted the government's efforts to sell bonds to finance the war; the farmers and merchants supplied British armies in Canada with meat and grain. In October, 1814, Massachusetts Federalists called a convention at which Connecticut, Rhode Island, Vermont, and New Hampshire were represented. This gathering at Hartford finally published a report recommending constitutional amendments (1) to omit slaves from the census on which representation was based; (2) to require a two-thirds vote of Congress to admit new states, impose commercial restrictions, or declare war; (3) to limit the President to a single term and prohibit the election of two persons in succession from the same state. Thus the dying Federalist party expressed its hostility to the Southern and Western supporters of Jeffersonian doctrines.

The Peace of Ghent. The negotiations which resulted in the Treaty of Ghent were powerfully influenced by the course of Great Britain's struggle with Napoleon as well as by the events in America.

EXTREME BRITISH DEMANDS. The British envoys at Ghent were instructed in August, 1814, to demand (1) cession to Canada of land in Maine and northern New York; (2) British control of the Great Lakes; (3) exclusion of American ships from the Newfoundland fisheries; (4) the creation of a northwestern state for the Indians south of the Great Lakes.

SUCCESS OF THE AMERICAN DELEGATES. The ability of the American representatives—Gallatin, J. Q. Adams, Clay, Bayard, and Russell—was great, but their diplomatic cards would have been poor had not the trend of events at the Congress of Vienna alarmed the British ministry, and the news of MacDonough's victory and Prevost's retreat changed its attitude.

TERMS OF THE TREATY. The treaty as finally signed provided merely for the cessation of hostilities and a return to conditions before the war. Such questions as boundaries and fisheries were referred to commissions for future adjustment. No mention was made of impressment, neutral rights, illegal blockades, or the right of search.

THE MOOD OF THE NATION. Although the war accomplished little toward the settlement of grievances against Great Britain which had caused the conflict, its effect on both Great Britain and the United States was salutary. Never again was the United States treated with that contempt which the British had shown before 1812; no longer were American political affairs completely dominated by the trend of European events; the disruptive forces of sectionalism and particularism for the moment gave way before the spirit of national self-sufficiency which the war years had engendered.

REVIEW QUESTIONS

1. Compare Secretary Gallatin's financial program with that of Alexander Hamilton.
2. Why did the Federalist party oppose the acquisition of Louisiana?
3. What was the nature of Jefferson's policy of peaceful coercion? Did it have a fair trial in the embargo?
4. Why were the "war hawks" so eager for war with Great Britain?
5. Explain New England's opposition to "Mr. Madison's War."
6. How do you explain the failure of the United States to conquer Canada?
7. What was the influence of the European situation upon the course of the negotiations at Ghent?
8. To what extent did the peace treaty settle the points at issue in the war?

Chapter XI

THE RISING NATIONAL SPIRIT

In the years immediately following the Treaty of Ghent most Americans seemed to be united in pride of country and in devotion to a common national purpose rather than to sectional interests. The mood, however, lasted less than a decade. The growth of national unity was a slow and, at times, a painful process for those whose first loyalty was to their particular regions of the country.

STRENGTHENING THE NATIONAL DEFENSE

The most obvious lesson of the War of 1812 had been the weakness of the defenses of the nation and the need for more adequate protection against possible foes along the nation's borders or across the sea.

An Enlarged Military Establishment. Congress made provision for a standing army of 10,000 men, and the President named Jacob Brown and Andrew Jackson, with the rank of major general, to command the Northern and Southern departments. Coastal defenses were improved, the coast guard was enlarged, and new warships were built. Congress became much more generous in appropriations for preparedness against war.

Protection of the Frontier. One important feature of the plans of the nationalistic leaders was the protection of the country's outposts along the frontiers of settlement.

SUPPRESSING INDIAN UNREST. Harrison's victories in the Northwest during the War of 1812 were followed by several treaties whereby the northern tribes permitted lands in Michigan, Indiana, and Illinois to be opened to settlement. In the Southwest the Seminoles in Florida joined the dispossessed Creeks in harassing border settlements and precipitated the First Seminole War (1817–18), which Andrew Jackson waged with vigor and success.

THE ACQUISITION OF FLORIDA. Jackson's zeal in prosecuting the Seminole War caused him to invade Florida and seize Spanish forts. Secretary of State Adams used the occasion as a pretext to demand that Spain control the Florida Indians or sell the province. Fearful that he could no longer hold the colony, King Ferdinand of Spain sold Florida (1819) on condition that the United States government assume claims of American citizens against Spain up to $5,000,000.

ANGLO-AMERICAN CONVENTION OF 1818. American interests along the northwestern border were safeguarded in an agreement with the British government providing: (1) that the northern boundary of the United States west of the Lake of the Woods was the 49th parallel to the Rockies; (2) that the Oregon Country was to be held in joint occupation for ten years.

Nationalist Legislation. Many representatives in Congress responded to the demand that the nation promote the economic well-being of its citizens by improving transportation, establishing a sound banking system, and assisting manufacturers to meet competition from Europe.

PROGRAM OF INTERNAL IMPROVEMENTS. The growing population in the trans-Allegheny region, dependent upon the Mississippi and its tributaries for an outlet for its produce, demanded that the federal government undertake turnpike and canal projects in order to improve transportation facilities and lower freight costs on bulky commodities. The National or Cumberland Road was completed to Wheeling on the Ohio.

The Bonus Bill of 1817. Despite sectional rivalries and states' rights prejudices, Congress passed a bill, proposed by John C. Calhoun, to set aside the bonus ($1,500,000) to be paid to the government by the Bank and devote it to a comprehensive program of internal improvements. Madison's constitutional scruples against internal improvements at national expense caused him to veto the bill.

State Projects. The funds devoted to roads and canals came largely from state appropriations and private capital. New York started to dig the Erie Canal in 1817; Pennsylvania aided turnpike companies and canal promoters, as did New Jersey, Maryland, and Virginia.

CENTRALIZED FINANCE. A major problem for the nationalists was that of establishing a financial system which would insure a sound currency.

Inflationary Banking. After Congress failed to recharter the Bank of the United States (1811), state-chartered banks increased rapidly, from 88 in 1811 to 246 in 1816. Only in Massachusetts was there any effective restraint on the quantity of bank notes which these banks might issue. By 1816 currency in circulation was twice as large as it had been five years earlier.

Second Bank of the United States. To curb unsound banking practices and to check further inflation of the currency, Calhoun and Clay joined in securing a congressional charter for a Second Bank of the United States (1816). One fifth of its capital stock was subscribed by the federal government, while more than 31,000 citizens subscribed for four fifths. Through the issue of its own notes, the Bank managed to compel state banks to limit their issues and to maintain those issues at full face value.

ECONOMIC INDEPENDENCE. The experiences of the War of 1812 had reinforced the sentiment that American producers needed protection against foreign competitors.

Demand for Protection. Manufacturing in New England and the Middle Atlantic States had grown rapidly behind the protective barriers of embargo (1807–1809) and war (1812–1814). The probable "dumping" of British exports in American ports caused manufacturers to demand that they be protected by a high tariff in their home market. They were joined by growers of hemp in Kentucky and by sheep raisers in Ohio, New York, and Vermont.

The Tariff of 1816. Protectionists, who had a direct interest in keeping out foreign imports, received aid in Congress from some Southerners, led by Calhoun, who believed that the United States should make itself economically independent of Europe. In the tariff of 1816 they put high duties on woolen and cotton goods. No cotton imports were to be valued at less than twenty-five cents per yard. By this principle of "minimal valuation" coarse cotton fabrics were kept out of the country, and the American market fell into the hands of New England's cotton manufacturers.

A SPOKESMAN FOR NATIONALISM

The Supreme Court decisions reached while John Marshall was chief justice heartened the politicians of the nationalistic school and aroused resentment among older Jeffersonians, who cherished the states' rights philosophy of the Kentucky and Virginia Resolutions.

Influence of John Marshall. During the period that he was chief justice, Marshall wrote 519 of the Court's 1,106 opinions. A staunch Federalist, he used the power of the federal judiciary to foster nationalism, to protect the rights of property owners, and to curb the radical tendencies of the state legislatures. His decisions convinced many of his fellow citizens that the Constitution was not a mere compact among sovereign states.

The Prestige of the Federal Judiciary. The regime of Marshall firmly established the doctrine of judicial review and made the Supreme Court the arbiter in all disputes regarding the functioning of the American constitutional system.

In MARBURY v. MADISON (1803) the Court refused to permit Congress to define the functions and jurisdiction of the federal judiciary if such definition conflicted with the Court's interpretation of the Constitution.

In FLETCHER v. PECK (1810) the Court declared an act of the Georgia legislature unconstitutional because it conflicted with the Court's interpretation of the constitutional guarantee of the sanctity of contracts.

In MARTIN v. HUNTER'S LESSEE (1816) the Court maintained its right to review decisions of the state courts in cases where such decisions were challenged on the ground of conflict with the federal Constitution.

The Power of the Federal Government. In its review of state and federal legislation the Court accepted the doctrine of "implied powers" and used it with great consistency in enabling the national government to exercise powers which the Constitution seemed to grant only by implication.

In McCULLOCH v. MARYLAND (1819) the Court upheld the constitutionality of the act chartering the Second Bank of the United States and denied the right of the states to restrict the Bank's activity by taxing it.

In GIBBONS v. OGDEN (1824) Marshall wrote a far-reaching decision which denounced state interference with interstate commerce and presented an interpretation of congressional powers so broad that the national legislature could control a large part of intrastate as well as interstate and foreign commerce.

The Protection of Property. Fearful that the democratic state legislatures would resort to radical economic policies, Marshall scrutinized carefully legislation which seemed hostile to the property interests.

In Dartmouth College v. Woodward (1819) the Court held that the pre-Revolutionary charter of Dartmouth College was a contract and therefore could not be changed by the state of New Hampshire against the will of the College.

In Craig v. Missouri (1830) the Court refused to permit the state of Missouri to evade the constitutional prohibition against bills of credit, thus protecting the creditor class against inflation.

THE ERA OF GOOD FEELING

As the Republicans under Madison became converts to the nationalism of Washington and Hamilton, Federalist opposition completely collapsed. In 1820 James Monroe was re-elected president with only one dissenting vote in the electoral college.

The Monroe Doctrine. The nationalism of the "Era of Good Feeling" was expressed in foreign policy by the presidential message known as the Monroe Doctrine.

The European Background. At the Congress of Verona (1822) the representatives of the Quadruple Alliance, sponsored by Prince Metternich of Austria, considered a plan to restore to King Ferdinand of Spain the Spanish colonies in America which had lately revolted and declared their independence. Great Britain, enjoying a lucrative trade with the former Spanish colonies, refused to join Russia, Austria, Prussia, and France in such a policy. Canning, the British foreign minister, suggested that the United States join Great Britain in opposition to a policy of intervention in Spanish America.

Adams' Policy. John Quincy Adams, Monroe's Secretary of State, was alarmed by the threat of the Quadruple Alliance and angered by the Russian Tsar's edict of 1821 extending the boundary of Alaska southward and claiming the western coast of North America as a possible field of Russian colonization. Confident that the British government would support the United States, he urged Monroe to define the relation between the Old World and the New.

Monroe's Message to Congress. President Monroe's message of December, 1823, contained the statement of the Monroe Doctrine: (1) that the American continents were not to be considered as fields for future colonization by European powers; (2) that the attempt of any European monarchy to extend its political system to this hemisphere would be regarded as dangerous to our peace and safety;

(3) that the United States had no intention of interfering with the existing colonies of European powers; and (4) that the United States was not concerned with Europe's quarrels. Although the Monroe Doctrine was merely a presidential proclamation of the national right of self-defense, it was an impressive indication that the destiny of the New World was not to be guided by the Old.

Revival of Party Strife. Beneath the apparent political calm of the "Era of Good Feeling" new lines of party organization were taking shape, which foreshadowed the revival of political division in the nation.

THE ELECTION OF 1824. Four favorite sons were presented by their respective states as presidential candidates in 1824: Andrew Jackson of Tennessee, Henry Clay of Kentucky, William H. Crawford of Georgia, and John Quincy Adams of Massachusetts.

The Decision of the House. As no one of the candidates secured a majority in the electoral college, the election was thrown into the House of Representatives, where Henry Clay gave his support to John Quincy Adams.

The "Corrupt Bargain." When Andrew Jackson, who had received the largest number of electoral votes, learned that Clay had been named Secretary of State, he was persuaded that a political deal between Adams and Clay had robbed him of the presidency. His friends determined to insure his election in 1828.

DEMOCRATS VERSUS NATIONAL REPUBLICANS. The Jacksonian leaders gradually built a party around the personality of their hero, whom they called "Old Hickory." Such former Republican politicians as Calhoun, Crawford, and Van Buren joined the anti-administration forces after 1824, and, taking the name "Democrat," emphasized their return to fundamental Jeffersonian principles. The administration party, National Republican, supported the nationalistic program of Clay and Adams.

A FUTILE ADMINISTRATION (1825–1829). Frustration was the keynote of John Quincy Adams' administration. Congress refused to follow his nationalistic program of devoting federal revenues to the construction of roads and canals, the building of warships, and the endowment of educational institutions. The Senate quarreled with him over his proposal to send delegates to the Panama Congress of Latin American republics (1826); the Georgia legislature defied him in its treatment of the Cherokee Indians; and Canning's attitude thwarted all his attempts to settle outstanding differences between Great Britain and the United States.

THE ELECTION OF ANDREW JACKSON. The politicians who organized the campaign to discredit Adams, did a thorough job. Into the Jacksonian ranks they marshaled (1) Westerners who detected "aristocratic principles" in Adams' policies; (2) Southerners who were eager to defend states' rights; (3) Eastern wage earners who demanded recognition of their claims to political power. The campaign of 1828 resulted in victory for Jackson, as he carried all the Southern and Western states, Pennsylvania, and most of the electoral votes of New York.

REVIEW QUESTIONS

1. To what extent did the Republicans in the decade after the war of 1812 adopt the Federalist philosophy of government?
2. Discuss the constitutional principles which seem most important in the decisions of the Supreme Court while John Marshall was chief justice.
3. What European developments were responsible for the enunciation of the Monroe Doctrine in 1823?
4. How do you account for the nationalism of Monroe's administrations?
5. In what sense did the election of 1824 terminate the "Era of Good Feeling"?
6. Why was John Quincy Adams unable to carry out the nationalistic program which he had devised for his administration?
7. How did party groupings change after the election of 1824?

CHAPTER XII

JACKSONIAN DEMOCRACY

The election of Andrew Jackson was but one manifestation of the powerful influences throughout the nation which were bringing a decline in aristocratic privilege and a democratizing of political and economic institutions.

THE WESTWARD MOVEMENT

The flow of settlers into the great Mississippi Valley reached remarkable proportions in the twenty years after the Treaty of Ghent. This migration, unlike most other colonizing movements, was not sponsored by great land companies or promoted under government auspices, but was primarily the movement of individual family groups.

The Growing Power of the West. The rapid growth in population of the region west of the Appalachian Mountains brought many new states into the Union: Kentucky (1792), Tennessee (1796), Ohio (1803), Louisiana (1812), Indiana (1816), Mississippi (1817), Illinois (1818), and Alabama (1819). The votes of this "western bloc" in Congress were especially important in settling questions relating to Indian policies, the public lands, and internal improvements.

CAUSES OF WESTWARD MIGRATION. Among the forces that lured settlers into the West, or drove them from the East, were the following: (1) the fascination of adventurous living on the frontier; (2) the chance to secure fertile land at low prices ($1.25 an acre in 1820); (3) the desire to escape from the political, social, and religious discriminations of the Eastern communities; and (4) the pressure of economic depression, especially the Panic of 1819, with the consequent unemployment in Eastern cities. The westward-moving groups were augmented by foreigners, fleeing from the consequences of the Napoleonic wars in Europe.

86

THE ROUTES OF TRAVEL. The majority of Western settlers, traveling in family groups, reached their respective destinations by stage coach, wagon, or horseback over rough roads, or by river craft and canal boats. The overland routes into the Mississippi Valley were innumerable, but four natural highways were important: (1) the Wilderness Road through Cumberland Gap into the Kentucky country tapped the Virginia and Carolina territory; (2) the Cumberland Road from Maryland across the mountains reached the Ohio at Wheeling; (3) the Lancaster Turnpike from Philadelphia ran into the road which crossed the mountains at Bedford and reached the Ohio at Pittsburgh; (4) the Genessee Road from Albany to Buffalo served many New Englanders.

THE FRONTIERSMEN. Although many in the East regarded the emigrants to the West as social misfits not worthy "to live in regular society," such a view was probably inspired by resentment over the loss of population and prestige suffered by the Eastern states. In the checkered pattern of Western life the influence of the industrious farmer, seeking a better home for his family, was dominant.

Expansionists and the Missouri Controversy. A sharp cleavage between the interests of the free-labor farmers of the northern Mississippi Valley and the slave-owning planters of the southern section became apparent in the controversy over the admission of Missouri to the Union.

THE TALLMADGE AMENDMENT. When the territory of Missouri applied (1818) for admission to the Union, James Tallmadge of New York proposed that the new state be created on condition that the further introduction of slaves be prohibited and that all children born to slave parents within the state be free at the age of twenty-five.

CONGRESSIONAL DEBATES. The Tallmadge amendment, which was accepted by the House but defeated in the Senate, caused a spirited controversy. The representatives of the states in which slavery was legal were fighting for the right to take their property into the nation's territory beyond the Mississippi, while the representatives of the free states, in which gradual emancipation by statute or constitutional provision was in process, were determined to prevent slavery from spreading. The spokesmen for the slave states did not defend their labor system on ethical grounds, but argued that in a union of equal states Congress had no power to impose a limitation upon any state and that each state should be free to enter the Union with or without slavery as it desired.

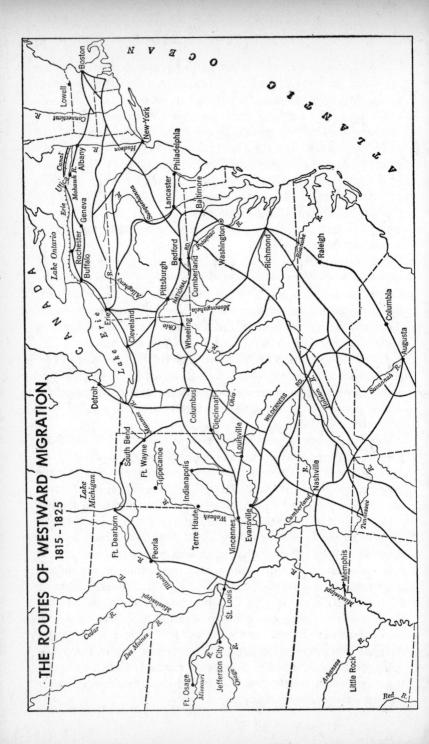

THE ROUTES OF WESTWARD MIGRATION
1815 - 1825

THE MISSOURI COMPROMISE. The Missouri question was settled in 1820 by a compromise which provided: (1) that Missouri should be admitted as a slave state; (2) that Maine should be admitted as a free state, thus keeping slave and free states evenly divided in the Union; (3) that slavery should be excluded from all the Louisiana Purchase territory north of latitude 36° 30′ except in Missouri itself. The South and Southwest voted solidly for the Compromise, while fifteen Northern Republicans supported it, probably because they feared that slavery restriction was being used in the free states as a political device to revive the Federalist party.

THE ADVENT OF THE PEOPLE'S POWER

By the time of Andrew Jackson's election, men and women in the United States were talking about the possibility of transforming their nation into a commonwealth in which every citizen would have a chance to make the most of any individual talents that nature had bestowed.

Western Traits and Ideals. It is difficult to generalize about Western society; yet certain characteristics of this era were distinctive. The Western pioneers were of necessity resourceful, self-reliant, and aggressive. Having equalitarian tendencies, they hated political privilege, financial monopoly, and social distinction; they resented governmental restrictions; and they distrusted professional competence in any form of power. They demanded a government responsive to the popular will as expressed through representatives elected by universal manhood suffrage.

POLITICAL REFORMS. The Western states generally came into the Union with constitutions which provided for frequent elections, removal of religious and property qualifications for the suffrage, and effective popular control of the executive and the judiciary.

DECLINE OF ARISTOCRACY. Even in the aristocratic strongholds of the East, the influence of the frontier democracy was felt. One state after another modified its fundamental law in order to democratize its government. Massachusetts (1820) and New York (1821) widened the suffrage; and Delaware (1831), Mississippi (1832), and Georgia (1833–1835) granted manhood suffrage to white citizens.

Eastern Wage Earners. In the ranks of the new democracy marched thousands of the workingmen in the industrial centers of the Eastern states.

LABOR IN POLITICS. By 1825 every Northern state except Rhode Island had granted white manhood suffrage. Laborers, therefore, had the franchise, but they made little headway in organizing an American labor party. Workingmen's parties strove for social legislation in such states as New York, Pennsylvania, Rhode Island, and Massachusetts. Since the federal government had slight control over matters in which they were interested, they were halfhearted in their attempts to form a national party.

LABOR DEMANDS. The program of organized labor was concerned less with wages and hours than with status. It contained such demands as: (1) free public education; (2) abolition of imprisonment for debt; (3) anticonvict-labor laws; (4) mechanics' lien laws to protect laborers from dishonest contractors; and (5) recognition of the right of collective bargaining.

Political Methods. The democratic movement wrought changes in the electoral process as well as in the organization and functioning of the political parties.

ELECTING THE PRESIDENT. The demand for the popular election of the President resulted in the transfer of the power to choose the presidential electors from the state legislatures to the qualified voters. By 1832 only South Carolina still permitted the legislature to name the electors. Likewise, the nomination of party candidates was taken out of the hands of the party's representatives in Congress (congressional caucus) and vested in a national convention of delegates chosen by local partisans. The Anti-Masonic party held the first national nominating convention in 1831, but the method was well established by 1840.

PARTY ORGANIZATIONS. The national nominating convention, supposedly democratic, really became the crowning glory of the professional politicians, who were shepherding the new voters and building up their local political machines by enrolling the urban wage earners. Public office became the reward for partisan service, and rotation in government jobs became not only desirable but necessary, in order to satisfy the claims of party workers. The boss and his machine had arrived.

DEMOCRATIC POLITICS

These democratic tendencies in national politics were powerful factors in the election of Andrew Jackson, the first President from the new West.

Andrew Jackson—Democrat. The hero of New Orleans—courageous, vigorous, and impetuous—interpreted his office as a direct mandate from the people to use the full power of the national government in curbing privilege and monopoly.

THE SPOILS SYSTEM. With the Westerner's contempt for the trained expert, Jackson combined a desire to reward his supporters with federal appointments. Accordingly, he removed competent as well as incompetent men long in office, in order to make room for the workers who were building the Jackson "machine."

THE "KITCHEN CABINET." Jackson's cabinet advisers, save Van Buren, were inconsequential. The President never established close contact with Congress; instead, he surrounded himself with political and personal friends who formed an intimate circle. To this "Kitchen Cabinet" belonged William B. Lewis, Isaac Hill, and Amos Kendall.

Social and Political Intrigue. John C. Calhoun, the Vice-President, expected to exercise controlling influence in the administration, as four of his political followers were in the cabinet.

THE "EATON MALARIA." Trouble in administration circles arose over the refusal of the cabinet members' wives led by Mrs. Calhoun, to accept Peggy Eaton, wife of the Secretary of War. Like a disease this social quarrel weakened the influence of the Calhounites with the President, who gallantly championed the cause of the Eatons.

THE QUARREL WITH CALHOUN. While the Eaton episode was troubling the political leaders, the "Kitchen Cabinet" let Jackson know that at the time of the First Seminole War (1818), Secretary of War Calhoun had suggested that General Andrew Jackson be court-martialed for his invasion of Florida. Between the President and the great South Carolinian personal friendship ceased.

THE REORGANIZATION OF THE CABINET. In 1831 Jackson effected an almost complete change in the personnel of his cabinet, thus terminating Calhoun's influence. Calhoun himself soon resigned the vice-presidency and became a senator from South Carolina.

Western Interests. The frontier democracy expected Jackson to be particularly vigilant in defending its interests.

INDIAN AFFAIRS. Jackson's policy toward the Indians was based upon the removal of all tribes to the region beyond the Mississippi. More than ninety treaties during his presidential terms compelled the Indians to surrender millions of acres and move west. Trouble developed with several tribes: (1) the Sacs and Fox in Illinois under Black Hawk were crushed by the Illinois militia (1832); (2) the

Cherokee nation in Georgia resisted the attempt to infringe their treaty rights and were not finally dispossessed until 1838; (3) the Seminoles likewise refused to accept a treaty of removal, and their chieftain, Osceola, opened hostilities which did not terminate until 1842 (Second Seminole War). Herding the Indians into reservations, designated by the United States government, brought tragedy to many tribes. Some were driven westward at the point of a bayonet, resentful that they had lost their lands to superior force and determined to resist in any way possible the advance of the white man.

LAND POLICIES. The West desired certain reforms in the national land system, urging that Congress make a progressive reduction in the price of public land unsold after a given period. Senator Thomas Hart Benton of Missouri had Jackson's support in his campaign for a general pre-emption law, but not until 1841 did Congress permit the head of a family to settle on a piece of land (160 acres) and purchase it, without competitive bids, at the minimum government price. The administration opposed Clay's proposal that the proceeds from the public lands be distributed to the states.

INTERNAL IMPROVEMENTS. The Jacksonian politicians refused to accept a policy of indiscriminate appropriation of government funds for internal improvements. In 1830 the President vetoed a bill authorizing the federal government to subscribe to the stock of the Maysville and Lexington (Kentucky) Turnpike, and set forth his states' rights view of the matter.

The New Sectionalism. The quarrel between Jackson and Calhoun had a deeper significance than appeared on the surface. It was closely associated with the spirited controversy over the protective tariff and the fundamental question of the nature of the Union.

THE SOUTH AND THE TARIFF. During the decade following the enactment of the protective tariff of 1816, South Carolina became the political leader of the Southern opposition to the protective tariff.

South Carolina's Economic Position. When Calhoun had advocated protection (1816), he had expected his state to share in the industrial expansion of the nation. But South Carolina, like most of the lower South, became wedded to cotton growing. As production increased, prices fell and her slowly increasing population declined in the economic scale, unable to compete with producers on the better lands of the Southwest. South Carolina planters blamed their plight largely on the protective tariff, which increased their cost of production and the prices of the imports that they consumed but conferred no benefit on them.

The Protectionist Movement. The years of South Carolina's decline marked a steady growth of protectionist sentiment (1816–1830), as Eastern industrialists joined the farmers of the middle states and the West in support of Clay's nationalistic program. The protectionist bill of 1820 failed by one vote in the Senate, while the act of 1824 provided for a general upward revision of rates. A convention at Harrisburg (1827) recommended higher duties to protect the woolen industry.

The "Tariff of Abominations" (1828). The tariff legislation of 1828 resulted from an attempt of the Jackson men in Congress to persuade both protectionist and low-tariff men that their leader was "safe" on the tariff question. Southern supporters of Jackson, led by Calhoun, permitted rates to be pushed to excessive levels in certain schedules in the hope that the Adams men in New England would finally defeat the bill. When the act, even with its objectionable features, became law, the Southerners were in a rebellious mood.

THE EXPOSITION AND PROTEST. Fearful that his state's hostility to the tariff might point the road to the dissolution of the Union, Calhoun devised a formula, known as nullification, as a check on mere majority rule in the nation. Based on the theory that the Constitution was a compact between sovereign states, nullification proposed that a state convention, as the agent of state sovereignty, should have the right to decide whether an act of Congress was constitutional. The remedy for an unconstitutional act was a state ordinance preventing its enforcement. Accordingly, the South Carolina legislature passed a series of eight resolutions condemning the 1828 tariff as unconstitutional. But Calhoun, then a candidate for Vice-President on the ticket with Jackson, urged his state not to attempt nullification until it learned what the new administration would do concerning the tariff.

SOUTHERN BID FOR WESTERN SUPPORT. The South was willing to give the West a free hand in disposing of the public lands if the West would support the South in opposition to protection.

The Foot Resolution. The proposal of Senator Foot (Connecticut) that Congress investigate the desirability of limiting public land sales aroused Senator Benton (Missouri), who denounced the attempt of Eastern manufacturers to restrict the growth and prosperity of the Western states. Senator Robert Hayne of South Carolina supported Benton and opened a general attack upon New England (1830).

The Webster-Hayne Debate. Webster answered Hayne's slur on the patriotism of New England, and the argument drifted from the question of public lands to the constitutional basis of the Union. Hayne elaborated on South Carolina's doctrine of nullification, and Webster branded it as a menace to the perpetuity of the national government.

ATTEMPTED NULLIFICATION. South Carolinians watched with ill-concealed impatience the deliberations of Congress over the tariff from 1830 to 1832.

Tariff of 1832. The tariff act which Jackson signed on July 14, 1832, maintained Clay's protectionist principles, though the rates were slightly lower than the act of 1828. The "nullifiers" in South Carolina promptly carried a resolution in the state legislature for a state convention to consider the momentous question of nullification.

The Ordinance of Nullification (November 24, 1832). The state convention in South Carolina passed an ordinance declaring the tariff acts of 1828 and 1832 null and void, prohibiting the collection of customs duties within the state after February 1, 1833, and threatening secession if the national government used force.

Jackson's Threat of Coercion. President Jackson was determined to enforce the federal laws. He warned South Carolina that nullification was incompatible with the maintenance of the Union, stationed warships in Charleston harbor, transferred artillery to Fort Moultrie, and held troops in readiness.

The Compromise (1833). Calhoun, fearful of civil war, and Clay, anxious to thwart Jackson's policy, co-operated in securing a compromise on the tariff question. Congress enacted a Force Bill, authorizing the President to use the army and navy to collect duties, at the same time that it passed a new tariff law, providing for a gradual scaling down of all schedules until they should reach 20 per cent ad valorem within ten years.

CONTROLLING THE POWER OF FINANCE

During the same week that he signed the Tariff of 1832, Jackson make a significant move in his war on the Bank of the United States by vetoing the bill to grant a new charter to that institution.

Jackson's Hostility to the Bank. In his attitude toward the Bank, Jackson represented the resentment of the debtor West over (1) the Bank's refusal to countenance inflation and (2) the high interest rates charged by the Bank's branches. Furthermore, the President regarded the Bank as a privileged corporation inimical to democratic principles, and he suspected it of anti-Jackson political activity. His first two messages to Congress (1829 and 1830) attacked the institution.

The Election of 1832. Henry Clay, eager to make Jackson's attitude toward the Bank an issue in the election of 1832, persuaded Nicholas Biddle, president of the institution, to apply for a renewal of the Bank's charter, though the old charter would not expire until 1836.

JACKSON'S VETO MESSAGE. The Bank Bill passed both houses of Congress, but was vetoed by the President in a strong message denouncing the institution and its practices. He maintained (1) that the Bank was unconstitutional; (2) that it had become a dangerous monopoly; (3) that its stock was concentrated in the hands of Eastern industrialists and foreign capitalists; (4) that its policies were hostile to the interests of the small banks throughout the West.

THE JACKSON-CLAY CAMPAIGN. Clay, who was nominated by the National Republicans, believed that he could defeat the President on the Bank issue. But he had sadly miscalculated the trend of popular prejudices. Despite Clay's organization of the financial interests and the conservative classes, Jackson was triumphantly re-elected in 1832, with Van Buren (whom the Senate had refused to confirm as minister to Great Britain) as Vice-President.

The Removal of Deposits. Jackson interpreted his re-election as a mandate to destroy the "monster," as he called the Bank. Furthermore, he became convinced that Biddle had mismanaged the Bank's affairs and that the institution was no longer solvent. He determined to cease using the Bank as a depository for the funds of the federal government. Under the Secretary of the Treasury, Roger B. Taney, the governmental surpluses were drawn out of the Bank of the United States and deposited with "pet banks," which were state banks selected by the administration.

The Panic of 1837. The closing years of Jackson's presidential career were marked by a phenomenal prosperity in which were rooted the causes of the financial panic and economic depression that began in 1837.

FUNDAMENTAL FACTORS IN THE PANIC. In a sense the causes of the Panic of 1837 were implicit in the rapid growth and expansion of the population of the United States.

Land Speculation. The steady increase in land sales reached "boom" proportions in 1835 and 1836, as the building of canals and railroads opened new areas to a rapidly growing population. Prices of town lots as well as farm lands reflected the exuberant confidence in the future of the nation.

Investments in Internal Improvements. State governments vied with private capitalists in promoting turnpike, canal, and railroad construction, gauged not to present needs but to the possibilities of future growth.

Expansion of Credit Facilities. The speculative mania was encouraged by the rapid expansion of credit through the instrumentality of state banks, which loaned their unsecured bank notes freely to finance land sales and internal improvement projects. Inflation was further stimulated by the willingness of foreign investors to purchase state bonds and the stocks of railroad and canal companies.

Lack of Liquid Assets. The obvious result of the fictitious prosperity (1835–1837) was to convert an excessive amount of the nation's capital into such forms as land not yet brought under cultivation, canals not yet completed, and railroads not yet prepared to haul freight or passengers.

THE SPECIE CIRCULAR (1836). Jackson and his advisers finally realized that the apparent prosperity was based largely upon inflated land values and unsecured bank notes. In order to check inflation and to protect the government revenues, the President issued the Specie Circular, which forbade the federal land offices to receive anything but specie in payment for government lands. By this order a definite curb was placed upon speculative land ventures, and at the same time the value of the state bank notes sharply declined.

THE FINANCIAL CRASH. The collapse of the credit system became complete as European creditors attempted to realize in the open market on their American securities. Eastern banks, which were pressed to meet foreign obligations, called for the loans advanced to Western and Southern banks. At the same time the government was calling upon the "pet banks" for its surplus funds, in order to make the loans to the various states which were authorized under the bill providing for distribution of the surplus. Banks either suspended specie payments or closed their doors; factories and shops closed; the plight of the unemployed became the more acute as a result of the crop failure of 1837.

ADMINISTRATION REMEDIES. Government revenues from customs and land sales fell off so rapidly that the Van Buren administration approved the issue of $10,000,000 in treasury notes as an emergency measure. The fourth installment of the surplus was not distributed to the states. After a long fight in Congress the Independent Treasury Act (1840) was signed, whereby the government was divorced from the banking system and subtreasuries were created in the important cities as depositories of government funds. But there was no wonder-working power in the administration's remedies.

REVIEW QUESTIONS

1. What was the significance of Andrew Jackson's election in 1828?
2. How do you explain the rapid acceleration of westward migration after 1815?
3. Why did the slavery issue become significant in the controversy over the admission of Missouri?
4. Why was the quarrel between Jackson and Calhoun a momentous one in the political history of the American people?
5. Explain the fundamental questions at issue in the famous debate between Webster and Hayne.
6. Discuss the attitude of each of the following toward South Carolina's Ordinance of Nullification: Andrew Jackson, Henry Clay, Daniel Webster.
7. What was the basis of Andrew Jackson's hostility to the Bank of the United States?
8. How do you explain Calhoun's opposition to the protective tariff in 1828 in the light of his support of the tariff of 1816?
9. Explain the relation of each of the following to the Panic of 1837: (a) the distribution of the surplus, (b) the Specie Circular, (c) the rapid increase in public land sales, (d) the investment of foreign capital in the United States.

Chapter XIII

THE FRUITS OF MANIFEST DESTINY

Even before the continent of North America had been completely explored and mapped, some Americans were determined that the boundaries of the United States must include all the territory that Providence intended them to occupy. In the middle decades of the nineteenth century this restless spirit of expansion came to be known as "manifest destiny." If the idea was not new, it was sponsored more vigorously by the government of the United States than at any other time in its history.

THE CONSERVATIVE WHIGS

The desire for expansion cut across party lines, but the Democrats were apt to be more responsive to it than their new political rivals, the Whigs. It was hostility to the methods and policies of President Jackson, whom they called "King Andrew I," that held the Whig party together.

The Anti-Jackson Forces. Between 1834 and 1836 the Whig organization took form. Its nucleus was the remnant of National Republicans of the Clay-Adams school.

In addition it came to include: (1) conservatives who resented Jackson's attacks on monopoly, and particularly his war against the Bank; (2) native Americans who were hostile to the growing foreign population and believed that most of the naturalized citizens were members of the Democratic party; and (3) states' rights advocates who had broken with the Democrats because of Jackson's handling of the nullification controversy.

Whig Strategy. The Whig leaders formulated no program of principles, but contented themselves with sharp criticism of the Jacksonians.

THE ELECTION OF 1836. Jackson's influence in 1836 was powerful enough to insure the election of his candidate, Martin Van Buren, who had been his Secretary of State and his Vice-President. The Whigs hoped to throw the election into the House of Representatives by voting for different candidates in several sections of the country— Daniel Webster in New England, William Henry Harrison in the Northwest, and Hugh White in the Southwest—but their attempt failed.

"Tippecanoe and Tyler, Too." In 1840 the Whigs made political capital out of the Panic of 1837, tracing the depression to Jackson's policies and blaming Van Buren for his failure to take adequate action.

Nomination of Harrison. In 1840 the Whig party deserted its logical leader, Henry Clay, and chose William Henry Harrison, the hero of Tippecanoe. They presented their candidate as a "man of the people" in contrast to Van Buren, whom they denounced as the aristocratic leader of the Eastern Democrats.

Tyler and the Whigs. To strengthen their party in the South, the Whigs gave the vice-presidential nomination in 1840 to John Tyler, a states' rights Virginian, who hated Andrew Jackson, but was really no friend of the policies championed by Clay and Webster. In a campaign remarkable for noise and the constant display of coonskin caps, cider barrels, and miniature log cabins, the Whigs outshouted and outvoted the Democrats.

War within the Whig Ranks. Within five weeks of his inauguration, Harrison was dead and John Tyler had succeeded to the presidential office. The new President was determined to lead his party, but he was soon challenged by Henry Clay, the powerful spokesman for the Whigs in Congress.

Clay's Program (1841). As soon as Congress assembled in special session, Clay presented a series of resolutions, which he insisted represented the party's legislative program. The proposals included: (1) repeal of the Independent Treasury Act and the charter of a new Bank of the United States; (2) the enactment of a protective tariff; and (3) the distribution to the states of the proceeds from the sale of public lands. It was a program reminiscent of the National Republicans of 1825.

An Obstinate President. The Whigs succeeded in repealing the Independent Treasury Act, but they could not draft a bank bill acceptable to President Tyler, who had constitutional scruples against such a national institution. He vetoed two bank bills, and Congress abandoned the struggle. After much wrangling over tariff schedules, Tyler finally signed the act of 1842, which was moderately protective, but he refused to permit the tariff to go into effect unless Clay abandoned his plan to distribute the land sales to the states.

Reorganization of the Cabinet. Tyler's refusal to accept Clay's program brought open war between the President and the Whig leaders in Congress. Clay's followers in the cabinet resigned and were replaced by political friends of the President, who seemed to be determined to build a third party of dissatisfied Whigs and old-line Democrats.

THE DIPLOMACY OF EXPANSION

At the time of Tyler's controversy with the Whigs, Daniel Webster, Secretary of State, did not resign, because he was engaged in momentous negotiations with Great Britain.

Anglo-American Controversies. The two chief questions at issue between the United States and Great Britain were the dispute concerning the boundary between Maine and New Brunswick and the unsatisfactory joint occupation of the Oregon Country. Minor, but irritating, grievances were: (1) the *Caroline* affair, in which Canadians had destroyed the American ship *Caroline* during the insurrection of 1837, because they suspected that the ship belonged to filibusterers; (2) the *Creole* case, involving a cargo of slaves who mutinied and put into port in the Bahamas, where they were freed by the British authorities; (3) the practice of the British squadrons off the African coast in searching American ships which they believed guilty of engaging in the slave trade; (4) resentment of British investors over the action of several states in repudiating their debts.

The Webster-Ashburton Treaty (1842). When the Peel ministry replaced that of Melbourne (1841), Great Britain indicated its willingness to discuss existing disputes in a friendly spirit. Lord Ashburton was sent to Washington to conduct negotiations with Webster. The terms of the treaty (1) settled the Maine-New Brunswick boundary by defining a compromise line, which gave the United States 7,000 of the 12,000 square miles in dispute, and (2) established a cruising convention which provided for patrolling squadrons off the African slave coast. The *Creole* case and the Oregon question were not solved in the treaty, but Ashburton apologized for the attack on the *Caroline*. The conversations between the diplomats greatly improved relations between the countries which they represented.

The Acquisition of Texas and Oregon. The success of the Webster-Ashburton negotiations was particularly fortunate in view of the increasing demands of the expansionists that the United States acquire Texas and Oregon, regions in which Great Britain was involved.

THE TEXAN REPUBLIC. The Mexican province of Texas, which had been colonized by emigrants from the United States, declared its independence on March 2, 1836.

Migration into Texas. In 1821 Moses Austin secured a patent from the Spanish authorities to establish three hundred families in Texas. His son, Stephen F. Austin, carried forward the project and received confirmation of the grant from Mexican officials, after Mexico had won its independence from Spain. His first settlement was made in December, 1821. Soon other colonizers were recipients of generous land grants. By 1830 nearly 20,000 Americans, chiefly from Tennessee, Mississippi, and Louisiana, had settled in Texas.

Revolution. Grievances on the part of the Anglo-American settlers against the Mexican authorities soon became serious. The Texans (1) desired to retain the English language and their Anglo-American traditions; (2) resented the Mexican laws suspending land contracts, imposing duties on imported goods, and forbidding foreigners to enter the province; and (3) feared that the Mexican government would abolish slavery. Mexico did abrogate the law against foreign immigration, but a crisis came in 1835, when Santa Anna's government reduced Texas to a military district in the province of Coahuila.

Texan Independence. The Texan movement for provincial autonomy quickly developed into a war for independence, which was won at the Battle of San Jacinto, when Santa Anna's forces were routed by the Texans under General Sam Houston. President Santa Anna was compelled to acknowledge the independence of the province, but the Mexican government refused to honor the presidential signature.

THE ANNEXATIONISTS. Although the treaty of 1819 with Spain contained provisions whereby the United States surrendered all claim on Texas, many Americans believed that the province would some

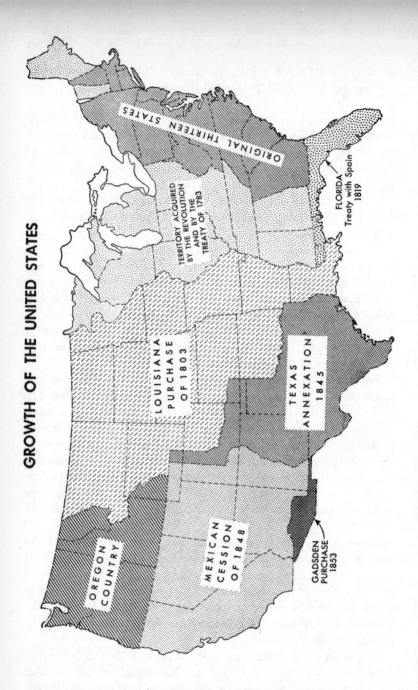

GROWTH OF THE UNITED STATES

ORIGINAL THIRTEEN STATES

FLORIDA
Treaty with Spain
1819

TERRITORY ACQUIRED
BY THE REVOLUTION
AND BY THE
TREATY OF 1783

LOUISIANA
PURCHASE
OF 1803

TEXAS
ANNEXATION
1845

OREGON
COUNTRY

MEXICAN
CESSION
OF 1848

GADSDEN
PURCHASE
1853

day be added to United States territory. John Quincy Adams (1827) and Andrew Jackson (1829, 1835) tried to purchase it from Mexico.

Controversy over Annexation. The great majority of Texans desired annexation to the United States, but there was determined opposition to such a project from the antislavery forces, who charged the Southern slaveholders with conspiring to create several slave states out of Texas in order to insure Southern control of the federal government. The controversy could end only in war with Mexico. On the other hand, the movement for expansion was supported by (1) expansionists who regarded it as the nation's destiny to occupy the whole continent; (2) slaveholders who were eager to acquire territory suitable for the extension of the plantation economy of the South; (3) those who feared that an independent Texas might become an undesirable neighbor or a region under the economic control of Great Britain; and (4) a small group of speculators who were interested in Texas land and depreciated Texas bonds.

Calhoun's Treaty (1844). Jackson recognized the independence of Texas (1837), but he left the question of annexation to his successor. Van Buren displayed little interest in the matter. Tyler made the issue his own after his quarrel with the Whigs. When he appointed Calhoun as Secretary of State (1843) the annexation of Texas became the chief policy of the administration. Calhoun negotiated a treaty of annexation, but it was defeated by a decisive vote in the Senate (June, 1844).

Campaign of 1844. Henry Clay, who was unanimously nominated by the Whigs, expected that his Democratic opponent would be Martin Van Buren, a foe of annexation. To remove the Texas issue from the campaign, Clay wrote his famous "Raleigh letter" advising against the acquisition of Texas. The Democrats, however, blocked Van Buren's nomination and chose as their candidate James K. Polk, an ardent expansionist, who ran on a platform calling for the reannexation of Texas and the reoccupation of Oregon. Antislavery Whigs, irritated by Clay's evasive pronouncements concerning Texas after his nomination, cast many votes for James G. Birney, the candidate of the Liberty party, and Polk was elected.

Annexation of Texas. Tyler interpreted Polk's election as an endorsement of his own expansionist policy. He sponsored a joint resolution for the annexation of Texas, which Congress passed just three days before Tyler left the presidency. Texas finally accepted the terms of annexation and by December, 1845, had drafted a constitution under which it was admitted to the Union.

OREGON. In the campaign of 1844 the expansionists managed to make the annexation of Texas more palatable to Northern voters by linking it with the acquisition of Oregon, a region west of the Rockies, stretching from Spanish territory to Russian Alaska.

American Claims. Late in the eighteenth century Spain, Russia, France, and Great Britain all set forth vague claims to the Oregon Country. The government of the United States early in the nineteenth century based its claims upon (1) the explorations of Captain Robert Gray, who in 1792 discovered and named the Columbia River; (2) the expedition of Lewis and Clark (1805–1806); and (3) the establishment of John Jacob Astor's trading post, Astoria (1811).

Anglo-American Agreement. The British claims to the territory were equally well founded. An attempt in 1818 to define the possessions of each nation resulted in a compromise which provided for a ten-year period of joint occupation. Actually, the arrangement gave the representatives of the Hudson's Bay Company control of the region. Joint occupation, however, was renewed in 1827 for an indefinite period, with the provision that either nation might terminate the treaty by giving a year's notice.

Oregon's Adventurers. Prior to 1830 the contact of the United States with Oregon was limited to the visits of trappers and traders. During the next two decades migration into Oregon was stimulated by several forces: (1) the propaganda of enthusiasts like Hall J. Kelley, who organized a society for the settlement of the territory; (2) the activities of businessmen like Nathaniel Wyeth, who demonstrated by his overland trips (1832, 1836) the practicability of a wagon route to the Oregon Country; (3) the missionary enterprises among the Indians of the Northwest established by the Methodists, Presbyterians, and Catholics.

Treaty of 1846. The steady stream of migrants, which reached considerable proportions in 1843, gave point to the demands of the extremists that the United States acquire all of Oregon. The slogan became "Fifty-four forty or fight," referring to the northern boundary of Oregon. After considerable diplomatic maneuvering, however, the Polk administration finally agreed to a treaty which divided Oregon, and fixed the 49th parallel as the northern boundary of the United States between the Rockies and the Pacific.

POLK AND THE MEXICAN PROBLEM

The settlement of the Oregon question with Great Britain was facilitated by the fact that in the spring of 1846 United States relations with Mexico had reached the breaking point and the Polk administration momentarily expected the outbreak of hostilities.

Polk's Peace Efforts. President Polk insisted that his policy was one of conciliation so far as Mexico was concerned, but his pacific gestures were nullified by his determination to defend American annexation of Texas, which Mexico refused to recognize, and by his desire to add to United States territory the province of California, which Mexico refused to sell.

THE SLIDELL MISSION. In the autumn of 1845 Polk sent John Slidell as a special envoy to Mexico with instructions (1) to offer to assume claims of United States citizens against Mexico if the Mexican government would recognize the Rio Grande rather than the Nueces as the southern boundary of Texas; (2) to offer $5,000,000 additional for the cession of New Mexico; (3) to offer $25,000,000 additional for the cession of both California and New Mexico. Slidell was to conduct his negotiations in such manner as to promote cordial relations with Mexico.

MEXICAN POLICY. Political disturbances in Mexico made Slidell's task doubly difficult. The temper of the country was so hostile to the United States that two Mexican presidents refused to receive Polk's envoy. To patriotic Mexicans it seemed as if the United States, having stolen Texas, was plotting to disrupt their nation completely. They willingly followed their irate leaders in demanding war against the northern enemy.

The Mexican War. Discouraging reports from Slidell caused Polk to order General Zachary Taylor, "Old Rough and Ready," to advance from the Nueces to the Rio Grande. As soon as the President learned that Mexican forces had crossed the Rio Grande, he informed Congress that war existed by the act of Mexico itself (May 11, 1846).

OUTBREAK OF HOSTILITIES. Congress, accepting Polk's statement that Mexico had assumed the role of aggressor, authorized the President to raise an army of 50,000 men, and voted $10,000,000 of war appropriations. The Western and Southern states responded enthusiastically, but the Northeast was apathetic. New England abolitionists were most severe in their criticism of the administration's policy.

CAMPAIGNS OF OLD ROUGH AND READY. Although Taylor's strategy was often faulty, his campaigns in northern Mexico were almost uniformly successful. Victories at Palo Alto and Resaca de la Palma enabled him to enter Matamoros in May, 1846. By the end of the year he had captured Monterey, Saltillo, and Victoria and was holding a front two hundred miles long. His position was seriously threatened in February, 1847, when Santa Anna discovered that part of the American force had been diverted to Scott's command. Taylor, however, withstood the assault at Buena Vista, and his small army remained undisturbed during the remainder of the war.

CONQUEST OF CALIFORNIA. Mexican control in California and New Mexico, which was merely nominal, was easily overthrown. (1) Commodore Sloat of the Pacific fleet, and his successor Commodore Stockton, captured San Francisco, Monterey, and Los Angeles. (2) A group of American settlers under William B. Ide seized the town of Sonoma and proclaimed a republic under the "Bear Flag." Captain John C. Frémont, a topographical engineer in the service of the United States, assumed the leadership of these insurgents and the Stars and Stripes replaced the Bear Flag. (3) In June, 1846, Colonel S. W. Kearney set out from Fort Leavenworth, Kansas, took Santa Fe, and entered San Diego, California, in December. Stockton and Frémont co-operated with him in removing the last evidence of Mexican authority.

SCOTT'S MARCH ON MEXICO CITY. In November, 1846, the Polk administration decided to attack Mexico City by way of Vera Cruz and gave command of the expedition to General Winfield Scott. Scott's advance was stubbornly resisted, but his decisive victory at Cerro Gordo (April 17–18, 1847) scattered the Mexican forces. Engagements at Contreras, Churubusco, Molino del Rey, and Chapultepec brought the Americans into the Mexican capital.

TREATY OF GUADALUPE-HIDALGO. Nicholas P. Trist, chief clerk of the state department, whom Polk had sent secretly to Mexico, arranged the terms of the treaty of peace with the Mexican commissioners. Mexico agreed (1) to recognize the Rio Grande as the Texan boundary; (2) to cede New Mexico and California to the United States in return for $15,000,000 and the assumption by the United

States government of American citizens' claims against Mexico up to $3,250,000. The Senate ratified the treaty by a narrow margin on March 10, 1848.

The Election of 1848. One important result of the Mexican War was the elevation of General Zachary Taylor to the presidency of the United States.

TAYLOR VS. CASS. Despite their strictures on the Mexican War the Whigs nominated General Taylor, who was resentful over the manner in which he had been treated by a Democratic administration. The party was determined to win by capitalizing the popular enthusiasm for the hero of Buena Vista. It adopted a platform which was merely an expression of confidence in Taylor. The Democrats, meanwhile, had nominated Senator Lewis Cass of Michigan and had adopted a platform which endorsed the conduct of the Mexican War, but was evasive on all other questions.

THE FREE-SOIL PARTY. The Democrats were torn by factional dissension, notably in New York State, where the "Hunkers" or administration group were bitterly opposed by the "Barnburners," a faction supporting political reform and antislavery principles. The Barnburners refused to support Cass and nominated former President Van Buren. Their candidate received the support of the old Liberty party and a new group of Free-Soilers who were unalterably opposed to the extension of slavery into the territories.

WHIG VICTORY. In New York the Democratic defection was so large that Van Buren ran ahead of Cass, thus giving the state to the Whigs. Taylor's narrow margin in the electoral college was symbolic of the slight difference between the two major parties, both of which were carefully evading the pressing issue of the expansion of slavery.

The Mexican Cession. Shortly after the signing of the Treaty of Guadalupe-Hidalgo word came from California that gold had been discovered in the Sacramento Valley. It was the signal for a phenomenal migration to the Pacific Coast.

THE FORTY-NINERS. Fortune-hunters who sought a new El Dorado had a choice of three routes: (1) the overland road across the plains and through the passes of the Rockies; (2) the Isthmus of Panama route; or (3) the long voyage around Cape Horn. Within two years of the discovery of gold more than 90,000 adventurers had been drawn to California, and the territory, having drafted a constitution, was demanding admission into the Union. Its heterogeneous population, from all parts of the world and every social class, was grappling successfully with the problem of political organization.

TERRITORY OF UTAH. The gold rush materially aided the Mormon

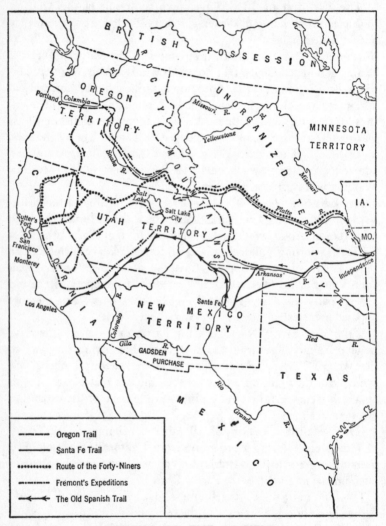

TRAILS TO THE PACIFIC

settlements in the vicinity of Great Salt Lake. The members of this religious sect, established by Joseph Smith in 1830, had followed their leader, Brigham Young, into the region in 1847, when it still belonged to Mexico. Young's colony was a halfway station on the overland route to California. In 1850 it became the territory of Utah and Young was appointed its first governor.

Isthmian Canal Projects. The Forty-niners emphasized the importance of a canal or railroad across the Isthmus of Panama. In 1846 the United States had negotiated a treaty with New Granada (Colombia) for an exclusive right of way across the isthmus. Two years later American capitalists began the construction of a railroad. Both British and American promoters were interested in a canal across Nicaragua. In 1850 the United States and Great Britain signed the Clayton-Bulwer Treaty, whereby each agreed not to obtain exclusive control over a Central American canal, nor to erect fortifications commanding it, nor to colonize any part of Central America. The neutrality of any canal constructed by private capital was jointly guaranteed.

The Gadsden Purchase. The acquisition of the Mexican Cession and the rapid growth of California gave impetus to the transcontinental railroad projects. In 1853 James Gadsden, a South Carolina railroad president, was sent to Mexico, where he conducted negotiations for the purchase of some thirty thousand square miles in the Gila Valley which offered the best southern route for a railroad to the Pacific.

REVIEW QUESTIONS

1. Who were the Whigs? What significance do you attach to their campaign methods in 1840?
2. What evidence of the influence of Hamiltonian theories do you find in the Whig legislative program of 1841?
3. How did John Tyler justify his refusal to accept the policies championed by the powerful Whig politicians?
4. The Webster-Ashburton Treaty removed important obstacles from the path of those expansionists who desired the annexation of Texas and the occupation of Oregon. Discuss.
5. How do you explain the failure of the United States to annex Texas as soon as it had declared its independence?
6. Why did territorial expansion become a significant issue in the presidential election of 1844?
7. Do you think Polk's policy in dealing with Mexico was justifiable? Why?
8. What political consequences of the Mexican War were evident in the election of 1848?

Chapter XIV

AMERICAN SOCIETY AT MID-CENTURY

Mid-century America was predominantly rural, its landscape criss-crossed by dirt roads which still carried much of its commerce and many of its travelers. Divided by sectional differences, most of its people were yet happy in their enjoyment of the present and confident about their progress in the future. Five times as many of them lived on farms as in the towns and cities.

INDUSTRY ON THE MARCH

The nation had already felt the influence of those changes in manufacturing, transportation and communication that are usually called the Industrial Revolution. The direction of its future development was unmistakable.

Population Trends. The census of 1850, with its elaborate compilations, revealed the remarkable growth of the population and its sectional distribution.

ENUMERATION. The nucleus of 3,929,000 in 1790 had grown to 12,866,000 in 1830 and to 23,191,000 in 1850.

DISTRIBUTION. In 1790 nearly 95 per cent of the population lived east of the Alleghenies, but in 1850 this percentage had decreased to 55. The rate of growth between 1830 and 1850 was 10 per cent for the Northeast, 40 per cent for the South and Southwest, and 75 per cent for the Northwest.

IMMIGRATION. Growth in population was due chiefly to the rapid reproduction of native stock. Between 1820, when statistics were first accurately kept, and 1830 less than 500,000 foreigners came to American shores. Five times as many came in the next two decades, most of them from Great Britain, Ireland, and the Germanies. By 1850, 12 per cent of the population was foreign-born. The United

States became an asylum for those who fled from unsatisfactory labor conditions in Great Britain, from famine in Ireland, or from political revolutions and economic depression on the Continent.

URBAN GROWTH. At the close of the Revolution only five cities in the country had more than eight thousand inhabitants. In 1850 there were 141 such cities representing every section of the nation. They contained 16 per cent of the total population. Already they were struggling with such problems as sanitation, transportation, public health, fire protection, and public safety. The "Native Americans" blamed the foreign groups for the growth of political corruption, social disorder, and religious bigotry. In 1850 the Nativists formed the Order of the Star Spangled Banner, which within a few years developed into the powerful Know-Nothing party.

Growth of Manufacturing. From the day in 1790 that Samuel Slater completed the first cotton mill, the growth of machine industry was rapid. By 1850 the annual output of United States mills and factories had reached a value of $1,055,511,000 and had surpassed the value of agricultural products.

RISE OF THE FACTORY SYSTEM. The forces which had wrought great industrial changes in Great Britain late in the eighteenth century were retarded in the United States by (1) the fact that the nation's capital was invested in agriculture, land speculation, or foreign trade; (2) the fear of capitalists that American factories could not compete with English industries; (3) the scarcity of an adequate supply of skilled and unskilled labor; (4) the lack of knowledge concerning machines and manufacturing processes (hard to obtain because of English laws prohibiting the export of new machines and the emigration of skilled mechanics); (5) the restricted local market due to poor transportation facilities. The most important factors in overcoming these initial obstacles were: (1) the phenomenal growth of population and its expansion across the continent; (2) the rapid improvement of transportation facilities after 1820; (3) the accumulation of capital for industrial investment which was accelerated by the transfer of funds from shipbuilding and foreign trade during the Napoleonic wars.

IMPROVED EQUIPMENT AND METHODS. Before the War of 1812 English spinning and carding machinery had been introduced in the American cotton industry. The generation following 1815 was prolific in the invention and improvement of machines for the textile

and metal industries. Francis C. Lowell and Paul Moody perfected
the power loom (1814); John Goulding improved the carding machine (1826); Frederick Geissenhainer smelted iron ore with an-

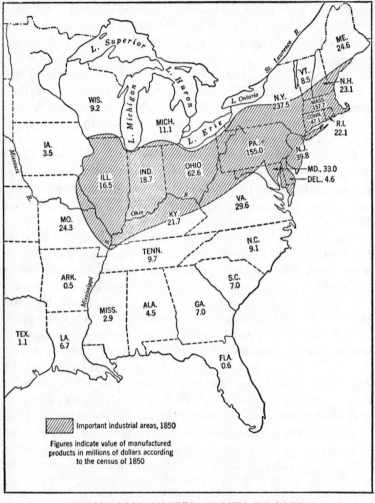

INDUSTRIAL UNITED STATES IN 1850

thracite coal (1833); Elias Howe invented the sewing machine
(1846); and William Kelly independently discovered the Bessemer
method of steel production.

New Forms of Power. Oliver Evans converted the low-pressure steam engine of James Watt into a more effective high-pressure engine (1803), but steam replaced water power slowly as the motive force in American factories. In 1830 more than one third of the plants in Pennsylvania used steam, but in New England less than 10 per cent had abandoned water power. Wood remained the principal fuel until the Civil War, but after 1820 the use of coal increased rapidly.

Distribution of Manufactures. Southern New England, southern New York, New Jersey, eastern Pennsylvania, and eastern Maryland comprised the first industrial area. It excelled in textiles, textile machinery, engines, boots and shoes, clothing, glassware, etc. The area which later achieved importance, after 1840, included western New York, western Pennsylvania, Ohio, Indiana, and Illinois. Except in Maryland and sections of Virginia, manufacturing made little progress in the South prior to 1865.

Size and Ownership of Factories. With few exceptions the early factories and mills were small establishments owned by individual proprietors, partners, or joint-stock companies. The corporate form of organization, which increased in importance after 1815, was used more frequently in New England than elsewhere. Stock ownership in corporations was usually confined to a small group.

Transportation and Communication. A factor of paramount influence in the expansion of industrial enterprises was the development of transportation and communication during the first half of the nineteenth century.

Agencies of Transportation. As population flowed into the Mississippi Valley the insistent demand for transportation facilities was answered in a variety of ways.

Turnpikes. With the completion of the Philadelphia and Lancaster Turnpike in 1794 the nation began to convert its dirt roads into passable highways. For thirty years private companies, often with state aid, constructed local and interstate roads, at times earning considerable profits. The most important federal project was the national road from Cumberland, Maryland, to Wheeling on the Ohio (opened 1817).

Rivers. The use of the rivers as natural highways was revolutionized with the invention of the steamboat. The successful run of Fulton's *Clermont* up the Hudson (1807) was the prelude to the widespread use of steamboats, especially on inland waters. In 1860 there were more than a thousand plying the waters of the Mississippi and its tributaries.

Canals. The steamboat on the island rivers did not solve the demand for east-west transportation facilities. Eastern cities tried to reach the trade of the West by means of canals. New York City forged ahead of its rivals in the decade after the completion of the Erie Canal (1825–1835). Philadelphia, Baltimore, and Charleston experimented with the same method. Pennsylvania financed a system of canals between Philadelphia and Pittsburgh (1826–1834). By 1850 more than 3,200 miles of canals had been dug in the United States.

Railroads. At the height of the canal craze came the railroad. The first pretentious project was sponsored by Baltimore merchants and bankers who incorporated the Baltimore and Ohio Railroad in 1827. In 1830 there were 32 miles of railroad in the country; in 1840 there were 2,818 miles; in 1850 more than 9,000 miles. The companies received generous grants of land and stock subscriptions from the various states and indirectly from the federal government. By 1860 the trunk lines had bound the Northeast and Northwest together with bands of steel.

THE TELEGRAPH. The invention of the electric telegraph was of tremendous significance in the expansion of the railroad systems. Samuel F. B. Morse succeeded in making this means of communication practicable in 1837, but the first telegraph line of consequence was not constructed until 1843. By 1860 more than 50,000 miles of telegraph united the country east of the Rocky Mountains, and the next year San Francisco was brought into the network.

Agriculture. Less striking, but no less significant than the expansion in industry and transportation, was the steady growth of agricultural activity.

NEW FARMING METHODS. Although the abundance of cheap and fertile land was responsible for careless and wasteful methods among American farmers, the early decades of the nineteenth century were marked by new ventures in land fertilization, crop rotation, and scientific stockbreeding. Many societies for the promotion of agriculture followed the establishment of the first one at Philadelphia in 1785. Among the champions of better husbandry none were more important than Robert R. Livingston, who imported merino sheep, Elkanah Watson, whose Berkshire system was the forerunner of the county fair, Robert H. Gardiner, who founded the Gardiner Lyceum (1823) as the first American school of agriculture, and Edmund Ruffin, whose original work on soil fertility was still authoritative at the close of the nineteenth century.

AGRICULTURAL MACHINERY. The invention of agricultural machinery was America's answer to the problem raised by the scarcity of farm labor, which resulted from the drift of population into the cities and the great migration into the West. Jethro Wood's cast-iron plow (1819), John Deere's steel plow (1839), and Cyrus McCormick's reaper (1834), together with horse rakes, mowing machines, cultivators, and mechanical threshers, lightened the farmer's labor and increased his product at the middle of the century.

PRODUCTION. Such staple commodities as corn, wheat, cotton, tobacco, and wool, as well as other crops, more than doubled in yield between 1830 and 1860. The South came to rely upon the West for its grain and livestock; New England and other parts of the East, in order to meet the competition of Western farms, turned to stock-raising, dairying, and truck gardening.

FORCES OF SOCIAL PROGRESS

American society during the first half of the nineteenth century was permeated by an optimistic faith in the perfectibility of man. It experimented widely, if not always wisely, with reform programs which were designed to emancipate the human spirit and improve social conditions.

Utopian Communities. Many of the reform movements were manifest in the formation of idealistic communities to revolutionize economic organization.

NEW HARMONY. Robert Owen, the English philanthropist, founded a community at New Harmony, Indiana, in 1824. His economic ideas and educational system might have succeeded had he been less radical on religion and marriage. The fame of New Harmony led to the establishment of a dozen similar ventures.

FOURIER'S PHALANXES. In 1841 Albert Brisbane popularized the principles of the French philosopher Charles Fourier, who advocated the organization of society on the basis of phalanxes or groups, not to exceed 1,800 persons, co-operating in industry, science, and art. More than thirty phalanxes were established in various states. The most famous was Brook Farm, originally founded by a group of New England transcendentalists and other intellectuals, including Nathaniel Hawthorne.

ICARIAN COMMUNITIES. The communistic proposals of Étienne Cabet were put to the test by his French followers in 1848, when they founded a colony on the Red River in Texas. Moving to Illinois the following year, they became the center from which communities were established in Missouri, Iowa, and California.

Religious Radicalism. Religious influences were powerful in opening new horizons for this generation of Americans, but at times they became manifest in fantastic forms.

SECTARIAN COMMUNISM. Into the nineteenth century survived many of the sects which had founded religious communities in the eighteenth century. There were the Pietists (1694) and the Dunkers (1732) in Pennsylvania; the Shakers had founded their first community at Watervliet, New York, in 1776. Other German sects of prominence were the Harmony Society (1805), the Separatists (1817), and the Amana Society (1859).

PERFECTIONISTS. The religious society organized by John Humphrey Noyes at Putney, Vermont, established a famous and successful community at Oneida, New York. The Perfectionists retained their communal organization until 1881.

THE MILLERITES. The sort of religious emotionalism which characterized the great revivals of the early nineteenth century was apparent in the response to the teachings of William Miller, who in 1832 began to preach the immediate second coming of Christ. His summons to a new way of life stirred multitudes in all parts of the country, many of whom made serious preparation for the end of the world in 1844.

Humanitarian Reforms. The forces of revealed religion were present in the great movements for social reform which this generation undertook in the belief that it was rapidly approaching its goal of a perfect society.

AIDING THE UNFORTUNATES. In their desire to remove all the barriers which hindered human progress the humanitarians paid especial attention to those who were physically or mentally handicapped. (1) In 1816 Thomas H. Gallaudet opened the first school for the teaching of deaf-mutes at Hartford, Connecticut. (2) Perkins Institute for the Education of the Blind (1829) represented the desire to open new avenues for these unfortunates. (3) The erection of the state asylum for the insane at Worcester, Massachusetts (1833), and the wonderful work of Dorothea Dix after 1841 revolutionized the treatment and care of the mentally ill and defective.

REVISING THE PENAL SYSTEM. The attacks against the injustice and barbarity of the penal system were directed particularly toward the following reforms: (1) the abolition of imprisonment for debt; (2) the modification of penal codes to remove inhuman punishments; (3) the provision of decent facilities in workhouses and jails; (4) the adoption of a sound program for the reformation of criminals.

FIGHTING INTEMPERANCE. The crusade against intemperance, which had been initiated by the writings of Benjamin Rush and Lyman Beecher, assumed formidable proportions after the creation of the American Temperance Society at Boston in 1826. Local auxiliaries and state societies, supported by the churches, enrolled thousands in the ranks of the signers of the temperance pledge. At first the reformers relied upon persuasion to effect their purposes, but in the decade of the forties many began to urge restrictive and prohibitory legislation against the liquor traffic as the best way to promote temperance. The Maine law of 1851, sponsored by Neal Dow, was the first state enactment forbidding the manufacture, importation, or sale of intoxicating beverages.

THE CAMPAIGN FOR WOMEN'S RIGHTS. The participation of women in the humanitarian reforms was the immediate occasion for the campaign to remove the political and economic discriminations against them. The demand for civil rights, stressed by Lucretia Mott, Margaret Fuller, and Elizabeth Cady Stanton, brought changes in the laws of several states concerning woman's control of her property after marriage. The Woman's Rights Convention, held at Seneca Falls, New York, in 1848, was the first of several national conventions which demanded that women be given the ballot, that they be accorded equal opportunity with men to secure an education and to earn a living, and that all legal discrimination against them be removed.

Education. The cumulative effect of the forces favoring popular education was seen in the foundations of a public school system which were laid in the generation before the Civil War.

SECONDARY SCHOOLS. Although this period was marked by the growth of private schools, notably the academies, its most distinctive feature was the widespread acceptance by the various states of the fact that elementary education should be free, compulsory, and tax-supported. Massachusetts, under the leadership of Horace Mann from 1837 to 1848, set an example in organizing a system of secondary schools which was not lost on other states. Mann was a pioneer in broadening the curriculum, in creating professional morale among the teachers, and in providing ways and means of training teachers. In 1850 there were 80,000 elementary schools with 3,300,000 pupils and 6,000 high schools and academies with 250,000 students.

COLLEGES. The chief trends in higher education were reflected in the rapid increase in denominational colleges, the slow but steady growth of collegiate endowments, and the gradual expansion of the educational offering. The institutions of higher learning remained, however, primarily concerned with the training of youth for the Christian ministry.

PROFESSIONAL TRAINING. Although most doctors and lawyers received their professional education through a system of apprenticeship, schools of medicine and law were established with increasing frequency in connection with the liberal arts colleges. Scientific and technical training was excellent at such schools as Rensselaer Institute, West Point Military Academy, Sheffield at Yale, and Lawrence at Harvard.

THE CULTURAL HERITAGE

The artistic contributions of the period were comparatively slight, as one might expect from the proportion of time and interest given to territorial expansion, political controversy, business activity, and social and economic reforms.

Literature. In literature alone, of all the arts, there were significant achievements during the period.

NEW ENGLAND RENAISSANCE. The revival of intellectual interests in New England in comparison with the sterility of the earlier periods took on the aspects of a "renaissance." Boston became the intellectual center of the country. Sectionalism dominated the writings of most of the New England schools; historians like Palfrey, Ticknor, Bancroft, Hildreth, Prescott, and Motley either wrote the history of foreign lands or displayed a New England bias in dealing with their own country. Parkman's classic volumes were an exception. Few of the literary group in Massachusetts—Hawthorne, Thoreau, Whittier, Longfellow, Lowell, or Holmes—were as typical of the rising

America as Emerson, but even Emerson's fame did not rest upon any profound understanding, revealed in his writings, of the contemporary scene. He was, however, an outstanding exemplar of his generation's buoyant confidence in human perfectibility.

WRITERS OF THE MIDEAST. The literary groups in New York and Philadelphia revealed none of the unifying traits which characterized the New England school. Irving's romanticism differed from that of Cooper; Herman Melville's sense of futility was not akin to Walt Whitman's rebellion against his environment. The artistry of Edgar Allan Poe was unique in American letters.

THE SOUTH. The writers of the South were preoccupied with the defense of slavery. Even the greatest Southern novelist of the period, William Gilmore Simms, allowed his literary craftsmanship to suffer as he strove to win the approval of the slaveholding aristocracy of his section.

Painting. None of the portrait painters of the period following 1830 were as great in their art as Copley and Stuart of an earlier day. Probably the greatest advance was made in landscape painting by the artists of the "Hudson River School." New York became the principal art center of the country, especially after the formation of the National Academy of Design in 1828.

Sculpture and Architecture. The Greek influence was predominant both in sculpture and architecture during this period. American sculptors, most of whom secured their training in Italy, as did Hiram Powers and Thomas Crawford, produced little that was noteworthy and nothing that was really American in spirit. The architects, likewise, busy with the American phase of the world-wide Greek revival, followed classical forms whether they were designing country houses or state capitals. Too often their work seemed incongruous against its American background.

Music. In the field of musical art the American contribution was slight but certain developments were noteworthy: (1) the influence of the German choral societies in bringing some of the greatest music of the Old World to the New; (2) the improvement of church music through the work of such compilers as Lowell Mason; (3) the adaptation of Negro folk music in the songs of Stephen C. Foster; and (4) the growth of interest in musical art with the introduction of music into the schools.

The Theater. Although the theater gained in standing as popular prejudice was slowly overcome, its repertory showed little change. The actors were almost all English, but Edwin Forrest, Edwin Booth, and Charlotte Cushman were winning more than national fame. Relatively few plays by American playwrights were produced.

SCIENTIFIC ACHIEVEMENTS

Much more significant than their artistic accomplishments were the achievements of Americans in the field of science.

Pure Science. While it is easy to overestimate the contributions of Americans in the field of scientific research, the work of several scholars was noteworthy. J. J. Audubon in ornithology, Asa Gray in botany, Louis Agassiz in geology and zoology, Joseph Henry in physics, and Benjamin Silliman in chemistry earned international reputations.

Applied Science. The application of scientific principles to production, transportation, and communication in the era before the Civil War was the beginning of that process of mechanization which went forward so rapidly in the United States after 1865. One of the great "breakthroughs" was the introduction of the principle of interchangeable parts after Eli Whitney's pioneer work.

Medicine. An important contribution made by Americans in the field of applied science was the introduction of the use of anesthetics in surgery. In 1844 Horace Wells, a Connecticut dentist, demonstrated that nitrous oxide could be used as an anesthetic; C. W. Long, a Georgia physician, published in 1849 his conclusions concerning the use of ether to deaden pain; W. T. G. Morton, a Boston dentist, performed the first successful operation on an etherized patient in 1846.

REVIEW QUESTIONS

1. Discuss the factors which retarded industrial development in the United States at the close of the eighteenth century.
2. What social problems were aggravated by the increased foreign migration between 1820 and 1850?
3. What conditions were responsible for the rapid development of the railroad in the United States?
4. Do you discover any social philosophy which seems to be fundamental in the reform movements of the first half of the nineteenth century?

5. How do you account for the widespread interest in popular education? In what ways was this interest manifested?
6. What is meant by the "New England Renaissance"?
7. What American contributions in the field of the fine arts do you consider most significant?

CHAPTER XV

SLAVERY AND SECTIONALISM

For the people of the United States the decade between 1850 and 1860 was a period of uneasy truce between the sections. While most leaders seemed to believe that conflict between North and South was not inevitable, concern for the nation's future mounted with each passing year.

THE ANTISLAVERY IMPULSE

The controversy over slavery, which became acute after the Mexican War, was deeply rooted in American economic and social life.

Free and Slave States. By the middle of the eighteenth century slavery had become universal in English America, but as the nation entered upon its independent existence, the institution seemed to be declining.

GRADUAL EMANCIPATION IN NORTHERN STATES. Although slavery was indirectly recognized in the Constitution and Congress was forbidden to interfere with the importation of slaves for a period of twenty years, many of the states were already taking legal action against involuntary servitude. In 1780 the Massachusetts constitution by implication abolished slavery, and in the same year the Pennsylvania legislature made provision for gradual emancipation. New York declared in 1799 that all children born to slaves should be free after a period of apprenticeship. Gradual emancipation became the policy of all the Northeastern states.

NORTHWEST ORDINANCE. The Ordinance of 1787, which organized the Northwest Territory (see p. 54), barred slavery from the territories which were later to comprise the states of Ohio, Indiana, Illinois, Michigan, and Wisconsin. Thus the region east of the Mississippi came to be divided between slave and free territory.

SOUTHERN CRITICISM OF SLAVERY. At the close of the eighteenth century sentiment in the Southern states was far from unanimous in support of slavery. Free labor was more important than slave labor in the western districts of many Southern states. Planters like Washington, Jefferson, and George Mason doubted the economic value of the institution and feared its divisive influence in national affairs, as well as its moral evils. Most Southerners did not oppose the Act of Congress prohibiting the foreign slave trade (1808); some were the leaders in the work of the American Colonization Society (1817), which attempted to colonize free Negroes in Liberia.

The Rise of Cotton. The most important factor in fastening the grip of slavery upon the South was the expansion of cotton culture in the nineteenth century.

WHITNEY'S COTTON GIN (1793). Eli Whitney's invention of a machine to remove the seeds from raw cotton without injuring the fibre made it possible for Southern planters to produce profitably both the sea-island cotton of the coastal plain and the short-staple cotton which grew well in the uplands.

EXPANSION OF SLAVERY. The profitable nature of cotton culture and the abundance of uncultivated land on which cotton could be grown soon brought a sharp rise in the demand for Negroes to work cotton plantations. This demand was further increased by the opening of the river valleys of Louisiana to sugar culture. As slavery expanded, the system changed from that of the small plantation with a few slaves to the large plantations with a gang system of enforced labor. Southern planters turned from the raising of grains, rice, and tobacco to the cultivation of cotton and sugar cane.

The Proslavery Argument. The doubts concerning the economic desirability of slavery vanished with the expansion of cotton culture, and by 1830 the publicists and statesmen of the slave states had abandoned their criticism of an enforced labor system and were beginning to defend it as the sound basis of social organization. Their arguments, which may be traced in the writings of President Thomas R. Dew of William and Mary College, Chancellor William Harper of the Supreme Court of South Carolina, and Governor James H. Hammond of South Carolina, stressed (1) the historical and scriptural justification of slavery; (2) the economic advantages of the institution; and (3) the social benefits that it conferred upon the dominant white population.

The Antislavery Crusade. Southern apologists had many supporters in the free states, especially among the business interests associated with Southern trade; but sentiment in the North became gradually more critical of human bondage.

EARLY ANTISLAVERY SOCIETIES. Prior to 1830 the antislavery societies carried on their work in so moderate a spirit that their leaders found it possible to organize units in the slave states. Both Benjamin Lundy, the Quaker, and James G. Birney, the slaveholder, preached gradual emancipation to audiences in the Southern states.

GARRISONIAN ABOLITIONISTS. A sharp change in the temper of the opponents of slavery became manifest after William Lloyd Garrison began to publish the *Liberator* (1831). The Garrisonians scorned gradual emancipation and demanded the immediate abolition of slavery without compensation to the owners of slaves. So vigorous was their language that they aroused resentment even in the free states.

SOUTHERN REACTION. Within the slave states the attitude of the extreme abolitionists became a pretext for more determined insistence upon the legal and constitutional rights of the slaveholder. Abolitionists were charged with conspiring to stir up servile insurrection in the South, when the Nat Turner Insurrection broke out in Virginia (1831). Southern Congressmen demanded that abolitionist material be barred from the mails and persuaded the House of Representatives in 1836 to refuse to hear or take action upon antislavery petitions ("gag rule").

DIVISIONS OVER SLAVERY ISSUE

The most alarming feature of the slavery controversy was the struggle between the two sections over the status of slavery in the new territory acquired either by purchase or conquest.

The Missouri Compromise. The solution of the slavery question in the Louisiana Territory (see p. 89) had apparently been based upon the assumption that a political balance between the two sections of the country was both desirable and possible. The acquisition of both Oregon and Texas in the expansionist movement of the forties (see p. 101) was an attempt to maintain the semblance of equality between slave and free territory as the American people moved their borders westward.

The Compromise of 1850. The acquisition of the Mexican Cession and the rapid settlement of California during the gold rush specifically raised the issue of slavery extension at a time when the

Free-Soil party was trying to make opposition to slavery in the territories a political principle in the North.

THE WILMOT PROVISO. In 1846 David Wilmot, a Northern Democrat, introduced a resolution to the effect that slavery should be forever barred from any territory acquired from Mexico as a result of war or purchase. The resolution may have reflected the resentment of Northern Democrats over the preponderant Southern influence in the councils of the Polk administration, but it precipitated a bitter struggle in Congress, where it passed the House but was defeated in the Senate.

HOLDING EXTREMISTS IN CHECK. When California drafted a constitution and applied for admission into the Union as a free state, threats of disunion were heard. Various solutions of the slavery question in the Mexican Cession were proposed: (1) that the Missouri Compromise line be extended to the Pacific; (2) that Congress leave the matter to the decision of the federal courts; (3) that any decision regarding slavery be left to the people of the territory when they should be ready for statehood; and (4) that Congress take steps to protect the slaveholder as he went into the territory with his slave property.

CLAY'S RESOLUTIONS. In January, 1850, Henry Clay introduced in the Senate a series of resolutions, five of which finally became the basis of the settlement known as the Compromise of 1850. The provisions were: (1) California was to be admitted as a free state; (2) the slave trade, but not slavery, was to be abolished in the District of Columbia; (3) Congress was to enact a more effective fugitive slave law; (4) the public debt of Texas acquired before 1845 was to be paid by the United States as an indemnity for the state's relinquishment of its claims to a part of New Mexico; (5) territorial governments were to be established in New Mexico and Utah with the provision that either might be admitted to the Union with or without slavery, as they might determine.

SUPPOSED FINALITY OF THE COMPROMISE. The sectional truce was opposed by proslavery extremists like Calhoun, and by antislavery men like Seward and Chase. It received the support of conservative Northerners like Webster, and the more moderate representatives of Southern opinion. Politicians, North and South, insisted that the Compromise of 1850 was the final settlement of the slavery question.

THE ELECTION OF 1852. The Democrats nominated Franklin Pierce, a New Englander sympathetic to the South (a "doughface") and promised to defend the principles of the Compromise of 1850 against every attack. They won a resounding victory over the Whigs, who had chosen Winfield Scott, a hero of the Mexican War (p. 106) as their candidate. Scott, who was suspected of strong antislavery sentiments, received only 42 out of 296 electoral votes.

THE RUPTURE OF THE SECTIONAL TRUCE

The efforts of cautious political leaders and conservative businessmen could not maintain the uneasy truce of 1850, especially after Senator Stephen A. Douglas of Illinois sponsored the Kansas-Nebraska Bill in 1854.

Fugitive Slave Law. Antislavery groups in the North were incensed over the provisions of the Fugitive Slave Law passed in 1850. They denounced it because it failed to provide for a jury trial in the case of suspects, because it applied to slaves who had fled from their masters years before, and because it permitted federal officials to compel any citizen to aid in the apprehension and return of fugitives. Mass meetings in Northern cities resolved that they would not obey the law, while state legislatures finally passed "personal liberty laws" which prohibited the use of local jails for the confinement of fugitives. Southerners indignantly accused the North of deliberate intent to violate the Compromise.

Projects for Slavery Extension. Northerners, in turn, insisted that the South was keeping the slavery issue alive by its attempts to secure additional territory. They pointed to: (1) the filibustering expeditions of General Narciso Lopez in Cuba (1850–1851), which were supported by influential Southerners; (2) the notorious Ostend Manifesto (1854), signed by Pierre Soulé, James Buchanan, and John Y. Mason, diplomatic representatives of the United States, which covertly suggested that their country should seize Cuba; and (3) the military activities of William Walker in Nicaragua, which seemed to have the support of Southern extremists.

Repeal of the Missouri Compromise. The most fateful factor in undoing the sectional truce over the slavery issue was the Kansas-Nebraska Act (1854), repealing the Missouri Compromise which, since 1830, had been regarded as a settlement of the slavery question in the Louisiana Purchase Territory.

Douglas' Motives. Stephen A. Douglas, who proposed the repeal of the Missouri Compromise and the creation of the territories of

Nebraska and Kansas, has often been accused of trying to promote his presidential ambitions by winning the support of Southern Democrats. Other considerations, however, probably influenced him.

Demands of Missouri Planters. In the Senate, Atchison of Missouri pressed hard for a bill that would open the area west of his state to settlement, without any restriction against slavery. This required repeal of the Missouri Compromise.

Popular Sovereignty. Douglas, who had no moral convictions against human slavery, believed that the most democratic way to solve the issue was to allow the people of any new territory to decide whether or not they wished to legalize slavery in their boundaries.

Railroad Politics. Atchison, Douglas, and many of their associates in Congress were anxious to use the organization and settlement of the Nebraska region as a means of stimulating the growth of the Northwest and of promoting the building of a transcontinental railroad which would have its eastern terminal points in St. Louis and Chicago.

SHIFTING PARTY ALLEGIANCE. The political results of the Kansas-Nebraska Act were far-reaching. Many voters, alarmed by the conflict over slavery in the new territories, came to the conclusion that neither of the older parties—Democrats and Whigs—truly represented their views.

The Divided Whigs. In the Northern states some Whigs (Conscience Whigs) repudiated the Kansas-Nebraska Bill and all affiliation with proslavery members of their party. They fought the pro-Southern wing (Cotton Whigs) for control of the party.

The Anti-Nebraska Democrats. Many Northern Democrats left their party in protest against the Kansas-Nebraska Bill. Some of them joined with groups of Conscience Whigs in strengthening temporarily the Free-Soil party. As the two major parties began to break asunder, the American party (Know-Nothings) had a brief period of success with its program calling for restrictions on the foreign-born.

The Emergence of the Republicans. The most significant political development, however, was the formation of the Republican party. Recruited from the ranks of the Free-Soilers, Anti-Slavery Whigs, and Anti-Nebraska Democrats, the party was purely sectional in its appeal, for its cardinal principle was opposition to the extension of slavery anywhere within the territories of the United States.

Warfare in Kansas. The principle of popular sovereignty, which Douglas had written into the Kansas-Nebraska Bill, was put to the test on the soil of the Kansas Territory.

ARMED FREE-SOILERS AND BORDER RUFFIANS. Antislavery as well as proslavery forces sent their armed representatives into Kansas. The proslavery men, supported by residents of Missouri who rode across the border ("Border Ruffians"), elected a majority of the territorial legislature (1855) and established a government at Shawnee Mission; the free-soil men held a convention at Topeka and framed a constitution barring slavery. President Pierce decided to support the Shawnee government.

"BLEEDING KANSAS." Tension within the territory led to civil war in 1856. The free-state men fortified their capital, Lawrence, and it was wrecked by proslavery adherents. In retaliation John Brown led a small band in an attack on a settlement near Pottawatomie Creek, where five proslavery men were murdered. Guerrilla warfare continued despite the presence of United States troops in the territory.

THE LECOMPTON CONSTITUTION (1857). President Buchanan promised to restore order in Kansas and to give the bona fide settlers an opportunity to express their views on slavery. Nevertheless, he supported the Lecompton Constitution, which was drawn by the proslavery faction in such fashion that voters could vote only on the question of the *further* admission of slaves. Slave property within the territory was safeguarded by the constitution, regardless of whether further introduction of slaves was authorized.

Election of 1856. The Kansas strife was at its height in 1856, when the new Republican party made its first appeal to the country. It vigorously denounced the Kansas-Nebraska Act and the Democratic policy in Kansas. Since the party membership was confined to the North, and the organization was in its first presidential campaign, the Republicans were elated that their candidate, John C. Frémont, received 114 electoral votes against 174 for the successful Democrat, James Buchanan.

GROWTH OF THE REPUBLICAN PARTY

With the emergence of the Republican party as the major opponent of the Democrats the drift toward disunion was accelerated. Divergent social attitudes, based upon radically different economic systems, North and South, thwarted every effort at conciliation.

Panic of 1857. Republican politicians used the business depression which became evident soon after Buchanan was inaugurated as a means of discrediting the Democrats in those districts where unemployment was greatest. Manufacturers argued that the low-tariff policy of the Democrats had failed to protect them against British competition. In Pennsylvania, for example, Republican support of a high tariff probably helped in the election of 1858, when every Democratic congressman in the state was turned out of office.

The Dred Scott Decision (1857). In an attempt to settle the slavery controversy by judicial decision the Supreme Court merely succeeded in increasing the hostile feeling between the two sections.

THE SUPREME COURT'S OPINION. Dred Scott, a slave residing in Missouri, had been taken by his master into the free state of Illinois and later into the northern part of the Louisiana Purchase, where slavery had been forbidden by the Missouri Compromise. Scott sued for his freedom and the case finally reached the Supreme Court. The majority opinion, written by Chief Justice Taney, held that no Negro slave or descendant of a slave could be a citizen of the United States and that therefore Scott could not bring suit in the federal courts. More important was the additional ruling in which the Court announced that Congress had no right to prohibit slavery in the territories and that the Missouri Compromise had been null and void from the day of its enactment.

SIGNIFICANCE OF THE DECISION. The decision delighted the South, which now saw slavery protected by constitutional guarantees in every part of the national territories. The Republican party, which was demanding congressional legislation against slavery in the territories, was placed for the moment on the defensive.

The Lincoln-Douglas Debates (1858). The slavery question in the light of the Dred Scott decision was the momentous issue in the celebrated debates between Abraham Lincoln and Stephen A. Douglas.

DOUGLAS' POPULARITY. The Northern Democrats followed Douglas in his acceptance of the Dred Scott decision as good law and in his insistence that it in no way vitiated the principle of popular sovereignty as the solution of the slavery issue. After Douglas quarreled with the Buchanan administration over the Lecompton Constitution and demanded a fair trial for popular sovereignty in Kansas, even some of the Republicans rallied to his support and urged his re-election to the Senate from Illinois.

THE FREEPORT DOCTRINE. Abraham Lincoln, after a disappointing career as a Whig politician, emerged as a powerful leader of the Western Republicans. Convinced that Douglas and his doctrines were more dangerous for Republican principles than even the demands of the extreme Southerners, Lincoln accepted the Republican nomination for the Senate against Douglas and challenged his opponent to a series of debates. At Freeport he compelled Douglas to admit that in spite of the Dred Scott decision the people of a territory might exclude slavery. The Democratic leader explained that although slavery might be "legal" in a territory it could not exist where the people failed to enact legislation "friendly" to it. Such an explanation merely emphasized the gulf between Douglas and the Southern Democrats, who were demanding complete protection for their institution.

LINCOLN'S LEADERSHIP. The debates with Douglas made Lincoln one of the foremost spokesmen of the Republican party. His friends began to organize the campaign which was to bring him the presidential nomination in 1860.

John Brown's Raid (1859). This attempt of a fanatic abolitionist to stage a slave insurrection was ended after he and his little band that had seized the arsenal at Harpers Ferry were captured by United States marines. Brown was hanged in December, 1859. To many Southerners the raid appeared as "the invasion of a state by a murderous gang of abolitionists bent on inciting slaves to murder helpless women and children." They regarded it as the result of the principles which the Republican party was advocating. On the other hand, to Northern abolitionists, including Emerson and Thoreau, Brown was a hero and martyr.

Antislavery Literature. During this period the institution of slavery was increasingly attacked in books and newspapers circulated throughout the free states. The most effective works in arousing abolitionist sentiment were *Uncle Tom's Cabin* (1852), a novel by Harriet Beecher Stowe, which portrayed the evils of slavery, and *The Impending Crisis in the South; How to Meet It* (1857), a book by Hinton Rowan Helper, a North Carolinian, which cited the bad effects of slavery on Southern white workers and farmers. Rarely, however, was there a description of the degrading effect of slavery on the black race and on their white masters. Few listened to the eloquent words of such free Negroes as Frederick Douglass portraying the anguish of their fellow blacks still held in bondage.

The Election of 1860. The presidential election of 1860 marked the first national victory for the Republican party, which polled practically all its votes in the free states of the North.

THE DEMOCRATIC SCHISM. The refusal of the Democratic Convention to accept a proslavery platform caused the delegates from the lower South to bolt and nominate John C. Breckinridge of Kentucky. The regular Democrats nominated Stephen A. Douglas of Illinois.

THE CONSTITUTIONAL UNIONISTS. The remnants of the old Whig party and the Know-Nothings united to form the Constitutional Unionists, who were committed to the maintenance of the Union and compromise on the slavery question. They chose John C. Bell of Tennessee as their candidate.

THE REPUBLICAN VICTORY. The Republican convention nominated Abraham Lincoln and reaffirmed its hostility to slavery in the territories. At the same time it sought to win favor with the agricultural and business interests by advocating a homestead act and a protective tariff. The contest in the free states was really between Lincoln and Douglas; in the slave states between Breckinridge and Bell. Although Lincoln received only 40 per cent of the popular vote, he led decisively in the electoral college with 180 votes against 72 for Breckinridge, 39 for Bell and 12 for Douglas.

REVIEW QUESTIONS

1. Explain the change in the attitude of the South toward slavery which became evident in the second quarter of the nineteenth century.
2. What was the defense of slavery offered by Southern apologists in the proslavery argument?
3. Why was it impossible for the moderates to maintain a sectional truce on the basis of the Compromise of 1850?
4. Discuss the political consequences of the repeal of the Missouri Compromise.
5. Explain Lincoln's attitude toward the decision of the Supreme Court in the case of Dred Scott.
6. What was the significance of John Brown's Raid?
7. How do you account for the victory of the Republican party in the election of 1860?

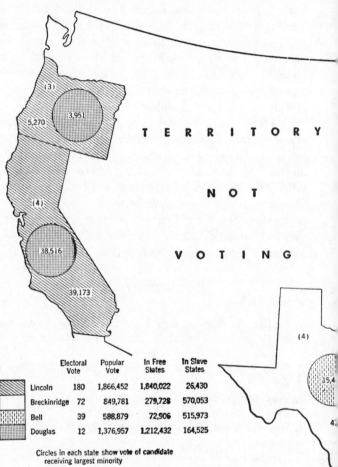

T E R R I T O R Y

N O T

V O T I N G

(3)

5,270

3,951

(4)

38,516

39,173

	Electoral Vote	Popular Vote	In Free States	In Slave States
Lincoln	180	1,866,452	1,840,022	26,430
Breckinridge	72	849,781	279,728	570,053
Bell	39	588,879	72,906	515,973
Douglas	12	1,376,957	1,212,432	164,525

Circles in each state show vote of candidate
  receiving largest minority

Numbers in parenthesis in each state show
  electoral vote

(4)

15,4

4

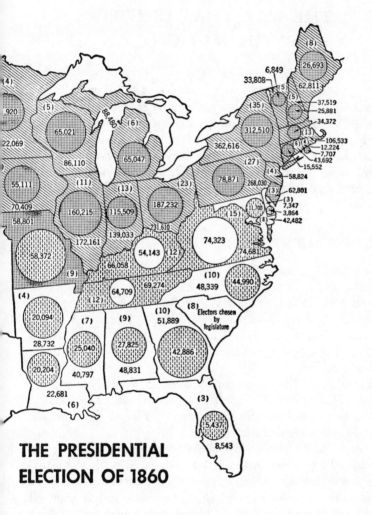

THE PRESIDENTIAL ELECTION OF 1860

Chapter XVI

THE WAR THAT UNIFIED
THE NATION

The civil strife that threatened to destroy the United States between 1861 and 1865 was a national tragedy; but it was more than that. It drew a sharp line across the life of the American people and set their faces toward enduring unity. It proved that a nation "conceived in liberty and dedicated to the proposition that all men are created equal" can endure and grow powerful, in ideas as well as resources.

THE MOVEMENT FOR SOUTHERN INDEPENDENCE

South Carolina made the election of Abraham Lincoln the occasion for an ordinance of secession which was passed by a special convention on December 20, 1860. By February 4, 1861, the other six states of the lower South—Mississippi, Florida, Alabama, Georgia, Louisiana, and Texas—had left the Union and organized the Confederate States of America as a new nation with Jefferson Davis as President.

Secessionists. The movement for secession, which was opposed by some Southerners on the basis of principle and by others on grounds of expediency, had been gathering strength for a decade, especially in the cotton states.

Subordinate Position of the South. Southern leaders were disturbed by the evidence that their section was losing its commanding position in federal affairs. The political balance was destroyed between 1850 and 1860 as California, Minnesota, and Oregon—all free states—were admitted to the Union. All avenues for Southern expansion seemed to be closed. Southerners consequently feared that their inferior position would prevent them from protecting themselves against the economic power of the industrial North.

ALLEGED VIOLATIONS OF SOUTHERN RIGHTS. The secessionists charged the North with a series of acts which, they insisted, infringed upon the constitutional rights of the slave states. The list of grievances included: (1) the abolitionist propaganda; (2) the activities of the Underground Railroad in the Northern states; (3) the passage of personal liberty acts that impeded the retrieval of runaway slaves; and (4) the formation of a political party hostile to the basic Southern institution, slavery.

SOUTHERN FEAR OF THE REPUBLICAN PARTY. Although the Republican politicians maintained that their party would not interfere with slavery in the Southern states, such promises were not a guarantee against the possible control of the party machinery by the abolitionists. Furthermore, the Republican intention to exclude slavery from the territories would, if carried out, have resulted in a permanent majority of free states in Congress. Republican success meant the complete eclipse of the South so far as federal offices were concerned. In addition, the Republicans were championing (1860) a protective tariff, a homestead act, and a railroad to connect the Pacific Coast with the old Northwest—all measures which the South had consistently opposed.

ADVANTAGES OF AN INDEPENDENT SOUTH. The Southern extremists argued that their section would prosper more outside the Union because: (1) direct and unhampered trade with Europe could be established; (2) discriminatory taxes and tariffs could be abolished; (3) the African slave trade could be revived and the cost of labor lowered; (4) necessity would compel the development of manufacturing, banking, and commerce to meet the needs of an independent South.

POSSIBILITY OF PEACEFUL REVOLT AGAINST THE UNION. The more timid Southerners were reassured by the secessionists, who argued that the speed with which the South had recovered from the Panic of 1857 proved the economic power of cotton and the soundness of the plantation economy. The North, threatened with the loss of cotton and the Southern market, would not dare forcibly to oppose secession. If war came, the South could count upon the intervention of Great Britain, anxious to save her textile industries, and the support of the Ohio Valley, closely connected to the Cotton Kingdom by commercial ties.

Northern Reaction to Secession. Confused counsels marked the reaction of Northerners to the secession of the Southern states.

The abolitionists were glad to be rid of the "nefarious institution," slavery. There was strong opposition among the business interests with Southern connections to the idea of coercion in order to preserve the Union.

BUCHANAN'S VACILLATION. President Buchanan maintained that there was no constitutional right of secession, but he denied that there was any power vested in the federal government to compel the states to obey the laws of the Union. Surrounded by a cabinet in which Southern influence was predominant, he refused to send reinforcements to Fort Sumter or to take steps to collect customs and enforce the laws in the seceded states.

COMPROMISE ATTEMPTS. Numerous schemes for reconciliation were proposed during the winter of 1860–1861. The most important were the Crittenden Compromise and the Virginia Peace Convention.

Crittenden Compromise. The essence of the plan advocated by Senator J. J. Crittenden of Kentucky was contained in five "permanent" amendments to the Constitution: (1) protecting slavery in the states where it was legal; (2) sanctioning the domestic slave trade; (3) guaranteeing payment by the United States for escaped slaves; (4) forbidding Congress to abolish slavery in the District of Columbia without the consent of Virginia and Maryland; and (5) reviving the Missouri Compromise line. The Republicans at Lincoln's insistence refused to endorse any compromise which permitted the extension of slavery into any federal territory.

Peace Convention (1861). This gathering, sponsored chiefly by Virginians, contained representatives from thirty-three states who worked for a month to formulate a program of conciliation. Their final proposals, which differed little from the Crittenden Compromise, were virtually ignored by Congress.

LINCOLN'S POLICY

The evolution of Lincoln's policy was determined by his desire to unite the sentiment of the North behind the administration, his belief that some of the slave states would remain loyal to the federal government, and his refusal to permit secession to disrupt the Union.

Lincoln's Cabinet. In his selection of his cabinet advisers Lincoln attempted to secure a composite group reflecting the various opinions which would have to be reconciled to insure Republican success. William H. Seward of New York (State) represented the old antislavery Whigs; Salmon P. Chase of Ohio (Treasury) and Gideon Welles of Connecticut (Navy) had been anti-Nebraska Democrats; Simon Cameron of Pennsylvania (War) and Caleb Smith of Indiana (Interior) were leaders of important political machines; Edward Bates of Missouri (Attorney General) and Montgomery Blair of Maryland (Postmaster General) represented the border slave states.

Fort Sumter. Lincoln was determined to hold Forts Sumter and Pickens, but he hesitated to take any action which might be interpreted in the border slave states as an aggressive move against the Confederacy. His decision on April 6 to send provisions to Major Anderson and the troops in Fort Sumter confirmed the Confederate authorities in their opinion that the time had arrived to drive Federal forces from Charleston Harbor. The bombardment of Fort Sumter (April 12–13) ended Lincoln's hesitation. On April 15 he issued a proclamation calling upon the governors of the loyal states for 75,000 militia to serve for three months.

The Border Slave States. The appeal to arms which followed Sumter tested the loyalty of the border slave states to the Union. Virginia, Arkansas, North Carolina, and Tennessee seceded, casting their lot with the Confederacy. The capital of the Confederate States was moved from Montgomery to Richmond. In four other slave states—Delaware, Maryland, Kentucky, and Missouri—Unionist sentiment proved strong enough to prevent secession. In Maryland the vigor of the Union men, strongly supported by the administration, was responsible for holding the state in the Union. In Kentucky Lincoln's astute program for conciliation finally overcame the influence of the secessionist Governor Magoffin. In Missouri civil war broke out between the forces aligned with Governor Jackson, an ardent secessionist, and friends of the Union, who could count upon the loyalty of the German population.

The Belligerents. The superiority of the North in manpower and resources was great. The total population of the Confederacy was 8,700,000 (of whom 3,500,000 were slaves) while the North had a population of 22,700,000. In transportation facilities, industrial establishments, liquid capital, foodstuffs, the North likewise possessed a decided advantage. To offset the disparity, the South relied upon the great volume of cotton exports (if they could be maintained), the defensive character of the war, the superior training of its volun-

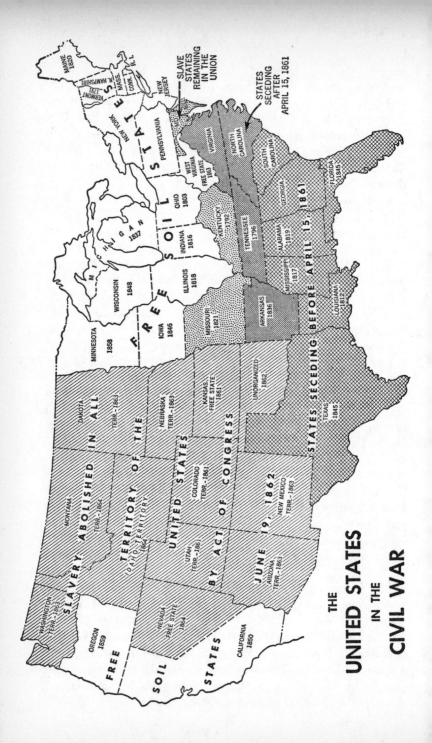

THE
UNITED STATES
IN THE
CIVIL WAR

tcers for the struggle, and the large number of competent military leaders who were available.

THE RESORT TO ARMS

The administration's program of offensive warfare came to include three principal objectives: the capture of Richmond, the control of the Mississippi River, and the effective blockade of the ports of the Confederacy.

"On to Richmond." The defensive strategy of the Southern commanders—Robert E. Lee, Joseph E. Johnston, and Thomas J. Jackson—withstood every attempt of Federal troops to take the Confederate capital during the early years of the war.

THE FIRST BATTLE OF BULL RUN (July, 1861). Northern forces under General Irvin McDowell, eager to seize Richmond, were checked by the Confederates at Bull Run, Virginia. The struggle between the two demoralized armies resulted in the rout of the Federal troops. The necessity of more adequate preparation for the combat was impressed upon both belligerents.

THE PENINSULAR CAMPAIGN (March-July, 1862). After Bull Run, George B. McClellan, fresh from a victorious campaign in West Virginia, was given command of the Army of the Potomac, which he reorganized, drilled, and equipped for the advance on Richmond. Ordered by the President to set his splendid army in motion, he finally decided to approach Richmond by way of Fortress Monroe and the peninsula between the York and James rivers. With the utmost caution he proceeded from Yorktown to White House, to Fair Oaks, and thence to within sight of Richmond, where he waited in vain for reinforcements. After meeting the Confederate counteroffensive successfully at Malvern Hill, he decided that his position was untenable and abandoned the campaign, just as Robert E. Lee took command of the Confederate troops.

THE BATTLE OF ANTIETAM. McClellan was removed from command, but after General John Pope had suffered a disastrous defeat at the hands of "Stonewall" Jackson in the Second Battle of Bull Run, the former leader of the Army of the Potomac was recalled to stop Lee's invasion of the North. The two armies met at Antietam (September 17, 1862), and Lee was compelled to retreat. McClellan failed to follow up his victory and Lincoln removed him once more, giving the command to General A. E. Burnside.

THE HIGH TIDE OF THE CONFEDERACY. Lee inflicted a disastrous defeat on Burnside at Fredericksburg (December, 1862), and at Chancellorsville (May, 1863) humiliated Burnside's successor, "Fighting Joe" Hooker.

Lee's Invasion of the North. During the early summer of 1863 Lee planned an invasion of the Northern states, which he hoped would so impress European statesmen that they would recognize the Confederacy. His task was more difficult because he had lost his greatest corps commander through the death of "Stonewall" Jackson at Chancellorsville.

Gettysburg (July 1–3, 1863). General George G. Meade, now in charge of the Army of the Potomac, managed to bring Lee's forces to battle in the little town of Gettysburg in southern Pennsylvania. It was the greatest battle of the war and marked the beginning of the end for the military forces of the Confederacy. The daring charge, led by General George Pickett, almost broke through the center of the Union lines, but reserves finally held the key positions and the magnificent effort of the Southern troops failed.

Defeat and Retreat. On July 4, 1863, Lee gave up his plan for invasion of the North and started his retreat into Virginia. Meade hesitated to attack and lost the chance to destroy the Army of Northern Virginia. But Lee had mounted the last Confederate offensive.

Opening the Mississippi. The federal government was far more successful in its efforts to secure control of the Mississippi than it was in its offensives against Richmond.

GRANT'S CAMPAIGNS. Early in 1862 General U. S. Grant secured General Halleck's permission to advance against the Confederate defenses on the Tennessee and Cumberland rivers. With the aid of river gunboats under Flag Officer Foote, he captured Fort Henry on the Tennessee and a few weeks later Fort Donelson on the Cumberland. He advanced up the Tennessee and withstood a vigorous Confederate attack on the bloody field of Shiloh (April 6–7, 1862).

CAPTURE OF NEW ORLEANS. Several weeks later Flag Officer David G. Farragut, commanding seventeen ships, ran past the shore batteries protecting New Orleans and secured control of the city. The Confederates were still in possession of the river between Vicksburg and Port Hudson.

FALL OF VICKSBURG. Late in the autumn of 1862 Grant began his long campaign against Vicksburg. Supported by Admiral Porter's gunboats, he managed after great effort to place his troops in such

CIVIL WAR CAMPAIGNS

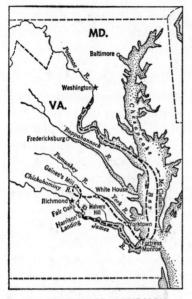

THE PENINSULAR CAMPAIGN

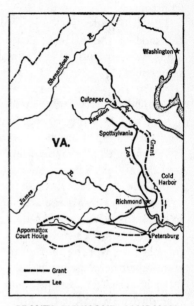

GRANT'S RICHMOND CAMPAIGN

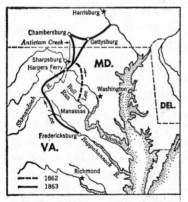

LEE'S INVASIONS of the NORTH

SHERMAN'S MARCH

a position as to besiege the city. For six weeks the Confederates held out, capitulating on July 4, 1863. The capture of Vicksburg gave the Federal forces complete control of the Mississippi and severed Arkansas, Louisiana, and Texas from the other sections of the Confederacy.

The Blockade. In April, 1861, President Lincoln proclaimed a blockade of the Atlantic Coast from South Carolina to Florida. Thus was inaugurated the attempt to starve the Confederacy into submission.

NORTHERN NAVAL SUPREMACY. At the outbreak of hostilities the South had no navy and virtually no merchant marine from which a navy could be improvised. The North, on the other hand, was constantly augmenting its squadrons. By the close of 1862 the federal navy controlled all the important ports except Wilmington, Charleston, and Mobile. The blockade-runners found it increasingly difficult to carry on their trade through ports in the West Indies.

MONITOR VERSUS MERRIMAC. The Confederates made a bold attempt to break the blockade when they reconstructed the frigate *Merrimac* as an ironclad and sent her into Hampton Roads (March 8, 1862) to demolish the wooden ships of the Federal navy. She might have accomplished her mission had it not been for the appearance of another ironclad, the *Monitor,* built for the United States government. The duel between the two was indecisive but the attempt to break the blockade was thwarted. Henceforth wooden ships were obsolete.

EFFECTS OF THE BLOCKADE. The steady pressure of the cordon of ships slowly starved the South. Rations were reduced; clothing, shoes, medicines were lacking; the transportation system broke down for want of replacements; general destitution made support of the armies in the field increasingly difficult.

The Closing Campaigns. After Gettysburg and Vicksburg the South fought valiantly but vainly to prevent the collapse of the Confederacy.

WAR IN THE WEST. Grant, Sherman, Sheridan, and Thomas cooperated in the autumn of 1863 to rescue Rosecrans, who was besieged at Chattanooga, and to win the battles of Lookout Mountain and Missionary Ridge. In the spring of 1864 Sherman began his invasion of Georgia and by September 1 had captured Atlanta.

SHERMAN'S MARCH TO THE SEA. While Thomas held the Confederates out of Tennessee, Sherman cut loose from his base of supplies and marched across Georgia to Savannah, which he entered on December 20, 1864.

GRANT's HAMMER BLOWS. With the Army of the Potomac under his direct supervision Grant advanced relentlessly toward Richmond in the famous Wilderness campaign of 1864. His powerful but costly frontal attacks on the Confederates finally brought him victory in the spring of the following year.

APPOMATTOX. The cumulative effects of the Confederate reverses on land and sea made it impossible for Lee to prolong the unequal combat. He surrendered his army at Appomattox Court House, Virginia, on April 9, 1865. Johnston's surrender to Sherman in North Carolina a few weeks later brought to an end the armed resistance of the Confederacy.

AMERICAN RELATIONS WITH EUROPE

The policies of European powers during the war years were matters of deep concern for the government of the United States and that of the Confederacy.

British Policy. The Confederacy entered the war with hope that England's dependence upon cotton would bring a speedy recognition of Southern independence. Lincoln devoted his efforts to prevent such action on the part of the British government.

FAILURE TO RECOGNIZE THE CONFEDERACY. Although Great Britain early accorded the Confederate government the rights of a belligerent, she failed to recognize the independence of the Confederate States of America. The reasons for the failure were numerous: (1) the hostility of the British working classes to the cause of the South; (2) the support accorded the North by British antislavery sentiment, especially after the Emancipation Proclamation; (3) the reliance of Great Britain on Northern wheat; (4) the failure of the South to win a decisive victory; and (5) the successful diplomacy of the Lincoln administration.

THE TRENT AFFAIR. The United States and Great Britain were brought to the verge of war in 1861 by the action of Captain Charles Wilkes in stopping the British steamship *Trent* on the high seas and removing J. M. Mason and John Slidell, who had been appointed Confederate commissioners to Great Britain and France respectively. The British government was insistent in its demands for liberation of the commissioners and a disavowal of the act. Lincoln tactfully met the British demands after the resentment in the United States over the British attitude had subsided.

CONFEDERATE CRUISERS. The Palmerston ministry, secretly sympathetic with the South, was extremely negligent in fulfilling its obligations as a neutral government. Cruisers intended for the Confederate service were constructed in British shipyards. In 1862 the *Florida, Alabama,* and *Shenandoah* were delivered to the Confederate government by intermediaries, and began their destructive attacks upon the merchant shipping of the North. The vigorous protests of Ambassador Charles Francis Adams in 1863 compelled the British government to detain several ironclads which were being constructed. Thereafter Great Britain was more scrupulous in enforcing her neutrality. The activity of the commerce-destroyers subsequently became the basis for *Alabama* claims against the British government.

Napoleon III. Napoleon's government in France paid scant attention to its obligations as a neutral. The Emperor tried vainly to persuade Great Britain and Russia to join him in forcing the United States to agree to an armistice. He permitted ships to be constructed for the Confederacy, and he assisted the Confederate commissioners to place the famous Erlanger loan. Taking advantage of the war, he violated the Monroe Doctrine by placing Maximilian of Austria on the throne of a Mexican Empire which had been created by French troops. He refused to withdraw from Mexico until the United States sent General Philip Sheridan to the Mexican border at the close of the Civil War.

Powers Friendly to the Union. Russia, Prussia, and the Scandinavian countries were favorably disposed toward the United States during the war. Russia made her attitude conspicuous by sending her fleets to visit New York and San Francisco. This gracious gesture in part explains why the United States was willing to purchase Alaska when Russia offered it to her at the close of the war.

THE BUSINESS OF WAR

The war imposed problems upon the governmental authorities, both North and South, the solution of which had far-reaching consequences.

Raising Forces. Both the Union and the Confederacy at first relied on volunteer troops induced by bounties; but as it became apparent that the war would be long and hard-fought, both enacted conscription laws. However, it was still possible to obtain exemption by hiring a substitute—a provision resented by many of the poor. In New York City the first draft drawings, in July, 1863, provoked riots so serious that troops had to be called from the army in the field to suppress them.

Filling the War Chest. Northern governmental revenues came chiefly from taxation, the issuance of legal-tender notes, and the borrowing of money.

TAXATION. Constant increases in custom duties carried the average ad valorem rate to 47 per cent. The Federal treasury collected more than $305,000,000 in duties. Internal revenue taxes and taxes on incomes amounted to $356,846,000.

LEGAL TENDERS. The reluctance of Northern politicians to impose burdensome taxes resulted in the resort to fiat money in the form of "greenbacks," which were legal tender for all debts, public and private. These notes, which were in the nature of a forced loan, depreciated in value as their amount increased and the fortunes of the government on the field of battle declined. At the close of the war $431,000,000 were in circulation.

BORROWING. The Lincoln government obtained more than three times as much from loans as from all other sources.

Bonds and Notes. Short-term loans were effected through treasury notes in small denominations, carrying interest as high as 7 per cent. The long-term bonds were issued with interest rates of 5 and 6 per cent.

National Bank Act (1863). This act promoted the sale of government bonds, but its primary purpose was to provide federal regulation for the banking system of the country. It provided for the creation of national banks, each of which was required to purchase federal bonds to the extent of one third of its capital stock and to deposit them with the Treasury. Against this security the bank might issue bank notes up to 90 per cent of the value of the bonds. These national bank notes gradually replaced the confused issues of the state banks, which were subjected to a 10 per cent tax in 1866.

SOUTHERN FINANCES. When the blockade prevented any substantial revenue from customs, the Confederate government resorted to requisitions on the states, but the method was disappointing. Comprehensive excises and heavy income taxes were imposed. Fiat money was issued, though it was not made legal tender for private debts. Bond issues, except the first in 1861, failed to produce much specie. The most important foreign loan was placed with Émile Erlanger, the Paris banker, in 1863 and was based upon cotton.

Prosperity of the North. After the financial panic and business uncertainty which marked the first months of the war the North prospered mightily. The general trend of its economic activity was reflected in the statistics showing (1) increased production of raw materials by farm and mine, (2) unprecedented output of manufactured goods, (3) growth of transportation facilities, and (4) expansion of trade and commerce. Fortunes were accumulated with great rapidity through financial speculations, lucrative war contracts, and judicious industrial investments. The fact that salaries and wages lagged behind prices brought poverty and suffering to some at a time when others were setting a standard of ill-advised extravagance.

Maintaining Morale. In the North as well as the South, the powers of the central government were stretched to meet the exigencies of war. Restraint of civil liberty was deemed necessary in order to quiet criticism of governmental policies.

LINCOLN'S WAR POWERS. Although early decisions of the Supreme Court had held that the writ of habeas corpus could be suspended only by act of Congress, Lincoln continually suspended the writ wherever he felt that the safety of the country demanded it. Even after Congress passed a law (March, 1863) providing that suspects could not be kept in prison more than twenty days without indictment by a grand jury, Lincoln continued to authorize political arrests and to uphold sentences by military tribunals. The Supreme Court (1866) held in the case of *ex parte Milligan* that the administration had violated constitutional rights by the military trial of a civilian in a place where the civil courts were open.

CONFEDERATE POLICIES. The Davis administration proceeded more cautiously in its exercise of war powers. The writ of habeas corpus was suspended under authorization of the Confederate Congress (February, 1862). So strong was the opposition in many of the states, where the state courts continued to issue the writ, that Congress in August, 1864, withdrew the President's authority. States' rights, which had been the basis of secession, made it difficult for the central government of the Confederacy to enforce its decisions.

Political Dissensions. Factional strife, which seriously embarrassed the Lincoln administration, developed during the war within the ranks of both political parties.

REPUBLICANS. In some sections a sharp division developed within the Republican party between the Radicals, who demanded the immediate abolition of slavery, and the Conservatives, who believed that abolition was subordinate to the preservation of the Union in the Republican program. Lincoln's conduct of the war was the subject of frequent attack by the Radicals.

DEMOCRATS. Many of the Democrats, generally known as "War Democrats," loyally supported the Lincoln government. The regular party organizations conducted political contests against Lincoln's supporters. A militant minority of Democrats, who were called "Copperheads," demanded peace without victory and bitterly attacked the President for his despotism. This faction, strong in the old Northwest, carried on its propaganda through secret orders such as the Knights of the Golden Circle, the Sons of Liberty, and the American Knights.

ADMINISTRATION SUPPORTERS. The Lincoln government was really supported by a coalition of Republicans and War Democrats. This fact was recognized in 1864 when Lincoln insisted that Andrew Johnson, a War Democrat, be named for second place on the ticket of the Union Republican party. The Democrats made substantial gains in the congressional elections of 1862 as a result of the dissatisfaction with the administration's attitude toward slavery, political arrests, and the conduct of the war. Many political observers believed that Lincoln could not be re-elected in 1864 in a campaign against General George B. McClellan, who had been nominated by the regular Democrats and their "Copperhead" allies. Timely military victories probably helped the President to secure 212 electoral votes to his opponent's 21.

Freeing the Slaves. Although the Lincoln administration insisted that the war was being waged to preserve the Union, the abolition of slavery finally was included in the list of war aims.

COMPENSATED EMANCIPATION. Lincoln's program with reference to slavery was based upon gradual emancipation with compensation and possible colonization of the free Negroes outside the United

States. He worked hard to persuade the representatives of the loyal slave states to accept emancipation with compensation on condition that the federal government bear part of the financial burden, but he failed. Congress did free the slaves in the District of Columbia and reimburse their owners (1862).

CONTRABAND. General B. F. Butler treated slaves who came into the Federal lines as contraband of war, because they were property used in war service, and confiscated them. The principle was applied by Congress in the first Confiscation Act (1861). Lincoln felt that the Second Confiscation Act (1862) was premature in its provision that the slaves of rebel masters, whether or not the slaves were used for war service, should be free of their servitude if they came within Federal lines.

EMANCIPATION PROCLAMATION (1863). Lincoln finally came to the conclusion that the freeing of the slaves might be used as a military punishment for the Confederate states. Immediately after the Battle of Antietam (September 22, 1862) he announced that on January 1, 1863, he would declare "forever free" the slaves in all the states which were still in arms against the authority of the federal government on that date. The effect of the Proclamation in Europe, especially in Great Britain, was highly favorable to the Northern cause. It had no immediate effect upon the military situation, however, except to unify sentiment in the slave states and to alienate some of the Northern conservatives from the administration.

THIRTEENTH AMENDMENT. In December, 1863, the House of Representatives received a resolution for a Thirteenth Amendment to the Constitution prohibiting slavery within the United States or any place subject to its jurisdiction. Not until January, 1865, could the necessary two-thirds majorities in Congress be obtained. The amendment was then referred to the state legislatures, three fourths of which ratified by December, 1865. Thus the abolition of slavery was made final and legal.

Tragedy. The tragic years of war were almost over when, on April 14, 1865, the President of the United States was stricken by an assassin's bullet. Lincoln's assailant was the actor John Wilkes Booth, a Southern sympathizer, temporarily deranged by the collapse of the Confederate cause. He little realized that his deed would bring even greater grief to the prostrate South; for Lincoln's death removed the leader who was already planning for a new nation in a spirit of "malice toward none and charity for all."

REVIEW QUESTIONS

1. Why did the election of Abraham Lincoln become the pretext for South Carolina's secession in 1860?
2. Discuss Buchanan's attitude toward the constitutional basis of the doctrine of secession.
3. Why were the Republicans under Lincoln's leadership opposed to the Crittenden Compromise?
4. How did you account for the fact that four slave states remained loyal to the Union?
5. What change occurred in Lincoln's policy toward slavery during the course of the war?
6. How did the financial requirements of the government during the war years lead to the enactment of the National Banking Act of 1863?
7. What were the "greenbacks"? What justification was there for the issuance of "greenbacks"?
8. How do you explain the failure of the British government to recognize the independence of the Confederacy?
9. What factors do you consider most important in explaining the failure of the struggle for Southern independence?

Chapter XVII

REBUILDING THE POLITICAL STRUCTURE

The sectional animosities, which had been intensified by the ugly events of war, made it more difficult than most Americans had imagined to solve the problems of political reconstruction at the close of hostilities. Peace brought new patterns of life to both South and North.

THE DILEMMA OF RECONSTRUCTION

It required a long generation after Appomattox to reorganize state and local governments that had been destroyed in the collapse of the Confederacy, to re-establish normal relations between North and South, and to revive in many a rebellious community a sense of national loyalty.

The Tragedy of Dixie. Amidst the ruins of war, the states of the Confederacy had to begin the slow process of reshaping relations between races and among divided social groups, at the same time that they tried to regain their political place in the Union.

THE PHYSICAL SCARS. From Virginia to Texas the traveler in the first years of peace found physical destruction and human destitution on every side. The land between Washington and Richmond was described as a "desert." Atlanta, Columbia, Mobile, Richmond, and many smaller towns had been gutted by fires. Wherever plantation or village had escaped, it was invariably surrounded by the ruins of destroyed mills, bridges, dams, and railroad tracks. Fields overgrown with weeds proclaimed in many areas the complete breakdown of the economy.

DESTITUTION AND CONFUSION. For the moment, war had destroyed the basis of Southern society and thrown most of the population—both white and Negro—into confusion. Southern planters, once affluent and powerful, now faced the facts that the labor system had been destroyed, financial savings wiped out, and transportation and industry brought to a standstill. Even more difficult to resolve were the problems posed by the changing status of the Negro, as he made the slow transition from slave to wage earner. It was easier to repair war's physical wreckage than to create a new citizenry in a devastated land.

POLITICAL PROBINGS. Both North and South leaders, as well as the people generally, thought of the problems of reconstruction in political terms. Political reconstruction was imperative for the South, where most governmental processes, except for federal military control, had stopped with the collapse of the Confederacy. Northern leaders were as anxious as the Southerners to establish normal relations in the Federal Union for the lately rebellious states. They differed, bitterly at times, over the definition of "normal relations."

Framing a Reconstruction Policy.
Members of Congress, even before Lee's surrender, had turned their attention to political procedures for bringing the "states of the secession back into the Union." A few—very few—were inclined to be conciliatory toward the Confederate states. Most were determined that Southerners should pay a heavy penalty for secession—an illegal act. Some demanded that the entire South be treated as a "conquered province" which Congress had constitutional power to govern, using military force if necessary.

LINCOLN'S PLANS. President Lincoln brushed aside the "conquered province" theory, maintaining that since there was no constitutional right to secede, the states of the Confederacy had merely been "out of their proper practical relation" with the Union. The President acted to restore the states to their former status as quickly as possible. He (1) set up provisional governments in regions where Union armies were already in control; (2) issued a Proclamation of Amnesty and Reconstruction (1863) pardoning all (with a few exceptions) who would swear allegiance to the government of the United States and accept "all acts of Congress passed during the existing rebellion with reference to slaves"; and (3) authorized the establishment of a new government for any state if one-tenth of its qualified voters of 1860 would take the required loyalty oath.

CONGRESSIONAL REBUTTAL. Lincoln's conciliatory proposals brought quick response from congressional leaders (of his own party) who feared he would "let the South off too easily." In July, 1864, Congress passed the drastic Wade-Davis bill which (1) provided that a majority of white male citizens had to take a loyalty oath before a civil government could be organized in a seceded state and (2) excluded from the electorates of such states former Confederate officeholders and soldiers. Lincoln gave this bill a pocket veto, whereupon he was denounced by some congressmen for "dictatorial usurpation."

THE "JOHNSON GOVERNMENTS." President Lincoln's unfinished work fell into the hands of his successor, Andrew Johnson, who tried to give substance to Lincoln's plans. He granted amnesty to all former Confederates (except certain officers, political leaders, and large property-holders) who would take an oath to "support, protect and defend the Constitution." He set up provisional governments in seven former Confederate states, and authorized the loyal white citizens in these states to elect state legislatures, which were to repeal ordinances of secession, repudiate the Confederate state debts, and ratify the Thirteenth Amendment.

PRESIDENT JOHNSON VERSUS CONGRESS

Congress refused to seat the senators and representatives elected by the "provisional" state governments authorized by President Johnson. Instead, the Republicans in Congress, led by Thaddeus Stevens in the House and Benjamin Wade in the Senate, created a Joint Committee on Reconstruction, with fifteen members, which was empowered to examine all aspects of political reconstruction and make new proposals for congressional action.

Emergence of the Radicals. Opponents of Johnson's political program for reconstruction soon were named "Radicals" by the newspaper writers of the period. They were men of many motives but found common cause in hostility to Johnson.

MOTIVES OF THE RADICALS. High moral purpose and partisan self-interest were strangely blended in the plans and strategy of the Radical Republican leaders. Contemporary documents portrayed the following significant motives in building strength for the group: (1) the humanitarian desire to safeguard the interests of the Negro in the South; (2) the hope of Northern industrialists that the removal of Southern influence from Congress would promote legislation favorable to business enterprise; (3) resentment over the speedy return to power of the former Confederate politicians in Southern states; (4) the determination of Republican leaders to create a Republican party in the South; (5) the fear of executive encroachment on the authority of Congress; (6) last, but not least, personal animosity toward Johnson on the part of Congressmen who thought he was unworthy of the presidency.

CONGRESSIONAL LEGISLATION. Prodded by the Radical Republican leaders, Congress moved steadily in the direction of placing the Negro under the protection of the Federal government for so long a period of time as might be necessary. There was an implication that this protection would be maintained until the status of the Negro as a free man had been insured in the Southern states.

Freedmen's Bureau Bill (1866). Early in 1866 President Johnson vetoed a bill extending the life of the Freedmen's Bureau, which had been established in 1865. In July, 1866, a bill was repassed over the presidential veto, extending the powers of the Bureau to protect and provide for the emancipated slaves.

Civil Rights Act (1866). In April, 1866, President Johnson vetoed a Civil Rights Act, conferring citizenship on the Negro and assuring him equality with white citizens before the law. Congress passed the bill over the presidential veto.

The Fourteenth Amendment. In April, 1866, the Joint Committee on Reconstruction proposed the Fourteenth Amendment to the Constitution, which Congress promptly passed and referred to the states for ratification. By its provisions: (1) citizenship was conferred on every person born or naturalized in the United States, and state laws abridging civil rights were prohibited; (2) states which deprived the Negro of the ballot were to suffer a reduction of representation in Congress proportionate to the number denied the right to vote; (3) ex-Confederates were barred from holding national and state offices if they had filled similar posts before the war (this disability could be removed by a two-thirds vote in each house); (4) the Confederate debt was repudiated and the validity of the United States debt affirmed. Tennessee quickly ratified the amendment and was readmitted to the Union (1866). All the other states of the former Confederacy rejected this amendment on the advice of Johnson, who considered it beyond the constitutional power of Congress.

THE REIGN OF THE RADICALS

The victories of Radical Republican candidates in the Congressional elections of 1866 indicated that their political group had gained complete control of both houses of Congress.

The Reconstruction Acts (1867). Congress moved quickly

to drastic action, partly to punish states that had failed to ratify the Fourteenth Amendment. Over President Johnson's veto, it passed a Military Reconstruction Act, which was supplemented later in the year by acts outlining administrative and legal procedures. This legislation provided: (1) the ten states still unreconstructed were to be divided into five military districts with a major general in command of each; (2) constitutional conventions, elected by Negroes and loyal whites, were to frame constitutions providing for Negro suffrage; (3) these constitutions were to be acceptable to Congress; (4) qualified voters were to elect state legislatures pledged to ratify the Fourteenth Amendment; (5) with the ratification of the Fourteenth Amendment, the states could apply for representation in Congress.

Curbing Presidential Power. Aware that their program of action could be partially blocked by President Johnson, the Radical Republicans proceeded to limit presidential authority. The Tenure of Office Act (1867) required the Senate's consent for the removal of any official, including cabinet members, whose appointment had been made originally by the President with Senate approval. At the same time the Command of the Army Act virtually stripped the President of his functions as commander in chief of the nation's military forces.

IMPEACHMENT OF PRESIDENT JOHNSON. When the President fought back by removing a favorite of the Radicals, Edwin M. Stanton, from his post as Secretary of War, the House of Representatives impeached Johnson for "high crimes and misdemeanors."

TRIAL AND VERDICT (MARCH 5–MAY 26, 1868). The trial of the only president of the United States ever impeached was saved from the category of farce only by the dignified arguments of the attorneys for the defense. In the final vote seven Republican senators had the courage to vote for acquittal, thus wrecking Radical plans. Had one of the nineteen senators who voted for acquittal changed his vote, the Radicals would have been able to realize their goal, which was to make the President subservient to Congress and to alter the constitutional arrangement for separation of powers in the national government.

THE POLITICAL PAGEANT

Defeated in the trial of President Johnson, the Radical Republicans nevertheless moved on to important victories. They committed the Republican party not only to a vigorous reconstruction policy, but also to an economic program more favorable to the nation's manufacturing, banking, and railroad interests than to the agricultural leaders of the West and South.

The Grant Era. Fortunately for the Republican Party in 1868, Ulysses S. Grant was not opposed to the political and economic policies of the congressional Radicals. His victory over the Democratic nominee, Horatio Seymour, was won with three Southern states still under military occupation and with 700,000 newly enfranchised Negroes voting almost unanimously for the North's greatest military leader.

THE PRESIDENT. Grant's sterling qualities on the battlefield did not enable him to cope with the problems of the presidential office. His years in the White House suffered not from militarism but from political incompetence. He might have found help had he turned more frequently to such cabinet members as Hamilton Fish (State), J. D. Cox (Interior) or E. R. Hoar (Attorney General); but he preferred to consult with such politicians as Roscoe Conkling (N. Y.) and B. F. Butler (Mass.), who believed that the spoils of office should go to the victors in the political battle.

CORRUPTION IN VARIOUS FORMS. Though President Grant was personally and officially honest, he permitted dishonest men to use him and his high office for their own purposes. Too often he was naïve in his judgment of men and motives. Americans were distressed by a lengthening list of unsavory episodes: (1) "Black Friday" (September 24, 1869), when Jim Fisk and Jay Gould, using Grant's prestige, tried to corner the nation's gold supply; (2) the Crédit Mobilier, involving Vice-President Schuyler Colfax, which profited illegally through the construction of the Union Pacific Railroad; (3) the Whiskey Ring, including Grant's private secretary, which conspired to cheat the government of internal revenue taxes on distilled liquor; (4) the Belknap Fraud, in which the family of Grant's Secretary of War gained large profits from the assignment of trading posts in the Indian Territory; (5) the Sanborn Contracts, which caused Secretary of the Treasury Richardson to resign in order to escape censure; (6) the District of Columbia Ring, whereby the governor of the District, appointed and defended by Grant, handed out "honest graft" to his business associates.

The Reformers. By 1872 some leaders in the Republican party were in revolt against the low level of public ethics tolerated by

President Grant and his administration. A few had been charter members of the party in the years of its organization; others had been close to the Lincoln administration and were eager to persuade their fellow Republicans to return to the principles of the prewar years. They were joined by three larger groups: (1) those who felt that Grant had followed too harsh a line in the South; (2) those who desired reform of the civil service by a wider use of merit examinations; and (3) those who felt that Grant should lead Congress in a systematic reduction of tariff schedules.

THE LIBERAL REPUBLICANS. At a convention of reformers in Cincinnati in May, 1872, the name Liberal Republican was adopted. The delegates, however, ignored such dedicated reformers as Lyman Trumbull and Charles Francis Adams and named Horace Greeley, the gifted but eccentric editor of the *New York Tribune,* as their presidential candidate. Much to the surprise and amusement of the voters, the Democrats also named Greeley in the hope that fusion with the Liberal Republicans might enable them to defeat Grant, who had been nominated by the regular Republicans for a second term.

THE FIASCO OF 1872. Greeley's defeat was overwhelming—an evidence of his personal unpopularity rather than an expression of approval for Grant's policies. Politically inept the Liberal Republicans were, but their revolt made an impression on their party's leadership. In his second administration Grant moved slowly but perceptibly toward reform in civil service appointments, downward revision of tariff schedules, and a more liberal program of reconstruction in the states still under military governments.

THE DISPUTED ELECTION (1876)

After the failure of the Liberal Republican movement, Horatio Seymour, former governor of New York, remarked: "Our people want men in office who will not steal, but who will not interfere with those who do." By 1876, however, the leaders of both political parties believed that the time for housecleaning had arrived. The Republicans particularly were eager to escape the scandals of the Grant administrations.

Tilden versus Hayes. Reformers in the Democratic party engineered the nomination of Samuel J. Tilden, who as governor of New York had broken the power of William Marcy Tweed, the grafting boss of Tammany Hall. Alarmed by the possibility that the Democrats might win on the issue of political morality, the Republicans turned to the able Governor of Ohio, Rutherford B. Hayes, whose career had been untouched by any hint of scandal.

THE INCONCLUSIVE BALLOTING. Though Tilden carried New York and several other Northern states in addition to the South, he was sure of only 184 electoral votes, one short of the necessary majority. Twenty electoral votes were in doubt, including those of South Carolina, Florida, and Louisiana, which were just passing from the control of carpetbaggers and Negroes into the hands of the native whites (see p. 158).

THE ELECTORAL COMMISSION. To avert any violence over the disputed ballots, Congress created a special Electoral Commission to settle the controversy. Three Republicans and two Democrats from the Senate, three Democrats and two Republicans from the House and five justices of the Supreme Court voted eight to seven (along party lines) in favor of Hayes on every disputed point. Hayes was declared elected by 185 to 184 electoral votes.

The Compromise of 1877. Even before the Electoral Commission was appointed, prominent Republican politicians had reached an agreement with certain conservative Democrats to make sure that the decision, if favorable to the Republicans, would be accepted. Often called the Compromise of 1877, this understanding assured Southern leaders that if Hayes was elected President, he would withdraw the troops from all Southern states and would approve the distribution of federal subsidies for railroads and other public works in the South. The final result, therefore, placed the states of the former Confederacy under the political control of their white citizens and made the South a solidly Democratic region for several generations (see p. 159).

THE REVIVING SOUTH

It is difficult to determine whether the severe policies of the federal government were responsible for the reshaping of Southern society in the postwar years. Less vigorous congressional control might have brought much the same political, economic, and social results.

Political Transition. For a decade the Reconstruction Acts of 1867 denied to the planter aristocracy that political power which it had enjoyed before the Civil War. Registration lists in the former Confederate states showed that there were 703,000 Negro, and only 627,000 white, voters in 1868.

THE "CARPETBAG GOVERNMENTS." As a result, politically inexperienced Negroes, who had little or no education, gave their support to Northerners who had come into the South to gain power and wealth (carpetbaggers) and to Southerners who hoped to secure lucrative contracts or political office by aiding the Congressional program (scalawags).

EXTRAVAGANCE AND CORRUPTION. The legislatures elected in many Southern states (1868–1869) indulged in fraudulent practices and extravagant expenditures which resulted in huge public debts and burdensome taxes. In North Carolina, for example, the public debt more than doubled in two years, while the tax rate in Louisiana during 1870 was three times the rate in the more populous state of Pennsylvania. However, a number of Northern legislatures of the period were also corrupt.

THE REFORMERS. Not lost in the welter of misgovernment were some Negro and white leaders who tried sincerely to make life better for the average Southern citizen. They persuaded Republican legislatures (1870–1875) to enact laws providing for more and better courts, establishing new hospitals and asylums, and setting up a public school system. Thus Negro legislators made a genuine contribution to the rebuilding of the area in which they were now legally full citizens but in effect second-class citizens.

The Restoration of White Supremacy. By 1869 most Southern states had ratified the Fourteenth Amendment and had been permitted to rejoin the Union. Virginia, Georgia, Mississippi, and Texas were not able to satisfy Congress until 1870, when they were readmitted on condition that their legislatures ratify the Fifteenth Amendment, which forbade any state to deny the right to vote to any person on the ground of "race, color, or previous condition of servitude."

THE KU-KLUX KLAN. The Southern whites turned to nonpolitical methods in their efforts to undo the results of Radical Reconstruction. Secret societies—the Ku-Klux Klan, the Knights of the White Camelia, the Boys of '76—were used as the instruments of a policy of terrorism designed to frighten the Negroes and compel them to renounce their new political power. The Klan, which became the most notorious of the organizations, was dominated in some districts by terrorists.

PEACEFUL COERCION. Southerners who disliked the violent tactics of the Klan and other secret societies turned to more subtle forms of coercion. Negroes were denied employment and were kept from the polls, not by force but by intimidation.

THE ENFORCEMENT ACTS. Southern resistance brought legislation for the enforcement of the congressional program. (1) An act of May, 1870, imposed heavy penalties for violations of the Fourteenth and Fifteenth Amendments; (2) an act of February, 1871, placed congressional elections under the control of the federal authorities; (3) the Ku-Klux Act of the same year gave the President military powers to suppress violence in the Southern states. (In 1871 President Grant used these powers to subdue the Klan in South Carolina.)

The Return of the Conservatives. In spite of the Fourteenth and Fifteenth Amendments and the "force acts" passed by Congress, the Radical Republicans lost ground in the South after 1870. By 1876 only South Carolina, Florida, and Louisiana were still in the hands of governments supported by military authority. A year later the political compromise over the disputed presidential election (see p. 157) resulted in the withdrawal of federal troops from the South; state governments still in Republican hands quickly fell to the Southern Democrats.

THE LEGACY OF RECONSTRUCTION

For most of the South the period of congressional Reconstruction was a tragic era from which recovery was painfully slow.

Political Readjustments. The most obvious political consequence of congressional policies in the South was the adherence of the great majority of Southern whites to the Democratic party.

THE SOLID SOUTH. In the immediate postwar years most Southerners came to believe that the Republican party as a whole was the party of the Negro and the corrupt white man, who despised the South. As a result many areas in the former slave states knew only the one-party system. Whoever captured the Democratic nomination was virtually sure of winning. Between 1876 and 1928 the Republican party rarely carried any of the former Confederate states in a national election.

THE "BOURBONS." Within the one-party system, the leaders of the Democrats came to be known as "Bourbons." This faction consisted of some of the old planter class and many native whites who had made money during the Reconstruction period.

DISFRANCHISEMENT OF THE NEGRO. By ways which avoided violence, the Democratic leaders steadily reduced the number of Negroes who could meet the qualifications for the suffrage. Several devices were used: (1) literacy and educational tests which most Negroes could not pass; (2) poll taxes and other property requirements; (3) the application of the "grandfather" clause granting the suffrage only to those whose fathers or grandfathers had voted before 1867. The last device, of course, barred the Negroes and still made it possible for uneducated "poor whites" to vote.

Economic Rehabilitation. The political confusion of the post-war decade retarded all the Southern states in their efforts to promote the economic well-being of their citizens.

THE DISRUPTION OF THE PLANTATION SYSTEM. The revolutionary changes effected by the war compelled the landholders of the Southern states to reduce the size of their plantations. Some sold off surplus acres, but the majority preferred to try a plan of cultivation on shares, with tenants who were unable to pay a cash rental. Owner and tenant entered into a partnership, one furnishing land, the other labor.

THE RISE OF THE MERCHANT. The cash necessary to finance this partnership was generally supplied by merchants or bankers who took mortgages on the crops as security for loans. It proved to be an expensive system of rural credits. Interest rates were high; farmers were compelled to confine their production to staples like cotton and tobacco; and the small farmers became virtually tenants of the merchant-creditors.

INDUSTRIAL DEVELOPMENT. As the South of the great plantations disappeared, a new industrial order arose. The exploitation of coal, iron, phosphates, and lumber slowly gathered momentum. The less prosperous elements in the rural districts drifted into the towns to work in factories located where cheap water power was available. The increase in railroad mileage began to keep pace with the output of coal and pig iron and with the multiplication of cotton spindles.

Social Tensions. It is difficult to measure the effect of the Reconstruction years in the process of social readjustment throughout the South.

THE STATUS OF NEGROES. The brief period of political power which Negro voters enjoyed in the South under the Radical Republican regimes probably increased tension between the native whites and the freedmen.

Resentment over Military Reconstruction. In many communities the bitterness engendered by military occupation and imposed government brought interracial conflicts that curbed the free development of the newly liberated Negro population.

Insecurity of Negro Workers. The breakup of the large plantations into smaller farms was by no means a social gain in every section of the South. Too often it meant that the freedman found it difficult to secure and hold a job. The Negroes who drifted into mill towns or who got employment in mines and factories found that their labor was exploited almost as vigorously as it had been during the years of slavery.

CLEAVAGES AMONG NATIVE WHITES. The small farmers, heavily in debt, and the tenants on larger plantations grew ever more hostile toward the "Bourbon" representatives of the old planter-aristocracy and the new merchant-capitalist groups.

The New South. The phrase "the New South" which Henry Grady of the *Atlanta Constitution* used to describe the efforts of Southerners to balance agriculture with new industries, told only part of the story at the close of the nineteenth century. There was a vigorous leadership trying to remake the South economically, but many critical problems remained: (1) the Southern economy had not escaped from control by Northern financiers; (2) Southern political leaders remained far more interested in sectional than in national problems; (3) too many white, as well as Negro, farmers still lived in poverty; (4) mindful of heavy losses during the war and Reconstruction years, most Southern voters refused to accept tax programs which would provide funds for the social services needed to rebuild from war's destruction.

THE BOOMING NORTH

While the South struggled with its tragic heritage, the North was moving toward ever greater economic strength. At the Philadelphia Exposition (1876), celebrating the centennial of their independence as a nation, Americans were amazed by the exhibits revealing their increasing wealth.

Beyond the Mississippi. Much of the national wealth during the decade following the Civil War was drawn from the trans-

Mississippi West. Grains from the Great Plains, livestock for the "cattle country," copper, lead, silver, and gold from Western mines—all gave impetus to the speculative investments of Eastern capitalists and to the economic boom throughout the North, which was only briefly deflated by the depression of 1873.

The Thrust of the Railroads. Eastern business interests, western mining companies, and the growing communities of the Pacific coast were quick to bind the various parts of the nation together with miles of steel rails. On May 10, 1869, the Union Pacific and Central Pacific railroads met near Ogden, Utah, with two engines "facing on a single track, half a world behind each back." This first transcontinental line was one of five built before 1877. The others were: Northern Pacific, Atlantic and Pacific, Texas and Pacific, and the Atchison, Topeka and Santa Fe. With numerous "feeder lines" the railroad network brought the manufacturer closer to the raw materials he needed and to the markets in which he sold his goods. It gave the city dweller easier access to the resources of farm and forest.

The Shape of the New Industrialism. By 1877 the characteristic features of "big business" in the United States were emerging. On every side there was abundant evidence of: (1) the growth of mass production; (2) the use of the corporate form of business organization; (3) the expansion of manufacturing enterprises into all parts of the nation; (4) rapidly mounting investment of domestic and foreign capital in the nation's industries and transportation and communication lines. Americans in 1877 realized that a second industrial revolution was beginning to transform their land.

REVIEW QUESTIONS

1. To what extent did Andrew Johnson follow Abraham Lincoln's policy in dealing with the reconstruction of the states that had formed the Confederacy?
2. How was the program of the congressional Radicals, as set forth in the Fourteenth Amendment, modified by the Reconstruction Acts of 1867?
3. In what sense was the election of 1868 a victory for the business and financial interests of the Northern states?
4. How do you explain the failure of the Radicals to secure a conviction in the impeachment proceedings against President Johnson?

5. If you had been a Southern planter during the years immediately following the collapse of the Confederacy, what economic problems would you have faced?

6. An eminent American historian has characterized the Civil War years as the period of a Second American Revolution. Do you see any justification for this statement?

7. What did Southern leaders have in mind when they wrote about the "New South"?

8. Discuss the significance of the Reconstruction period for present-day race problems in the United States.

9. If you had been qualified to vote in 1872, would you have voted for President Grant's re-election? Why?

10. During the post-Civil War years were American business leaders justified in consolidating small business enterprises into large-scale industries? Defend your answer.

EXAMINATIONS *

Mid-Term Examination

(One Hour)

Answer Question I and three additional questions.

I. State clearly the significance of any four of the following in the economic development of the United States.

    a. The Assiento (14)
    b. *Gibbons* v. *Ogden* (82)
    c. Eli Whitney (120, 123)
    d. Embargo Act (75)
    e. Samuel Slater (111)
    f. Treaty of San Lorenzo (65)
    g. Tariff of 1816 (81)
    h. *McCulloch* v. *Maryland* (82)

II. The results of the election of 1800 have often been described as "revolutionary." Do you agree with this description? Why? (67–68)

III. If you had been a member of the First Congress of the United States, would you have supported Alexander Hamilton's financial measures? Give an explanation of your vote. (61–62)

IV. Some American historians insist that the American Revolution was a social upheaval as well as a political revolt. Discuss the social and economic results of the Revolutionary years. (52–56)

V. How do you account for the decline of the Federalist party and its failure to win a national election after it was defeated by the Jeffersonians in 1800? (66–68, 72–73, 86–97)

VI. The colonial period of American history was a time of training in self-government, which Americans put to effective use when they had won their political independence. Do you agree with this statement? Why? (21–28, 37–42)

*The figures in parentheses refer to pages in the Outline where information relating to each question may be found.

Final Examination

(Three Hours)

Answer Question I and five other questions.

I. One of the great themes in the story of the American people, from the settlement of Jamestown to the close of the Civil War, was the broadening of the base of popular participation in government. Discuss as fully as possible. (22, 52–53, 58–60, 67–68, 89–90, 129–131, 147–148)

II. Why has the spirit of nationalism that followed the War of 1812 generally been described as "premature?" (79–83)

III. In what ways did the philosophy and purposes of Jacksonian democracy differ from those of the Jeffersonian democrats? (67–78, 86–97)

IV. What evidence of political continuity do you find in the programs of the Federalists, the Whigs, and the Republicans? (60–67, 72–73, 98–100, 103, 107, 128–131, 135)

V. For more than seventy-five years after the ratification of the Constitution the controversy over the nature of the federal union grew in intensity, culminating finally in Civil War. Indicate the relation of each of the following to that controversy: The Hartford Convention, the Kentucky and Virginia Resolutions, the South Carolina Ordinance of Nullification. (77, 67, 92–94)

VI. Compare and contrast the views toward the institution of slavery in the United States of Stephen A. Douglas and Abraham Lincoln. (126–131, 147–148)

VII. The humanitarian reforms of the first half of the nineteenth century were the answers of many Americans to the impact of industrial and urban growth. Discuss. (110–117)

VIII. One of the bitterest fruits of westward expansion was the intensification of the slavery controversy. Do you agree with this statement? Support your answer with specific incidents. (86–89, 122–130)

IX. Sectionalism and nationalism have often seemed to be conflicting forces in American history. Do you believe that the Civil War and Reconstruction diminished sectional animosities? Explain your answer. (150–162)

AMERICAN HISTORICAL DOCUMENTS

The reader's attention is called to the following basic documents of American history pertinent to the topics discussed in this volume. These documents are quoted or summarized in *American Historical Documents,* edited by Harold C. Syrett and published by Barnes and Noble, Inc.

The First Charter of Virginia (1606)

Smith's "Generall Historie of Virginia: The Fourth Booke" (1624)

The First Charter of Massachusetts (1629)

The Cambridge Agreement (1629)

Charter of Freedoms and Exemptions to Patroons (1629)

Bradford's "History of Plymouth Plantation" (1630–1648)

The Charter of Maryland (1632)

Fundamental Orders of Connecticut (1639)

Massachusetts "Body of Liberties" (1641)

Massachusetts School Law of 1642

New England's First Fruits: "Description of Harvard College" (1643)

"A Short Account of the Mohawk Indians" (1644)

The Bloody Tenent of Persecution . . . (1644)

Maryland Toleration Act (1649)

Johnson's "Wonder-working Providence of Sions Saviour in New England" (1654)

"A Brief Description of the Province of Carolina" (1666)

Manifesto Concerning the Troubles in Virginia (1676)

"Some Account of the Province of Pennsilvania" (1681)

Thomas Brattle's Letter on the Salem Witchcraft Proceedings (1692)

Pennsylvania Charter of Privileges (1701)

Charter of Georgia (1732)

Zenger Case Defense (1735)

A Faithful Narrative of the Surprising Work of God, . . . (1737)

Albany Plan of Union (1754)

James Otis' Speech against Writs of Assistance (1761)

Treaty of Paris (1763)

Patrick Henry's "Treason" Speech (1765)

Resolutions of the Stamp Act Congress (1765)

Nonimportation Agreement of New York Merchants (1765)

Letters from a Pennsylvania Farmer (1767–1768)

Massachusetts Circular Letter (1768)

Declaration and Resolves of the First Continental Congress (1774)

Patrick Henry's "Liberty or Death" Speech (1775)

Mecklenberg County Resolutions (1775)

Declaration of the Causes and Necessities of Taking up Arms (1775)

Common Sense (1776)

Virginia Bill of Rights (1776)

The Declaration of Independence (1776)

Treaties with France (1778)

Articles of Confederation (1781)

Letters from an American Farmer (1782)

Treaty of Paris (1783)

Land Ordinance of 1785

Virginia Statute of Religious Liberty (1786)

Treaty with Morocco (1787)

Northwest Ordinance (1787)

The Constitution (1787)

Letters from the Federal Farmer to the Republican (1787)

The Federalist; Number 51 (1788)

Washington's First Inaugural Address (1789)

Judiciary Act of 1789

Report on the Public Credit (1790)

Jefferson's Opinion on the Constitutionality of the Bank (1791)

Hamilton's Opinion on the Constitutionality of the Bank (1791)

Report on Manufactures (1792)

Washington's Neutrality Proclamation (1793)

Chisholm v. *Georgia* (1793)

Jay's Treaty (1794)

Pinckney's Treaty (Treaty of San Lorenzo) (1795)

Washington's Farewell Address (1796)

XYZ Papers (1798)

Alien and Sedition Acts (1798)

Kentucky and Virginia Resolutions (1798)

Jefferson's First Inaugural Address (1801)

Louisiana Purchase Treaty (1803)

Marbury v. *Madison* (1803)

Proclamation on the Burr Conspiracy (1806)

Jefferson's Message on the Lewis and Clark Expedition (1806)

Act to Prohibit the Importation of Slaves (1807)

Neutrality Laws during the Napoleonic Wars (1807–1810)

Fletcher v. *Peck* (1810)

John Randolph's Speech against War with Great Britain (1811)

Madison's War Message (1812)

Treaty of Ghent (1814)

Report and Resolutions of the Hartford Convention (1815)

Charter of the Second Bank of the United States (1816)

Erie Canal Act (1817)

Rush-Bagot Agreement (1817)

Convention of 1818

Adams-Onís Treaty (1819)

Dartmouth College v. *Woodward* (1819)

"Irrepressible Conflict" Speech (1858)

John Brown's Last Speech (1859)

Ableman v. *Booth* (1859)

Davis Resolutions (1860)

South Carolina Ordinance of Secession (1860)

Crittenden Plan (1860)

Virginia (Peace Convention) Plan (1861)

Morrill Tariff (1861)

Lincoln's First Inaugural Address (1861)

Constitution of the Confederate States (1861)

Lincoln's Call for Volunteers (1861)

Homestead Act (1862)

Morrill Act (1862)

Pacific Railroad Act (1862)

Emancipation Proclamation (1863)

Lincoln's Gettysburg Address (1863)

Lincoln's Plan for Reconstruction (Ten Per Cent Plan) (1863)

Wade-Davis Bill (1864)

Lincoln's Second Inaugural Address (1865)

Freedmen's Bureau Act (1865)

Lincoln's Last Speech (1865)

Ex parte Milligan (1866)

First Reconstruction Act (1867)

Johnson's Veto of First Reconstruction Act (1867)

Tenure of Office Act (1867)

Alaska Purchase Act (1867)

Second, Third, and Fourth Reconstruction Acts (1867)

Mississippi v. *Johnson* (1867)

Ku-Klux Klan—Organization and Principles (1868)

Articles of Impeachment of Johnson (1868)

Burlingame Treaty (1868)

Texas v. *White* (1869)

Veazie Bank v. *Fenno* (1869)

Enforcement Acts (1870–1871)

Amnesty Act (1872)

Coinage Act (1873)

Slaughterhouse Cases (1873)

Specie Resumption Act (1875)

Civil Rights Act (1875)

Independent (Greenback) Platform (1876)

Decision of the Electoral Commission (1877)

Appendix B

PRESIDENTS AND SECRETARIES OF STATE

President	Term	Secretary of State	Year
1. George Washington	1789–1797	Thomas Jefferson	1789
		Edmund Randolph	1794
		Timothy Pickering	1795
2. John Adams	1797–1801	Timothy Pickering	
		John Marshall	1800
3. Thomas Jefferson	1801–1809	James Madison	1801
4. James Madison	1809–1817	Robert Smith	1809
		James Monroe	1811
5. James Monroe	1817–1825	John Q. Adams	1817
6. John Quincy Adams	1825–1829	Henry Clay	1825
7. Andrew Jackson	1829–1837	Martin Van Buren	1829
		Edward Livingston	1831
		Louis McLane	1833
		John Forsyth	1834
8. Martin Van Buren	1837–1841	John Forsyth	
9. William Henry Harrison	1841	Daniel Webster	1841
10. John Tyler	1841–1845	Daniel Webster	
		Hugh S. Legaré	1843
		Abel P. Upshur	1843
		John C. Calhoun	1844
11. James Knox Polk	1845–1849	James Buchanan	1845
12. Zachary Taylor	1849–1850	John M. Clayton	1849
13. Millard Fillmore	1850–1853	Daniel Webster	1850
		Edward Everett	1852
14. Franklin Pierce	1853–1857	William L. Marcy	1853
15. James Buchanan	1857–1861	Lewis Cass	1857
		Jeremiah S. Black	1860
16. Abraham Lincoln	1861–1865	William H. Seward	1861
17. Andrew Johnson	1865–1869	William H. Seward	
18. Ulysses S. Grant	1869–1877	Elihu B. Washburne	1869
		Hamilton Fish	1869

19. RUTHERFORD B. HAYES	1877–1881	William M. Evarts	1877
20. JAMES A. GARFIELD	1881	James G. Blaine	1881
21. CHESTER A. ARTHUR	1881–1885	James G. Blaine	
		F. T. Frelinghuysen	1881
22. GROVER CLEVELAND	1885–1889	Thomas F. Bayard	1885
23. BENJAMIN HARRISON	1889–1893	James G. Blaine	1889
		John W. Foster	1892
24. GROVER CLEVELAND	1893–1897	Walter Q. Gresham	1893
		Richard Olney	1895
25. WILLIAM McKINLEY	1897–1901	John Sherman	1897
		William R. Day	1898
		John Hay	1898
26. THEODORE ROOSEVELT	1901–1909	John Hay	
		Elihu Root	1905
		Robert Bacon	1909
27. WILLIAM H. TAFT	1909–1913	Philander C. Knox	1909
28. WOODROW WILSON	1913–1921	William J. Bryan	1913
		Robert Lansing	1915
		Bainbridge Colby	1920
29. WARREN G. HARDING	1921–1923	Charles E. Hughes	1921
30. CALVIN COOLIDGE	1923–1929	Charles E. Hughes	
		Frank B. Kellogg	1925
31. HERBERT C. HOOVER	1929–1933	Henry L. Stimson	1929
32. FRANKLIN D. ROOSEVELT	1933–1945	Cordell Hull	1933
		E. R. Stettinius	1945
33. HARRY S. TRUMAN	1945–1953	E. R. Stettinius	
		James F. Byrnes	1945
		George C. Marshall	1947
		Dean Acheson	1949
34. DWIGHT D. EISENHOWER	1953–1961	John Foster Dulles	1953
		Christian Herter	1959
35. JOHN F. KENNEDY	1961–1963	Dean Rusk	1961
36. LYNDON B. JOHNSON	1963–1969	Dean Rusk	
37. RICHARD M. NIXON	1969–1974	William P. Rogers	1969
		Henry Kissinger	1973
38. GERALD R. FORD	1974–1977	Henry Kissinger	
39. JIMMY CARTER	1977–1981	Cyrus R. Vance	1977
		Edmund Muskie	1980
40. RONALD REAGAN	1981–	Alexander Haig	1981
		George Schultz	1982

APPENDIX C

STATES, TERRITORIES, AND DEPENDENCIES

States

Original thirteen states indicated in capital letters

State	Settled	Area Sq. Mi.	Entered Union
Alabama	1702	51,060	1819
Alaska	1783	571,065	1959
Arizona	1580	113,575	1912
Arkansas	1685	52,499	1836
California	1769	156,573	1850
Colorado	1858	103,884	1876
CONNECTICUT	1635	4,899	1788
DELAWARE	1638	1,978	1787
Florida	1565	54,252	1845
GEORGIA	1733	58,274	1788
Hawaii	c.500	6,415	1959
Idaho	1842	82,708	1890
Illinois	1720	55,930	1818
Indiana	1733	36,185	1816
Iowa	1788	56,032	1846
Kansas	1727	82,048	1861
Kentucky	1775	39,863	1792
Louisiana	1699	45,106	1812
Maine	1624	31,012	1820
MARYLAND	1634	9,874	1788
MASSACHUSETTS	1620	7,867	1788
Michigan	1668	57,019	1837
Minnesota	1805	80,009	1858
Mississippi	1699	47,223	1817
Missouri	1764	69,138	1821
Montana	1809	145,736	1889
Nebraska	1847	76,612	1867
Nevada	1850	109,788	1864
NEW HAMPSHIRE	1623	9,014	1788
NEW JERSEY	1664	7,531	1787
New Mexico	1537	121,510	1912
NEW YORK	1614	47,939	1788
NORTH CAROLINA	1650	49,067	1789
North Dakota	1780	69,457	1889
Ohio	1788	40,972	1803

State	Settled	Area Sq. Mi.	Entered Union
Oklahoma	1889	68,887	1907
Oregon	1838	96,248	1859
PENNSYLVANIA	1682	45,007	1787
RHODE ISLAND	1636	1,058	1790
SOUTH CAROLINA	1670	30,272	1788
South Dakota	1794	76,378	1889
Tennessee	1757	41,762	1796
Texas	1686	262,840	1845
Utah	1847	82,339	1896
Vermont	1724	9,276	1791
VIRGINIA	1607	39,838	1788
Washington	1845	66,709	1889
West Virginia	1727	24,079	1863
Wisconsin	1670	54,705	1848
Wyoming	1834	97,411	1890

Territories and Dependencies

	Acquired	Area Sq. Mi.
Guam	1898—ceded to U. S. by Spain	209
Puerto Rico	1898—ceded to U. S. by Spain; became a self-governing Commonwealth, 1952	3,421
American Samoa	1899—annexed by treaty with Germany and Great Britain	76
Canal Zone	1904—leased in perpetuity from Panama	553
Virgin Islands	1917—purchased from Denmark	133
Midway, Wake, and other Pacific islands		42

Appendix D

A DECLARATION

BY THE REPRESENTATIVES OF THE UNITED STATES
OF AMERICA IN GENERAL CONGRESS ASSEMBLED

July 4, 1776 *

When, in the course of human events, it becomes necessary for one people to dissolve the political bands which have connected them with another, and to assume, among the powers of the earth, the separate and equal station to which the laws of nature and of nature's God entitle them, a decent respect to the opinions of mankind requires that they should declare the causes which impel them to the separation.

We hold these truths to be self-evident, that all men are created equal; that they are endowed by their Creator with certain unalienable rights; that among these are life, liberty, and the pursuit of happiness. That, to secure these rights, governments are instituted among men, deriving their just powers from the consent of the governed; that, whenever any form of government becomes destructive of these ends, it is the right of the people to alter or to abolish it, and to institute new government, laying its foundation on such principles, and organizing powers in such form, as to them shall seem most likely to effect their safety and happiness. Prudence, indeed, will dictate that governments long established should not be changed for light and transient causes; and, accordingly, all experience hath shown, that mankind are more disposed to suffer, while evils are sufferable, than to right themselves by abolishing the forms to which they are accustomed. But when a long train of abuses and usurpations, pursuing invariably the same object, evinces a design to reduce them under absolute despotism, it is their right, it is their duty, to throw off such government and to provide new guards for their future security. Such has been the patient sufferance of these colonies, and such is now the necessity which constrains them to alter their former systems of government. The history of the present King of Great Britain is a history of repeated injuries and usurpations, all having in direct object the establishment of an absolute tyranny over these States. To prove this, let facts be submitted to a candid world:

* Spelling, punctuation, and capitalization have been modernized.

He has refused his assent to laws the most wholesome and necessary for the public good.

He has forbidden his governors to pass laws of immediate and pressing importance, unless suspended in their operation till his assent should be obtained; and, when so suspended, he has utterly neglected to attend to them.

He has refused to pass other laws for the accommodation of large districts of people, unless those people would relinquish the right of representation in the legislature, a right inestimable to them and formidable to tyrants only.

He has called together legislative bodies at places unusual, uncomfortable, and distant from the depository of their public records, for the sole purpose of fatiguing them into compliance with his measures.

He has dissolved representative houses repeatedly for opposing with manly firmness his invasions on the rights of the people.

He has refused for a long time, after such dissolutions, to cause others to be elected; whereby the legislative powers, incapable of annihilation, have returned to the people at large for their exercise; the state remaining in the meantime exposed to all the dangers of invasion from without, and convulsions within.

He has endeavored to prevent the population of these States; for that purpose obstructing the laws for naturalization of foreigners, refusing to pass others to encourage their migration hither, and raising the conditions of new appropriations of lands.

He has obstructed the administration of justice, by refusing his assent to laws for establishing judiciary powers.

He has made judges dependent on his will alone, for the tenure of their offices, and the amount and payment of their salaries.

He has erected a multitude of new offices, and sent hither swarms of officers to harass our people, and eat out their substance.

He has kept among us, in times of peace, standing armies, without the consent of our legislatures.

He has affected to render the military independent of and superior to the civil power.

He has combined with others to subject us to a jurisdiction foreign to our constitution, and unacknowledged by our laws; giving his assent to their acts of pretended legislation:

For quartering large bodies of armed troops among us:

For protecting them, by a mock trial, from punishment for any murders which they should commit on the inhabitants of these States:

For cutting off our trade with all parts of the world:

For imposing taxes on us without our consent:

For depriving us, in many cases, of the benefits of trial by jury:

For transporting us beyond seas to be tried for pretended offences:

For abolishing the free system of English laws in a neighboring province, establishing therein an arbitrary government, and enlarging its boundaries so as to render it at once an example and fit instrument for introducing the same absolute rule into these colonies:

For taking away our charters, abolishing our most valuable laws, and altering fundamentally the forms of our governments:

For suspending our own legislatures, and declaring themselves invested with power to legislate for us in all cases whatsoever.

He has abdicated government here, by declaring us out of his protection and waging war against us.

He has plundered our seas, ravaged our coasts, burnt our towns, and destroyed the lives of our people.

He is at this time transporting large armies of foreign mercenaries to complete the works of death, desolation, and tyranny, already begun with circumstances of cruelty and perfidy scarcely paralleled in the most barbarous ages, and totally unworthy the head of a civilized nation.

He has constrained our fellow citizens, taken captive on the high seas, to bear arms against their country, to become the executioners of their friends and brethren, or to fall themselves by their hands.

He has excited domestic insurrections amongst us, and has endeavored to bring on the inhabitants of our frontiers, the merciless Indian savages, whose known rule of warfare is an undistinguished destruction of all ages, sexes, and conditions.

In every stage of these oppressions, we have petitioned for redress in the most humble terms; our repeated petitions have been answered only by repeated injury. A prince, whose character is thus marked by every act which may define a tyrant, is unfit to be the ruler of a free people.

Nor have we been wanting in attention to our British brethren. We have warned them, from time to time, of attempts made by their legislature to extend an unwarrantable jurisdiction over us. We have reminded them of the circumstances of our emigration and settlement here. We have appealed to their native justice and magnanimity, and we have conjured them, by the ties of our common kindred, to disavow these usurpations, which would inevitably interrupt our connections and correspondence. They, too, have been deaf to the voice of justice and consanguinity. We must, therefore, acquiesce in the necessity which denounces our separation, and hold them, as we hold the rest of mankind, enemies in war, in peace, friends.

We, therefore, the representatives of the United States of America, in general Congress assembled, appealing to the Supreme Judge of the world for the rectitude of our intentions, do, in the name, and by the authority of the good people of these colonies, solemnly publish and declare, that these united colonies are, and of right ought to be, free and independent states: that they are absolved from all allegiance to the British Crown, and that all political connection between them and the state of Great Britain is, and ought to be, totally dissolved; and that, as free and independent states, they have full power to levy war, conclude peace, contract alliances, establish commerce, and to do all other acts and things which independent states may of right do. And, for the support of this declaration, with a firm reliance on the protection of Divine Providence, we mutually pledge to each other our lives, our fortunes, and our sacred honor.

CONSTITUTION OF THE UNITED STATES *

Adopted September 17, 1787
Effective March 4, 1789

WE the people of the United States, in order to form a more perfect union, establish justice, insure domestic tranquillity, provide for the common defense, promote the general welfare, and secure the blessings of liberty to ourselves and our posterity, do ordain and establish this Constitution for the United States of America.

ARTICLE I

SECTION 1. All legislative powers herein granted shall be vested in a Congress of the United States, which shall consist of a Senate and House of Representatives.

SECTION 2. 1. The House of Representatives shall be composed of members chosen every second year by the people of the several States, and the electors in each state shall have the qualifications requisite for electors of the most numerous branch of the State legislature.

2. No person shall be a Representative who shall not have attained to the age of twenty-five years, and been seven years a citizen of the United States, and who shall not, when elected, be an inhabitant of that State in which he shall be chosen.

3. Representatives and direct taxes [1] shall be apportioned among the several States which may be included within this Union, according to their respective numbers, which shall be determined by adding to the whole number of free persons, including those bound to service for a term of years, and excluding Indians not taxed, three fifths of all other persons.[2] The actual enumeration shall be made within three years after the first meeting of the Congress of the United States, and within every subsequent term of ten years, in such manner as they shall by law direct. The number of Representatives shall not exceed one for every thirty thousand, but each State shall have at least one Representative; and until

* Spelling, punctuation, and capitalization have been modernized.

[1] See the 16th Amendment.

[2] See the 14th Amendment.

such enumeration shall be made, the State of New Hampshire shall be entitled to choose three, Massachusetts eight, Rhode Island and Providence Plantations one, Connecticut five, New York six, New Jersey four, Pennsylvania eight, Delaware one, Maryland six, Virginia ten, North Carolina five, South Carolina five, and Georgia three.

4. When vacancies happen in the representation from any State, the executive authority thereof shall issue writs of election to fill such vacancies.

5. The House of Representatives shall choose their speaker and other officers, and shall have the sole power of impeachment.

SECTION 3. 1. The Senate of the United States shall be composed of two Senators from each State, chosen by the legislature thereof,[1] for six years; and each Senator shall have one vote.

2. Immediately after they shall be assembled in consequence of the first election, they shall be divided as equally as may be into three classes. The seats of the Senators of the first class shall be vacated at the expiration of the second year, of the second class at the expiration of the fourth year, and of the third class at the expiration of the sixth year, so that one third may be chosen every second year; and if vacancies happen by resignation, or otherwise, during the recess of the legislature of any State, the executive thereof may make temporary appointments until the next meeting of the legislature, which shall then fill such vacancies.[1]

3. No person shall be a Senator who shall not have attained to the age of thirty years, and been nine years a citizen of the United States, and who shall not, when elected, be an inhabitant of that State for which he shall be chosen.

4. The Vice President of the United States shall be President of the Senate, but shall have no vote, unless they be equally divided.

5. The Senate shall choose their other officers, and also a president pro tempore, in the absence of the Vice President, or when he shall exercise the office of President of the United States.

6. The Senate shall have the sole power to try all impeachments. When sitting for that purpose, they shall be on oath or affirmation. When the President of the United States is tried, the Chief Justice shall preside; and no person shall be convicted without the concurrence of two thirds of the members present.

7. Judgment in cases of impeachment shall not extend further than to

[1] See the 17th Amendment.

removal from office, and disqualification to hold and enjoy any office of honor, trust, or profit under the United States; but the party convicted shall nevertheless be liable and subject to indictment, trial, judgment, and punishment, according to law.

SECTION 4. 1. The times, places, and manner of holding elections for Senators and Representatives shall be prescribed in each State by the legislature thereof; but the Congress may at any time by law make or alter such regulations, except as to the places of choosing Senators.

2. The Congress shall assemble at least once in every year, and such meeting shall be on the first Monday in December, unless they shall by law appoint a different day.

SECTION 5. 1. Each House shall be the judge of the elections, returns, and qualifications of its own members, and a majority of each shall constitute a quorum to do business; but a smaller number may adjourn from day to day, and may be authorized to compel the attendance of absent members, in such manner, and under such penalties as each House may provide.

2. Each House may determine the rules of its proceedings, punish its members for disorderly behavior, and, with the concurrence of two thirds, expel a member.

3. Each House shall keep a journal of its proceedings, and from time to time publish the same, excepting such parts as may in their judgment require secrecy; and the yeas and nays of the members of either House on any question shall, at the desire of one fifth of those present, be entered on the journal.

4. Neither House, during the session of Congress, shall, without the consent of the other, adjourn for more than three days, nor to any other place than that in which the two Houses shall be sitting.

SECTION 6. 1. The Senators and Representatives shall receive a compensation for their services, to be ascertained by law, and paid out of the Treasury of the United States. They shall in all cases, except treason, felony, and breach of the peace, be privileged from arrest during their attendance at the session of their respective Houses, and in going to and returning from the same; and for any speech or debate in either House, they shall not be questioned in any other place.

2. No Senator or Representative shall, during the time for which he was elected, be appointed to any civil office under the authority of the United States, which shall have been created, or the emoluments whereof

shall have been increased during such time; and no person holding any office under the United States shall be a member of either House during his continuance in office.

Section 7. 1. All bills for raising revenue shall originate in the House of Representatives; but the Senate may propose or concur with amendments as on other bills.

2. Every bill which shall have passed the House of Representatives and the Senate shall, before it become a law, be presented to the President of the United States; if he approve he shall sign it, but if not he shall return it, with his objections, to that House in which it shall have originated, who shall enter the objections at large on their journal, and proceed to reconsider it. If after such reconsideration two thirds of that House shall agree to pass the bill, it shall be sent, together with the objections, to the other House, by which it shall likewise be reconsidered, and if approved by two thirds of that House, it shall become a law. But in all such cases the votes of both Houses shall be determined by yeas and nays, and the names of the persons voting for and against the bill shall be entered on the journal of each House respectively. If any bill shall not be returned by the President within ten days (Sundays excepted) after it shall have been presented to him, the same shall be a law, in like manner as if he had signed it, unless the Congress by their adjournment prevent its return, in which case it shall not be a law.

3. Every order, resolution, or vote to which the concurrence of the Senate and House of Representatives may be necessary (except on a question of adjournment) shall be presented to the President of the United States; and before the same shall take effect, shall be approved by him, or being disapproved by him, shall be repassed by two thirds of the Senate and House of Representatives, according to the rules and limitations prescribed in the case of a bill.

Section 8. The Congress shall have power:

1. To lay and collect taxes, duties, imposts, and excises, to pay the debts and provide for the common defense and general welfare of the United States; but all duties, imposts, and excises shall be uniform throughout the United States;

2. To borrow money on the credit of the United States;

3. To regulate commerce with foreign nations, and among the several States, and with the Indian tribes;

4. To establish an uniform rule of naturalization, and uniform laws on the subject of bankruptcies throughout the United States;

5. To coin money, regulate the value thereof, and of foreign coin, and fix the standard of weights and measures;

6. To provide for the punishment of counterfeiting the securities and current coin of the United States;

7. To establish post offices and post roads;

8. To promote the progress of science and useful arts, by securing for limited times to authors and inventors the exclusive right to their respective writings and discoveries;

9. To constitute tribunals inferior to the Supreme Court;

10. To define and punish piracies and felonies committed on the high seas, and offenses against the law of nations;

11. To declare war, grant letters of marque and reprisal, and make rules concerning captures on land and water;

12. To raise and support armies, but no appropriation of money to that use shall be for a longer term than two years;

13. To provide and maintain a navy;

14. To make rules for the government and regulation of the land and naval forces;

15. To provide for calling forth the militia to execute the laws of the Union, suppress insurrections, and repel invasions;

16. To provide for organizing, arming, and disciplining the militia, and for governing such part of them as may be employed in the service of the United States, reserving to the States respectively, the appointment of the officers, and the authority of training the militia according to the discipline prescribed by Congress;

17. To exercise exclusive legislation in all cases whatsoever, over such district (not exceeding ten miles square) as may, by cession of particular States, and the acceptance of Congress, become the seat of the government of the United States, and to exercise like authority over all places purchased by the consent of the legislature of the State in which the same shall be, for the erection of forts, magazines, arsenals, dockyards, and other needful buildings; and

18. To make all laws, which shall be necessary and proper for carrying into execution the foregoing powers, and all other powers vested by this Constitution in the government of the United States, or in any department or officer thereof.

Section 9. 1. The migration or importation of such persons as any of the States now existing shall think proper to admit, shall not be prohibited by the Congress prior to the year one thousand eight hundred and eight, but a tax or duty may be imposed on such importation, not exceeding ten dollars for each person.

2. The privilege of the writ of habeas corpus shall not be suspended, unless when in cases of rebellion or invasion the public safety may require it.

3. No bill of attainder or ex post facto law shall be passed.

4. No capitation, or other direct, tax shall be laid, unless in proportion to the census or enumeration hereinbefore directed to be taken.[1]

5. No tax or duty shall be laid on articles exported from any State.

6. No preference shall be given by any regulation of commerce or revenue to the ports of one State over those of another; nor shall vessels bound to, or from, one State be obliged to enter, clear, or pay duties in another.

7. No money shall be drawn from the Treasury, but in consequence of appropriations made by law; and a regular statement and account of the receipts and expenditures of all public money shall be published from time to time.

8. No title of nobility shall be granted by the United States; and no person holding any office of profit or trust under them shall, without the consent of the Congress, accept of any present, emolument, office, or title, of any kind whatever, from any king, prince, or foreign state.

Section 10. 1. No State shall enter into any treaty, alliance, or confederation; grant letters of marque and reprisal; coin money; emit bills of credit; make anything but gold and silver coin a tender in payment of debts; pass any bill of attainder, ex post facto law, or law impairing the obligation of contracts; or grant any title of nobility.

2. No State shall, without the consent of the Congress, lay any imposts or duties on imports or exports, except what may be absolutely necessary for executing its inspection laws; and the net produce of all duties and imposts, laid by any State on imports or exports, shall be for the use of the Treasury of the United States; and all such laws shall be subject to the revision and control of the Congress.

3. No State shall, without the consent of Congress, lay any duty of tonnage, keep troops or ships of war in time of peace, enter into any

[1] See the 16th Amendment.

agreement or compact with another State, or with a foreign power, or engage in war, unless actually invaded, or in such imminent danger as will not admit of delay.

ARTICLE II

SECTION 1. 1. The executive power shall be vested in a President of the United States of America. He shall hold his office during the term of four years, and, together with the Vice President chosen for the same term, be elected, as follows:

2. Each State shall appoint, in such manner as the legislature thereof may direct, a number of electors, equal to the whole number of Senators and Representatives to which the State may be entitled in the Congress; but no Senator or Representative, or person holding an office of trust or profit under the United States, shall be appointed an elector.

3. The electors shall meet in their respective States, and vote by ballot for two persons, of whom one at least shall not be an inhabitant of the same State with themselves. And they shall make a list of all the persons voted for, and of the number of votes for each; which list they shall sign and certify, and transmit sealed to the seat of the government of the United States, directed to the President of the Senate. The President of the Senate shall, in the presence of the Senate and House of Representatives, open all the certificates, and the votes shall then be counted. The person having the greatest number of votes shall be the President, if such number be a majority of the whole number of electors appointed; and if there be more than one who have such majority, and have an equal number of votes, then the House of Representatives shall immediately choose by ballot one of them for President; and if no person have a majority, then from the five highest on the list the said House shall in like manner choose the President. But in choosing the President, the votes shall be taken by States, the representation from each State having one vote; a quorum for this purpose shall consist of a member or members from two thirds of the States, and a majority of all the States shall be necessary to a choice. In every case, after the choice of the President, the person having the greatest number of votes of the electors shall be the Vice President. But if there should remain two or more who have equal votes, the Senate shall choose from them by ballot the Vice-President.[1]

4. The Congress may determine the time of choosing the electors, and the day on which they shall give their votes; which day shall be the same throughout the United States.

5. No person except a natural born citizen, or a citizen of the United

[1] Superseded by the 12th Amendment.

States at the time of the adoption of this Constitution, shall be eligible to the office of President; neither shall any person be eligible to that office who shall not have attained to the age of thirty-five years, and been fourteen years a resident within the United States.

6. In case of the removal of the President from office, or of his death, resignation, or inability to discharge the powers and duties of the said office, the same shall devolve on the Vice President, and the Congress may by law provide for the case of removal, death, resignation, or inability, both of the President and Vice President, declaring what officer shall then act as President, and such officer shall act accordingly, until the disability be removed, or a President shall be elected.

7. The President shall, at stated times, receive for his services a compensation, which shall neither be increased nor diminished during the period for which he shall have been elected, and he shall not receive within that period any other emolument from the United States, or any of them.

8. Before he enter on the execution of his office, he shall take the following oath or affirmation:—"I do solemnly swear (or affirm) that I will faithfully execute the office of President of the United States, and will to the best of my ability, preserve, protect, and defend the Constitution of the United States."

Section 2. 1. The President shall be commander in chief of the army and navy of the United States, and of the militia of the several States, when called into the actual service of the United States; he may require the opinion, in writing, of the principal officer in each of the executive departments, upon any subject relating to the duties of their respective offices, and he shall have power to grant reprieves and pardons for offenses against the United States, except in cases of impeachment.

2. He shall have power, by and with the advice and consent of the Senate, to make treaties, provided two thirds of the Senators present concur; and he shall nominate, and by and with the advice and consent of the Senate, shall appoint ambassadors, other public ministers and consuls, judges of the Supreme Court, and all other officers of the United States, whose appointments are not herein otherwise provided for, and which shall be established by law; but the Congress may by law vest the appointment of such inferior officers as they think proper, in the President alone, in the courts of law, or in the heads of departments.

3. The President shall have power to fill up all vacancies that may happen during the recess of the Senate, by granting commissions which shall expire at the end of their next session.

SECTION 3. He shall from time to time give to the Congress information of the state of the Union, and recommend to their consideration such measures as he shall judge necessary and expedient; he may, on extraordinary occasions, convene both Houses, or either of them, and in case of disagreement between them with respect to the time of adjournment, he may adjourn them to such time as he shall think proper; he shall receive ambassadors and other public ministers; he shall take care that the laws be faithfully executed, and shall commission all the officers of the United States.

SECTION 4. The President, Vice President, and all civil officers of the United States, shall be removed from office on impeachment for, and conviction of, treason, bribery, or other high crimes and misdemeanors.

ARTICLE III

SECTION 1. The judicial power of the United States shall be vested in one Supreme Court, and in such inferior courts as the Congress may from time to time ordain and establish. The judges, both of the Supreme and inferior courts, shall hold their offices during good behavior, and shall, at stated times, receive for their services a compensation, which shall not be diminished during their continuance in office.

SECTION 2. 1. The judicial power shall extend to all cases, in law and equity, arising under this Constitution, the laws of the United States, and treaties made, or which shall be made, under their authority; to all cases affecting ambassadors, other public ministers, and consuls; to all cases of admiralty and maritime jurisdiction; to controversies to which the United States shall be a party; to controversies between two or more States; between a State and citizens of another State;[1] between citizens of different States; between citizens of the same State claiming lands under grants of different States, and between a State, or the citizens thereof, and foreign states, citizens, or subjects.

2. In all cases affecting ambassadors, other public ministers, and consuls, and those in which a State shall be party, the Supreme Court shall have original jurisdiction. In all the other cases before mentioned, the Supreme Court shall have appellate jurisdiction, both as to law and fact, with such exceptions, and under such regulations as the Congress shall make.

3. The trial of all crimes, except in cases of impeachment, shall be by jury; and such trial shall be held in the State where the said crimes shall have been committed; but when not committed within any State,

[1] See the 11th Amendment.

the trial shall be at such place or places as the Congress may by law have directed.

SECTION 3. 1. Treason against the United States shall consist only in levying war against them, or in adhering to their enemies, giving them aid and comfort. No person shall be convicted of treason unless on the testimony of two witnesses to the same overt act, or on confession in open court.

2. The Congress shall have power to declare the punishment of treason, but no attainder of treason shall work corruption of blood, or forfeiture except during the life of the person attainted.

ARTICLE IV

SECTION 1. Full faith and credit shall be given in each State to the public acts, records, and judicial proceedings of every other State. And the Congress may by general laws prescribe the manner in which such acts, records, and proceedings shall be proved, and the effect thereof.

SECTION 2. 1. The citizens of each State shall be entitled to all privileges and immunities of citizens in the several States.[1]

2. A person charged in any State with treason, felony, or other crime, who shall flee from justice, and be found in another State, shall on demand of the executive authority of the State from which he fled, be delivered up to be removed to the State having jurisdiction of the crime.

3. No person held to service or labor in one State, under the laws thereof, escaping into another, shall, in consequence of any law or regulation therein, be discharged from such service or labor, but shall be delivered up on claim of the party to whom such service or labor may be due.[2]

SECTION 3. 1. New States may be admitted by the Congress into this Union; but no new State shall be formed or erected within the jurisdiction of any other State; nor any State be formed by the junction of two or more States, or parts of States, without the consent of the legislatures of the States concerned as well as of the Congress.

2. The Congress shall have power to dispose of and make all needful rules and regulations respecting the territory or other property belonging

[1] See the 14th Amendment, Sec. 1.
[2] See the 13th Amendment.

to the United States; and nothing in this Constitution shall be so construed as to prejudice any claims of the United States, or of any particular State.

SECTION 4. The United States shall guarantee to every State in this Union a republican form of government, and shall protect each of them against invasion; and on application of the legislature, or of the executive (when the legislature cannot be convened) against domestic violence.

ARTICLE V

The Congress, whenever two thirds of both Houses shall deem it necessary, shall propose amendments to this Constitution, or, on the application of the legislatures of two thirds of the several States, shall call a convention for proposing amendments, which, in either case, shall be valid to all intents and purposes, as part of this Constitution, when ratified by the legislatures of three fourths of the several States, or by conventions in three fourths thereof, as the one or the other mode of ratification may be proposed by the Congress; provided that no amendment which may be made prior to the year one thousand eight hundred and eight shall in any manner affect the first and fourth clauses in the ninth section of the first article; and that no State, without its consent, shall be deprived of its equal suffrage in the Senate.

ARTICLE VI

1. All debts contracted and engagements entered into, before the adoption of this Constitution, shall be as valid against the United States under this Constitution as under the Confederation.[1]

2. This Constitution, and the laws of the United States which shall be made in pursuance thereof; and all treaties made, or which shall be made, under the authority of the United States, shall be the supreme law of the land; and the judges in every State shall be bound thereby, anything in the Constitution or laws of any State to the contrary notwithstanding.

3. The Senators and Representatives before mentioned, and the members of the several State legislatures, and all executive and judicial officers, both of the United States and of the several States, shall be bound by oath or affirmation to support this Constitution; but no religious test shall ever be required as a qualification to any office or public trust under the United States.

[1] See the 14th Amendment, Sec. 4.

ARTICLE VII

The ratification of the conventions of nine States shall be sufficient for the establishment of this Constitution between the States so ratifying the same.

Done in Convention by the unanimous consent of the States present the seventeenth day of September in the year of our Lord one thousand seven hundred and eighty-seven, and of the independence of the United States of America the twelfth. In witness whereof we have hereunto subscribed our names.

[Names omitted]

AMENDMENTS

First Ten Amendments passed by Congress Sept. 25, 1789.
Ratified by three fourths of the States December 15, 1791.

Articles in addition to, and amendment of, the Constitution of the United States of America, proposed by Congress, and ratified by the legislatures of the several States, pursuant to the fifth article of the original Constitution.

ARTICLE I

Congress shall make no law respecting an establishment of religion, or prohibiting the free exercise thereof; or abridging the freedom of speech, or of the press; or the right of the people peaceably to assemble, and to petition the government for a redress of grievances.

ARTICLE II

A well regulated militia, being necessary to the security of a free State, the right of the people to keep and bear arms shall not be infringed.

ARTICLE III

No soldier shall, in time of peace, be quartered in any house without the consent of the owner, nor in time of war, but in a manner to be prescribed by law.

ARTICLE IV

The right of the people to be secure in their persons, houses, papers, and effects, against unreasonable searches and seizures, shall not be violated, and no warrants shall issue, but upon probable cause, supported by oath or affirmation, and particularly describing the place to be searched, and the persons or things to be seized.

ARTICLE V

No person shall be held to answer for a capital, or otherwise infamous crime, unless on a presentment or indictment of a grand jury, except in cases arising in the land or naval forces, or in the militia, when in actual service in time of war or public danger; nor shall any person be subject for the same offense to be twice put in jeopardy of life or limb; nor shall be compelled in any criminal case to be a witness against himself, nor be deprived of life, liberty, or property, without due process of law; nor shall private property be taken for public use without just compensation.

ARTICLE VI

In all criminal prosecutions, the accused shall enjoy the right to a speedy and public trial, by an impartial jury of the State and district wherein the crime shall have been committed, which district shall have been previously ascertained by law, and to be informed of the nature and cause of the accusation; to be confronted with the witnesses against him; to have compulsory process for obtaining witnesses in his favor, and to have the assistance of counsel for his defense.

ARTICLE VII

In suits at common law, where the value in controversy shall exceed twenty dollars, the right of trial by jury shall be preserved, and no fact tried by a jury shall be otherwise reexamined in any court of the United States, than according to the rules of the common law.

ARTICLE VIII

Excessive bail shall not be required, nor excessive fines imposed, nor cruel and unusual punishments inflicted.

ARTICLE IX

The enumeration in the Constitution of certain rights shall not be construed to deny or disparage others retained by the people.

ARTICLE X

The powers not delegated to the United States by the Constitution, nor prohibited by it to the States, are reserved to the States respectively, or to the people.

ARTICLE XI
Passed by Congress March 4, 1794. Ratified February 7, 1795.

The judicial power of the United States shall not be construed to extend to any suit in law or equity commenced or prosecuted against one of the United States, by citizens of another State, or by citizens or subjects of any foreign state.

ARTICLE XII
Passed by Congress December 9, 1803. Ratified July 27, 1804.

The electors shall meet in their respective States, and vote by ballot for President and Vice President, one of whom, at least, shall not be an inhabitant of the same State with themselves; they shall name in their ballots the person voted for as President, and in distinct ballots the person voted for as Vice President, and they shall make distinct lists of all persons voted for as President, and of all persons voted for as Vice President, and of the number of votes for each, which lists they shall sign and certify, and transmit sealed to the seat of the government of the United States, directed to the President of the Senate; the President of the Senate shall, in the presence of the Senate and House of Representatives, open all the certificates and the votes shall then be counted; the person having the greatest number of votes for President shall be the President, if such number be a majority of the whole number of electors appointed; and if no person have such majority, then from the persons having the highest numbers not exceeding three on the list of those voted for as President, the House of Representatives shall choose immediately, by ballot, the President. But in choosing the President, the votes shall be taken by States, the representation from each State having one vote; a quorum for this purpose shall consist of a member or members from two thirds of the States, and a majority of all the States shall be necessary to a choice. And if the House of Representatives shall not choose a President whenever the right of choice shall devolve upon them, before the fourth day of March next following, then the Vice President shall act as President as in the case of the death or other constitutional disability of the President. The person having the greatest number of votes as Vice President shall be the Vice President, if such number be a majority of the whole number of electors appointed, and if no person have a majority, then from the two highest numbers on the list, the Senate shall choose the Vice President; a quorum for the purpose shall consist of two thirds of the whole number of Senators, and a majority of the whole number shall be necessary to a choice. But no person constitutionally ineligible to the office of President shall be eligible to that of Vice President of the United States.

ARTICLE XIII
Passed by Congress January 31, 1865. Ratified December 6, 1865.

SECTION 1. Neither slavery nor involuntary servitude, except as a punishment for crime whereof the party shall have been duly convicted, shall exist within the United States, or any place subject to their jurisdiction.

SECTION 2. Congress shall have power to enforce this article by appropriate legislation.

ARTICLE XIV
Passed by Congress June 13, 1866. Ratified July 9, 1868.

SECTION 1. All persons born or naturalized in the United States, and subject to the jurisdiction thereof, are citizens of the United States and of the State wherein they reside. No State shall make or enforce any law which shall abridge the privileges or immunities of citizens of the United States; nor shall any State deprive any person of life, liberty, or property, without due process of law; nor deny to any person within its jurisdiction the equal protection of the laws.

SECTION 2. Representatives shall be apportioned among the several States according to their respective numbers, counting the whole number of persons in each State, excluding Indians not taxed. But when the right to vote at any election for the choice of electors for President and Vice President of the United States, Representatives in Congress, the executive and judicial officers of a State, or the members of the legislature thereof, is denied to any of the male inhabitants of such State, being twenty-one years of age, and citizens of the United States, or in any way abridged, except for participation in rebellion, or other crime, the basis of representation therein shall be reduced in the proportion which the number of such male citizens shall bear to the whole number of male citizens twenty-one years of age in such State.

SECTION 3. No person shall be a Senator or Representative in Congress, or elector of President and Vice President, or hold any office, civil or military, under the United States, or under any State, who, having previously taken an oath, as a member of Congress, or as an officer of the United States, or as a member of any State legislature, or as an executive or judicial officer of any State, to support the Constitution of the United States, shall have engaged in insurrection or rebellion against the same, or given aid or comfort to the enemies thereof. But Congress may, by a vote of two thirds of each House, remove such disability.

SECTION 4. The validity of the public debt of the United States, authorized by law, including debts incurred for payment of pensions and bounties for services in suppressing insurrection or rebellion, shall not be questioned. But neither the United States nor any State shall assume or pay any debt or obligation incurred in aid of insurrection or rebellion against the United States, or any claim for the loss or emancipation of any slave; but all such debts, obligations, and claims shall be held illegal and void.

SECTION 5. The Congress shall have power to enforce, by appropriate legislation, the provisions of this article.

ARTICLE XV
Passed by Congress February 26, 1869. Ratified February 3, 1870.

SECTION 1. The right of citizens of the United States to vote shall not be denied or abridged by the United States or by any State on account of race, color, or previous condition of servitude.

SECTION 2. The Congress shall have power to enforce this article by appropriate legislation.

ARTICLE XVI
Passed by Congress July 2, 1909. Ratified February 23, 1913.

The Congress shall have power to lay and collect taxes on incomes, from whatever source derived, without apportionment among the several States, and without regard to any census or enumeration.

ARTICLE XVII
Passed by Congress May 13, 1912. Ratified April 8, 1913.

The Senate of the United States shall be composed of two Senators from each State, elected by the people thereof, for six years; and each Senator shall have one vote. The electors in each State shall have the qualifications requisite for electors of the most numerous branch of the State legislatures.

When vacancies happen in the representation of any State in the Senate, the executive authority of such State shall issue writs of election to fill such vacancies: *Provided,* That the legislature of any State may empower the executive thereof to make temporary appointments until the people fill the vacancies by election as the legislature may direct.

This amendment shall not be so construed as to affect the election or term of any Senator chosen before it becomes valid as part of the Constitution.

ARTICLE XVIII
Passed by Congress December 18, 1917. Ratified January 16, 1919.

SECTION 1. After one year from the ratification of this article, the manufacture, sale, or transportation of intoxicating liquors within, the importation thereof into, or the exportation thereof from the United States and all territory subject to the jurisdiction thereof for beverage purposes is hereby prohibited.

SECTION 2. The Congress and the several States shall have concurrent power to enforce this article by appropriate legislation.

SECTION 3. This article shall be inoperative unless it shall have been ratified as an amendment to the Constitution by the legislatures of the several States, as provided in the Constitution, within seven years from the date of the submission hereof to the States by the Congress.

ARTICLE XIX
Passed by Congress June 4, 1919. Ratified August 18, 1920.

The right of citizens of the United States to vote shall not be denied or abridged by the United States or by any State on account of sex.

Congress shall have power to enforce this article by appropriate legislation.

ARTICLE XX
Passed by Congress March 2, 1932. Ratified January 23, 1933.

SECTION 1. The terms of the President and Vice President shall end at noon on the 20th day of January, and the terms of Senators and Representatives at noon on the 3rd day of January, of the years in which such terms would have ended if this article had not been ratified; and the terms of their successors shall then begin.

SECTION 2. The Congress shall assemble at least once in every year, and such meeting shall begin at noon on the 3rd day of January, unless they shall by law appoint a different day.

SECTION 3. If, at the time fixed for the beginning of the term of the President, the President-elect shall have died, the Vice President-elect shall become President. If a President shall not have been chosen before the time fixed for the beginning of his term, or if the President-elect shall have failed to qualify, then the Vice President-elect shall act as President until a President shall have qualified; and the Congress may by law provide for the case wherein neither a President-elect nor a Vice President-elect shall have qualified, declaring who shall then act as President, or the manner in which one who is to act shall be selected, and such person shall act accordingly until a President or Vice President shall have qualified.

Section 4. The Congress may by law provide for the case of the death of any of the persons from whom the House of Representatives may choose a President whenever the right of choice shall have devolved upon them, and for the case of the death of any of the persons from whom the Senate may choose a Vice President whenever the right choice shall have devolved upon them.

Section 5. Sections 1 and 2 shall take effect on the 15th day of October following the ratification of this article.

Section 6. This article shall be inoperative unless it shall have been ratified as an amendment to the Constitution by the legislatures of three fourths of the several States within seven years from the date of its submission.

ARTICLE XXI
Passed by Congress February 20, 1933. Ratified December 5, 1933.

Section 1. The eighteenth article of amendment to the Constitution of the United States is hereby repealed.

Section 2. The transportation or importation into any State, Territory, or possession of the United States for delivery or use therein of intoxicating liquors in violation of the laws thereof, is hereby prohibited.

Section 3. This article shall be inoperative unless it shall have been ratified as an amendment to the Constitution by conventions in the several States, as provided in the Constitution, within seven years from the date of the submission hereof to the States by the Congress.

ARTICLE XXII
Passed by Congress March 21, 1947. Ratified February 27, 1951.

Section 1. No person shall be elected to the office of the President more than twice, and no person who has held the office of President, or acted as President, for more than two years of a term to which some other person was elected President shall be elected to the office of the President more than once. But this article shall not apply to any person holding the office of President when this article was proposed by the Congress, and shall not prevent any persons who may be holding the office of President, or acting as President, during the term within which this article becomes operative from holding the office of President or acting as President during the remainder of such term.

SECTION 2. This article shall be inoperative unless it shall have been ratified as an amendment to the Constitution by the legislatures of three-fourths of the several States within seven years from the date of its submission to the States by the Congress.

ARTICLE XXIII
Passed by Congress June 16, 1960. Ratified March 29, 1961.

SECTION 1. The District constituting the seat of Government of the United States shall appoint in such manner as the Congress may direct:

A number of electors of President and Vice President equal to the whole number of Senators and Representatives in Congress to which the District would be entitled if it were a State, but in no event more than the least populous state; they shall be in addition to those appointed by the states, but shall be considered, for the purpose of the election of President and Vice President, to be electors appointed by a state; and they shall meet in the District and perform such duties as provided by the twelfth article of amendment.

SECTION 2. The Congress shall have power to enforce this article by appropriate legislation.

ARTICLE XXIV
Passed by Congress August 27, 1962. Ratified January 23, 1964.

SECTION 1. The right of citizens of the United States to vote in any primary or other election for President or Vice President, for electors for President or Vice President, or for Senator or Representative in Congress, shall not be denied or abridged by the United States or any State by reason of failure to pay any poll or other tax.

SECTION 2. The Congress shall have the power to enforce this article by appropriate legislation.

ARTICLE XXV
Passed by Congress July 6, 1965. Ratified February 10, 1967.

SECTION 1. In case of the removal of the President from office or his death or resignation, the Vice President shall become President.

SECTION 2. Whenever there is a vacancy in the office of the Vice President, the President shall nominate a Vice President who shall take the office upon confirmation by a majority vote of both houses of Congress.

SECTION 3. Whenever the President transmits to the President pro tempore of the Senate and the Speaker of the House of Representatives his written declaration that he is unable to discharge the powers and duties of his office, and until he transmits to them a written declaration to the contrary, such powers and duties shall be discharged by the Vice President as Acting President.

SECTION 4. Whenever the Vice President and a majority of either the principal officers of the executive departments or of such other body as Congress may by law provide, transmit to the President pro tempore of the Senate and the Speaker of the House of Representatives their written declaration that the President is unable to discharge the powers and duties of his office, the Vice President shall immediately assume the powers and duties of the office as Acting President.

Thereafter, when the President transmits to the President pro tempore of the Senate and the Speaker of the House of Representatives his written declaration that no inability exists, he shall resume the powers and duties of his office unless the Vice President and a majority of either the principal officers of the executive department or of such other body as Congress may by law provide, transmit within four days to the President pro tempore of the Senate and the Speaker of the House of Representatives their written declaration that the President is unable to discharge the powers and duties of his office. Thereupon Congress shall decide the issue, assembling within 48 hours for that purpose if not in session. If the Congress, within 21 days after receipt of the latter written declaration, or, if Congress is not in session, within 21 days after Congress is required to assemble, determines by two-thirds vote of both houses that the President is unable to discharge the powers and duties of his office, the Vice President shall continue to discharge the same as Acting President; otherwise, the President shall resume the powers and duties of his office.

ARTICLE XXVI
Passed by Congress March 23, 1971. Ratified June 30, 1971.

SECTION 1. The right of citizens of the United States, who are eighteen years of age or older, to vote shall not be denied or abridged by the United States or any state on account of age.

SECTION 2. The Congress shall have the power to enforce this article by appropriate legislation.

INDEX GUIDE TO THE CONSTITUTION

PREAMBLE

ARTICLE I. The Legislative Department.
Organization of Congress and terms, qualifications, apportionment, and election of Senators and Representatives.
Procedure in impeachment.
Privileges of the two houses and of their members.
Procedure in lawmaking.
Powers of Congress.
Limitations on Congress and on the States.

ARTICLE II. The Executive Department.
Election of President and Vice President.
Powers and duties of the President.
Ratification of appointments and treaties.
Liability of officers to impeachment.

ARTICLE III. The Judicial Department.
Independence of the judiciary.
Jurisdiction of national courts.
Guarantee of jury trial.
Definition of treason.

ARTICLE IV. Position of the States and territories.
Full faith and credit to acts and judicial proceedings.
Privileges and immunities of citizens of the several States.
Rendition of fugitives from justice.
Control of territories by Congress.
Guarantees to the States.

ARTICLE V. Method of amendment.

ARTICLE VI. Supremacy of the Constitution, laws, and treaties of the United States.
Oath of office—prohibition of a religious test.

ARTICLE VII. Method of ratification of the Constitution.

AMENDMENTS

I. Freedom of religion, speech, press, and assembly; right of petition.

II. Right to keep and bear arms.
III. Limitations in quartering soldiers.
IV. Protection from unreasonable searches and seizures.
V. Due process in criminal cases.
Limitation on right of eminent domain.
VI. Right to speedy trial by jury, and other guarantees.
VII. Trial by jury in suits at law.
VIII. Excessive bail or unusual punishments forbidden.
IX. Retention of certain rights by the people.
X. Undelegated powers belong to the States or to the people.
XI. Exemption of States from suit by individuals.
XII. New method of electing President.
XIII. Abolition of slavery.
XIV. Definition of citizenship.
Guarantees of due process and equal protection against State action.
Apportionment of Representatives in Congress.
Validity of public debt.
XV. Extension of suffrage to colored persons.
XVI. Tax on incomes "from whatever source derived."
XVII. Popular election of Senators.
XVIII. Prohibition of intoxicating liquors.
XIX. Extension of suffrage to women.
XX. Abolition of "lame duck" session of Congress.
Change in presidential and congressional terms.
XXI. Repeal of 18th Amendment.
XXII. Limitation of President's terms in office.
XXIII. Extension of suffrage to District of Columbia in presidential elections.
XXIV. Abolition of poll tax requirement in national elections.
XXV. Presidential succession and disability provisions.
XXVI. Extension of suffrage to 18-year-olds.

SELECTED REFERENCES FOR
ADDITIONAL READING

Books indicated by an asterisk (*) have been reprinted in paperback.

CHAPTER I: OPENING A NEW WORLD

General Surveys:
Becker, Carl, *The Beginnings of the American People* (1915) *
'Brebner, J. B., *Explorers of North America, 1492–1806* (1933) *
Cheney, E. P., *The Dawn of a New Era, 1250–1453* (1936)

Special Studies:
Beazley, C. R., *Prince Henry the Navigator* (1895)
Bourne, E. G., *Spain in America, 1450–1580* (1904)
Bridenbaugh, Carl, *Vexed and Troubled Englishmen, 1590–1642* (1968)
Driver, H. E., *Indians of North America* (2nd ed., 1969)
Kirkpatrick, F. A., *The Spanish Conquistadores* (2nd ed., 1946) *
Morison, S. E., *Admiral of the Ocean Sea* (2 vols., 1942)
Munro, W. B., *Crusaders of New France* (1918)

CHAPTER II: THE COMING OF THE ENGLISH

General Surveys:
Andrews, C. M., *Colonial Folkways* (1919)
Craven, W. F., *The Southern Colonies in the Seventeenth Century* (1949)
Wertenbaker, T. J., *The First Americans, 1607–1690* (1927)
Wright, L. B., *The Atlantic Frontier* (1947) *

Special Studies:
Adams, J. T., *The Founding of New England* (1921) *
Mannix, D. P., and Cowley, Malcolm, *Black Cargoes: A History of the Atlantic Slave Trade, 1518–1865* (1962) *
Miller, Perry, *Roger Williams* (1953) *
Morison, S. E., *Builders of the Bay Colony* (1930) *
Willison, G. F., *Saints and Strangers* (1945) *
Wright, L. B., *First Gentlemen of Virginia* (1940) *

CHAPTER III: PROVINCIAL AMERICA

General Surveys:
Adams, J. T., *Provincial Society* (1927)
Bridenbaugh, Carl, *Cities in the Wilderness; The First Century of Urban Life in America, 1625–1742* (2nd ed., 1955) *
Parrington, V. L., *The Colonial Mind, 1620–1800* (Vol. I of *Main Currents in American Thought*) (1927) *
Savelle, Max, *Seeds of Liberty: Genesis of the American Mind* (1948) *
Wertenbaker, T. J., *The Golden Age of Colonial Culture* (2nd ed., 1949) *

Special Studies:
Crane, V. W., *Benjamin Franklin and a Rising People* (1954) *
Franklin, Benjamin, *Autobiography* (first published in 1868; reprinted in numerous editions) *
Gewehr, W. M., *The Great Awakening in Virginia, 1740–90* (1930)
Greene, E. B., *Religion and the State* (1941) *
Miller, Perry, *The New England Mind* (2 vols., 1953, 1954) *

CHAPTER IV: PROBLEMS OF IMPERIAL CONTROL

General Surveys:
Andrews, C. M., *The Colonial Background of the American Revolution* (rev. ed., 1931) *
Gipson, L. H., *The British Empire before the American Revolution,* Vol. I (1936)

Special Studies:
Bailyn, Bernard, *Origins of American Politics* (1968)
Dickerson, O. M., *American Colonial Government, 1696–1765* (1912)
Guttridge, G. H. *The Colonial Policy of William III* (1922)
———, *English Whiggism and the American Revolution* (1942) *

CHAPTER V: ANGLO-FRENCH STRUGGLE FOR SUPREMACY

General Surveys:
Costain, T. B., *The White and the Gold* (1954)
Parkman, Francis, *The Battle for North America* (condensation of Works), ed. John Tebbel (1948)
Wrong, G. M., *The Rise and Fall of New France* (1928)

Special Studies:
Bird, Harrison, *Battle for a Continent* (1965)
Pargellis, S. M., *Lord Loudoun in North America* (1933)
Parkman, Francis, *Montcalm and Wolfe* (2 vols., 1884) *

CHAPTER VI: CONFLICT OF INTERESTS WITHIN
             THE EMPIRE

General Surveys:
Becker, Carl, *The Eve of the Revolution* (1918)
Jensen, Merrill, *The Founding of a Nation: A History of the American
    Revolution, 1763–1776* (1968)
Miller, J. C., *The Origins of the American Revolution* (1943) *

Special Studies:
Burnett, E. C., *The Continental Congress* (1941) *
Miller, J. C., *Sam Adams: Pioneer in Propaganda* (1936) *
Morgan, E. S., and Morgan, H. M., *Stamp Act Crisis* (rev. ed., 1963) *
Peckham, H. H., *Pontiac and the Indian Uprising* (1947) *
Schlesinger, A. M., *The Colonial Merchants and the American Revolu-
    tion* (1918) *
Willison, G. F., *Patrick Henry and His World* (1965)

CHAPTER VII: REVOLUTION: POLITICAL AND SOCIAL

General Surveys:
Alden, J. R., *American Revolution, 1775–1783* (1954) *
Greene, E. B., *The Revolutionary Generation, 1763–90* (1943)
Jameson, J. F., *The American Revolution Considered as a Social Move-
    ment* (1926) *
Miller, J. C., *Triumph of Freedom, 1775–1783* (1948) *

Special Studies:
Adams, R. G., *Political Ideas of the American Revolution* (3rd ed.,
    1958)
Becker, Carl, *The Declaration of Independence* (1922) *
Bowen, C. D., *John Adams and the American Revolution* (1950) *
Flexner, James, *George Washington in the American Revolution* (1968)
Forbes, Esther, *Paul Revere and the World He Lived In* (1942) *
Morison, S. E., *John Paul Jones* (1959) *

Quarles, Benjamin, *The Negro in the American Revolution* (1961)
Van Doren, Carl, *Benjamin Franklin* (1938)
Ver Steeg, C. L., *Robert Morris: Revolutionary Financier* (1954)

CHAPTER VIII: ESTABLISHING THE NEW NATION

General Surveys:
Farrand, Max, *Fathers of the Constitution* (1921)
Fiske, John, *The Critical Period of American History, 1783–1789* (1888)
McLaughlin, A. C., *Foundations of American Constitutionalism* (1932) *
Rossiter, Clinton, *Political Thought of the American Revolution* (rev. ed., 1963) *

Special Studies:
Beard, C. A., *Economic Interpretation of the Constitution* (1913) *
Jensen, Merrill, *Articles of Confederation* (2nd ed., 1948) *
McLaughlin, A. C., *Confederation and the Constitution, 1783–1789* (1968)
Schuyler, R. L., *The Constitution of the United States* (1923)
Spaulding, E. W., *New York in the Critical Period, 1783–1789* (1932)
Van Doren, Carl, *The Great Rehearsal* (1948) *

CHAPTER IX: THE FEDERALIST REGIME

General Surveys:
Bassett, J. S., *The Federalist System* (1906)
Bowers, C. G., *Jefferson and Hamilton* (1925) *
Krout, J. A., and Fox, D. R., *The Completion of Independence* (1944)
Miller, J. C., *The Federalist Era, 1789–1801* (1960) *
White, L. D., *The Federalists* (1948) *

Special Studies:
Baldwin, Leland, *The Whiskey Rebels* (1939)
Flexner, J. T., *George Washington and the New Nation* (1970)
Freeman, D. S., *George Washington* (6 vols., 1948–1954; Vol. VII, completed by J. A. Carroll and M. W. Ashworth, 1957)
Miller, J. C. *Crisis in Freedom: The Alien and Sedition Acts* (1951) *
Schachner, Nathan, *Alexander Hamilton* (1946) *

CHAPTER X: THE JEFFERSONIANS

General Surveys:
Bowers, C. G., *Jefferson in Power* (1936) *
Koch, Adrienne, *Jefferson and Madison: The Great Collaboration* (1950) *
Malone, Dumas, *Jefferson the President* (1970)
Wiltse, C. M., *The Jeffersonian Tradition in American Democracy* (1935) *

Special Studies:
Beirne, F. F., *The War of 1812* (1949)
Brown, R. H., *Republic in Peril: 1812* (1964)
Forester, C. S., *The Age of Fighting Sail* (1956)
Pratt, J. W., *The Expansionists of 1812* (1949)
Sears, L. M., *Jefferson and the Embargo* (1927)
White, L. D., *The Jeffersonians* (1951) *

CHAPTER XI: THE RISING NATIONAL SPIRIT

General Surveys:
Babcock, K. C., *The Rise of American Nationality* (1906)
Dangerfield, George, *The Era of Good Feelings* (1952) *
Livermore, Shaw, *Twilight of Federalism: The Disintegration of the Federalist Party, 1815–1830* (1962)
Turner, F. J., *The Rise of the New West* (1906) *

Special Studies:
Bemis, S. F., *John Quincy Adams and the Foundations of American Foreign Policy* (1949)
Brooks, V. W., *The World of Washington Irving* (1944)
Corwin, E. S., *John Marshall and the Constitution* (1919)
James, Marquis, *Andrew Jackson, the Border Captain* (1933) *
Perkins, Dexter, *A History of the Monroe Doctrine* (rev. ed., 1955) *

CHAPTER XII: JACKSONIAN DEMOCRACY

General Surveys:
Ogg, F. A., *The Reign of Andrew Jackson* (1928)
Schlesinger, A. M., Jr., *The Age of Jackson* (1945) *
Turner, F. J., *The United States, 1830–1850* (1935)

Special Studies:

Billington, R. A., *The Protestant Crusade, 1800–1860* (1938)

Bowers, C. G., *Party Battles of the Jackson Period* (1922)

Foreman, Grant, *Indian Removal* (1932)

Fuess, C. M., *Daniel Webster* (2 vols., 1930)

James, Marquis, *Andrew Jackson, Portrait of a President* (1937) *

Robbins, R. M., *Our Landed Heritage, the Public Domain, 1776–1936* (1942) *

Taylor, G. R., *The Transportation Revolution, 1815–1860* (1951) *

Tyler, A. F., *Freedom's Ferment: Phases of American Social History from the Revolution to the Outbreak of the Civil War* (1944)

Van Deusen, J. G., *The Jacksonian Era: 1828–1848* (1959) *

Wiltse, C. W., *John C. Calhoun* (3 vols., 1944–1951)

CHAPTER XIII: THE FRUITS OF MANIFEST DESTINY

General Surveys:

Graebner, N. A., *Empire on the Pacific: A Study in American Continental Expansion* (1955)

Singletary, O. A., *Mexican War* (1960) *

Smith, J. H., *The War with Mexico* (2 vols., 1919)

Stephenson, N. W., *Texas and the Mexican War* (1921)

Special Studies:

DeVoto, Bernard, *Across the Wide Missouri* (1947) *

Nevins, Allan, *Frémont, Pathmarker of the West* (3rd ed., 1955)

James, Marquis, *The Raven: A Biography of Sam Houston* (1929) *

Wellman, P. J., *Glory, God and Gold* (1955)

White, S. E., *The Forty-Niners* (1918)

CHAPTER XIV: AMERICAN SOCIETY AT MID-CENTURY

General Surveys:

Curti, Merle, *Growth of American Thought* (3rd ed., 1964)

Ekirch, A. A., *The Idea of Progress in America, 1815–1860* (1944)

Gabriel, R. H., *The Course of American Democratic Thought* (2nd ed., 1956)

Special Studies:

Flexner, Eleanor, *Century of Stuggle: The Woman's Rights Movement in the United States* (1959) *

Hulbert, A. B., *The Paths of Inland Commerce* (1920)
Hunter, L. C., *Steamboats on the Western Rivers* (1949)
Perry, Bliss, *The American Spirit in Literature* (1918)
Thompson, Holland, *The Age of Invention* (1921)
Wittke, Carl, *We Who Built America; The Saga of the Immigrant* (rev. ed., 1964)

CHAPTER XV: SLAVERY AND SECTIONALISM

General Surveys:
Cole, A. C., *The Irrepressible Conflict* (1934)
Craven, A. O., *The Coming of the Civil War* (2nd ed., 1957) *
Nichols, R. F., *The Disruption of American Democracy* (1948)
Rozwenc, E. C., ed., *Causes of the American Civil War* (1961) *

Special Studies:
Dodd, W. E., *The Cotton Kingdom* (1919)
Elkins, S. M., *Slavery: A Problem in American Institutional and Intellectual Life* (2nd ed., 1968)
Macy, Jesse, *The Anti-Slavery Crusade* (1919)
Milton, G. F., *The Eve of Conflict: Stephen A. Douglas and the Needless War* (1934)
Nevins, Allan, *The Ordeal of the Union* (2 vols., 1947)
Owsley, F. L., *Plain Folk of the Old South* (1949) *
Sandburg, Carl, *Abraham Lincoln: The Prairie Years* (2 vols., 1926)
———, *Abraham Lincoln: The Prairie Years and the War Years* (3 vols., ????) *

CHAPTER XVI: THE WAR THAT UNIFIED THE NATION

General Surveys:
Catton, Bruce, *Centennial History of the Civil War* (3 vols., 1965) *
Leech, Margaret, *Reveille in Washington* (1941) *
Randall, J. G., and Donald, David, *Civil War and Reconstruction* (2nd ed., rev., 1969)

Special Studies:
Bishop, James, *The Day Lincoln Was Shot* (1955)
Catton, Bruce, *A Stillness at Appomattox* (1953) *
Nevins, Allan, *The Emergence of Lincoln* (2 vols., 1950) *
Quarles, Benjamin, *The Negro in the Civil War* (1953) *

Sandburg, Carl, *Abraham Lincoln: The War Years* (4 vols., 1939)
Strode, Hudson, *Jefferson Davis* (4 vols., 1955–1966)
Williams, T. H., *Lincoln and His Generals* (1952) *

CHAPTER XVII: REBUILDING THE POLITICAL STRUCTURE

General Surveys:

Bowers, C. G., *The Tragic Era* (1929) *
Carter, Hodding, *The Angry Scar: The Story of Reconstruction* (1959)
Dunning, W. A., *Reconstruction, Political and Economic* (1907) *
Franklin, J. H., *Reconstruction after the Civil War* (1961)
Kirkland, E. C., *Industry Comes of Age: Business, Labor and Public Policy* (1967) *
Stampp, K. M., *The Era of Reconstruction, 1865–1877* (1965) *

Special Studies:

Beale, H. K., *The Critical Year: A Study of Andrew Jackson and Reconstruction* (1930)
Brock, W. R., *An American Crisis* (1963) *
McKitrick, E. L., *Andrew Johnson and Reconstruction* (1960) *
Nevins, Allan, *Study in Power: John D. Rockefeller* (1953)
Taylor, G. R., and Neu, I. D., *The American Railroad Network* (1956)
Woodward, C. V., *Reunion and Reaction: The Compromise of 1877 and the End of Reconstruction* (1951) *

INDEX